PEOPLE FOR AND AGAINST GUN CONTROL

A Biographical Reference

Marjolijn Bijlefeld

The Greenwood Press "People Making a Difference" Series

GREENWOOD PRESS
Westport, Connecticut • London

Library of Congress Cataloging-in-Publication Data

Bijlefeld, Marjolijn, 1960–
    People for and against gun control : a biographical reference /
Marjolijn Bijlefeld.
        p.   cm.—(The Greenwood Press "People making a difference"
series, ISSN 1522–7960)
    Includes bibliographical references and index.
    ISBN 0–313–30690–7 (alk. paper)
    1. Gun control—United States.   I. Title.   II. Series.
HV7436.B54   1999
363.3'3'0973—dc21   98–53383

British Library Cataloguing in Publication Data is available.

Library of Congress Catalog Card Number: 98–53383
ISBN: 0–313–30690–7
ISSN: 1522–7960

First published in 1999

Greenwood Press, 88 Post Road West, Westport, CT 06881
An imprint of Greenwood Publishing Group, Inc.
www.greenwood.com

Printed in the United States of America

The paper used in this book complies with the
Permanent Paper Standard issued by the National
Information Standards Organization (Z39.48–1984).

10 9 8 7 6 5 4 3 2 1

Copyright Acknowledgments

The author and the publisher gratefully acknowledge permission to reprint excerpts from the following interviews conducted by Marjolijn Bijlefeld:

Madeleine (Lyn) Bates; Mike Beard; Carl C. Bell, MD; Kenneth V. F. Blanchard; Sarah Brady; Deane Calhoun at Youth ALIVE!; Sandy Chisholm; Katherine Kaufer Christoffel, MD, MPH; Philip J. Cook; Robert J. Cottrol; Preston K. Covey, PhD; U.S. Senator Larry E. Craig; Miguel A. Faria, Jr., MD; Richard J. Feldman; Alan M. Gottlieb; Daniel Gross; Stephen P. Halbrook; Marion P. Hammer; Scott Harshbarger, former Massachusetts Attorney General; Holley Galland Haymaker; Richard Haymaker; Dennis Henigan; Joshua Horwitz; Suzanna Gratia Hupp, DC; Phillip B. Journey; Jo Ann Karn; Don B. Kates, Jr.; Gary Kleck; C. Neal Knox; Dave Kopel; Marty Langelan, Langelan & Associates; Karen L. MacNutt; Carolyn McCarthy; Tanya K. Metaksa; Bryan Miller; Diane Nicholl; Sheriff Jay Printz; Michael A. Robbins; Andrés Soto; Steve Sposato; Joseph P. Tartaro; Peggy Tartaro; Stephen Teret; Lisa S. Thornton; Joy Turner; Linda Vasquez; Robert Walker; Douglas Weil, ScD; Garen Wintemute; James D. Wright; and Michael D. Yacino.

Contents

Series Foreword

Many controversial topics are difficult for student researchers to understand fully without examining key people and their positions in the subjects being debated. This series is designed to meet the research needs of high school and college students by providing them with profiles of those who have been at the center of debates on such controversial topics as gun control, capital punishment, and gay and lesbian rights. The personal stories—the reasons behind their arguments—add a human element to the debates not found in other resources focusing on these topics.

Each volume in the series provides profiles of people, chosen for their effective battles in support of or in opposition to one side of a specific controversial issue. The volumes provide an equal number of profiles of those on both sides of the debates. Students are encouraged to read stories from the two opposite sides to develop their critical thinking skills and to draw their own conclusions concerning the specific issues. They will learn about those people who are not afraid to stand up for their cause, no matter what it may be, and no matter what the consequences may be.

To further help the student researcher, the author of each volume has provided an introduction that outlines the history of the issue and the debates surrounding it, as well as explaining the major arguments and concerns of those involved in the debates. The pro and con arguments are clearly defined as are major developments in the movement. Students can use these introductions as a foundation for analyzing the stories of the people who follow.

Greenwood Press's hope is that each student will realize there are no easy answers to the questions these controversial topics raise, and that those on all sides of these debates have legitimate reasons for thinking, feeling, and arguing the way they do. These topics have become controversial because the people involved have very real, emotional stories to tell, and these stories have helped to shape the debates. Each profile provides information such as where and when the person was born, his or her family background, education, what pushed him or her into action, the contributions he or she has made to the movement, and the obstacles he or she has faced from the opposing factions. All this information is meant to help the student user critique the different viewpoints surrounding the issue and to come to a better understanding of the topic through a more personal venue than a typical essay can provide.

Introduction

The 50 people profiled in this volume are key figures in the gun control debate today. Among them are experts and activists seen or heard when the topic is discussed in the national media, along with others not well known outside their own communities. Major organizations such as the National Rifle Association, Second Amendment Foundation, Coalition to Stop Gun Violence, and Handgun Control Inc. each recommended people who had made important contributions to the debate. From there, the volume grew on its own and would have continued to do so were it not for space constraints. Almost everyone interviewed recommended another person with a different perspective or background. Nearly everyone who was asked to participate did so, but a few declined. The author is thankful to all those who allowed their stories to be shared.

This volume tries to put a human face on the often complicated and emotional debate over gun control. People are drawn to the issue for many reasons. Some have seen loved ones injured or killed, or are themselves victims of gun violence. Others see gun rights as a patriotic issue, a unique expression of the American character. To tamper with such rights, they feel, is to reject a part of the nation's history. Exploring this issue means wrestling with questions about individual rights, the role of government and law enforcement, and social issues such as gang violence and the need for safe communities in which to raise families.

Even the most staunch gun control activists don't see gun control as a panacea for society's problems. On the other side, even the most ardent gun rights activists don't expect that a fully armed society would be immune from all worries.

Adding to the complexity of this debate is the number of different levels where the two sides can disagree. What is the meaning of the Second Amendment? What is the difference between crime prevention and violence prevention? How valid are guns as weapons of self-protection? Can guns be made safer? Many of the people profiled here have spent years trying to answer these questions.

This volume shares 50 stories, each one unique. Expect to experience a range of emotions, and perhaps even have your mind changed several times over. It's hard not to sympathize with Stephen Sposato of California as he describes identifying his wife's body at the coroner's office after she was shot to death. After reading his profile, it will be easy to see what motivated him to support bans on assault weapons and to testify in favor of such laws before legislators in California and Washington, D.C.

Imagine the moment when Suzanna Gratia Hupp crouched behind a table in a Texas restaurant with her mother and father as a gunman methodically shot defenseless people. She would have had a clear shot at him at one point—but her gun was in her car. The gunman killed her parents that day. It's easy to see why gun rights is a priority in her work as a Texas state legislator.

For some, the decision to join the gun control debate was their way of reconstructing a life that had been turned upside down by gun violence. Sarah Brady, whose husband, Jim, was permanently disabled during the 1981 assassination attempt on President Ronald Reagan, is now the chair of Handgun Control, Inc. Before the shooting, her life centered on her three-year-old son and other duties of running the household. She never envisioned the role she'd play— or the admirers and enemies she'd earn.

Dan Gross gave up a successful advertising career to start PAX, an organization dedicated to reducing gun violence following a shooting that left his younger brother permanently disabled and a good friend dead. A lone gunman had stormed onto the observation deck of the Empire State Building and started shooting. Gross was watching a basketball game that February Sunday afternoon in 1997 before his father called with the news. "That was my last moment of sanity," he said, recalling the weeks that followed.

Joy Turner's son, Hank, fell victim to the war on California's streets—shot to death by gang members, even though he wasn't the intended target or a member of any gang. Turner relives her anguish regularly by taking her story to gang members in jails and to at-risk youth. There's no sugarcoating in her message. She tells the young men in raw, graphic language that their gang wars took her son and destroyed a part of her, too. Through her in-your-face ministry, she encourages them to redeem themselves. If they don't get out of the gangs, she tells them, "take out a life insurance policy. Don't make your mother or family pay for what you're doing. Don't make them have a car wash or go begging for some money to bury you."

Some people recall a moment of conversion, a realization that gun control or gun rights would be a topic to which they would devote much of their energy. For Neal Knox, who went on to play a pivotal role in helping the National Rifle Association become a lobbying powerhouse, the moment came decades before. As a young sergeant in the Texas National Guard, he heard a Belgian American friend tell of the horror of witnessing an entire family gunned down by Nazi soldiers because the father couldn't locate the pistol he had registered. His friend cried as he recounted the story, "Huge tears were rolling down his cheeks, making silver dollar size splotches on the dusty barrack's floor. That was my conversion from a casual gun owner to someone determined to prevent gun laws making such an outrage possible in this country," he said.

Even those who came to the issue through some professional or academic interest probably didn't expect it to become as consuming as it did. Many have had to forego other areas of study because firearms policy questions became increasingly compelling and complex.

Four physicians—Garen J. Wintemute, an emergency room physician, Katherine Kaufer Christoffel, a pediatrician, Carl C. Bell, a psychiatrist, and Lisa Thornton, a rehabilitation specialist—grew tired of seeing the shattered bodies and shattered lives caused by gun violence. Wintemute and Christoffel have taken on high profiles with their studies on gun violence, suicides, and unintentional injuries. They have also shouldered the criticisms of gun rights activists who argue that their methodology, conclusions, and motivations are flawed. But they say those criticisms actually spur them on. Thornton plays a less public role, but is no less confounded by Americans' attitudes toward guns. "It makes me angry because I don't understand this love affair with guns. Since I've entered pediatrics, I've been amazed by how much we hate our children. We give child safety lip service, but when it comes to saving the lives of kids, we're quick to say, 'I love my gun more,' " she said.

Academicians and researchers have entered the debate because they have seen some aspect of it not fully covered. James D. Wright, now a sociology professor at Tulane University, burst onto the gun control scene in the early 1980s. He once favored gun control, but his work studying criminals and the effectiveness of gun control laws made him rethink his position. While gun rights activists often cite his studies as support for their position, Wright calls himself an "agnostic" on the issue.

Indeed, there is room for disagreement even within the two sides of the debate. Some gun control activists are in favor of childproof or personalized handguns, for example. Others say such safety measures will only line the pockets of gun manufacturers. Gun owners also often have their own particular agendas—long gun owners, for example, might have few objections to handgun control measures.

Differences in strategies are also evident. Alan M. Gottlieb can afford to play the loose cannon because the small group he chairs—the Citizens Committee for the Right to Keep and Bear Arms, based in Bellevue, Washington—is so often in the shadow of the National Rifle Association. As a result, he can have a little more fun with the media and the public. For example, in 1996 he issued a press release that sarcastically declared, "Gun Lobby Endorses Clinton," because Clinton's pro-control activities were consolidating gun rights activists nationwide.

Most of these people have made tremendous personal sacrifices to further their cause. That's as true of ordinary people who keep their day jobs and stuff envelopes with legislative updates in the evenings as it is of those who have made the gun control issue a career. Marion Hammer, a Florida grandmother, struggled with giving up precious time with her growing grandchildren to take on the high-stress and high-profile position of president of the National Rifle Association. Jo Ann Karn, a Michigan grandmother, tried to ignore the small voice she heard during a Sunday sermon—the one that eventually led her to start a violence prevention program for teens in Holland, Michigan.

Whatever it was that drove these people to the debate, their commitment to it is clear. Yet as important as they are to the debate, gun control or gun rights represents only part of who and what they are. They are mothers, fathers, brothers, and sisters. They are academicians, researchers, engineers, physicians. Some are in it for a lifetime, others for a few years. And some may even change their views over the years.

That's part of the chemistry of the debate. As our impressions of crime in our communities change, so do people's feelings about gun control. We take up the issue when new gun legislation is proposed or when people feel threatened by crime. We turn to it to question why a troubled teenager had such easy access to a weapon used to shoot classmates, or why the United States has among the world's highest homicide rates. There are many questions. The answers are much more elusive.

This volume does not intend to show that one side is wrong and one is right. Instead, the profiles that follow can provide depth to the arguments and introduce new perspectives. And, despite their differences, these 50 people share a common trait: a commitment to making a safer society. But given the variety of ways they propose to accomplish that goal, it's clear the debate is far from settled.

THE ELEMENTS OF THE DEBATE

Nearly every formal debate on gun control at some point comes around to the Second Amendment to the U.S. Constitution. It reads, "A well-regulated militia, being necessary to the security of a free state, the right of the people to keep and bear arms shall not be infringed." The amendment was based on the English Bill of Rights, which reads, "That the subjects which are Protestants, may have arms for their defense suitable to their conditions, and as allowed by law" (enacted December 16, 1689).

During the development of the Constitution and Bill of Rights, Federalists and Anti-Federalists held conflicting views. Federalists favored a strong and active central government. Anti-Federalists feared that a strong federal government could easily evolve into a tyrannical one. Without a provision prohibiting a standing army, or allowing states to create their own militias, there would be no protection for the common man.

So what exactly did the framers mean when they selected this language for the Second Amendment? That's still debated today. It boils down to a "collective" versus an "individual rights" interpretation. The collective, or states' rights, view is primarily the pro–gun control view. Its interpretation focuses on the words "being necessary to the security of a free state." In order to protect themselves from a tyrannical government, states have the right to maintain militias. The right is a collective one, granted to the state, not to individual citizens of the state.

The individual rights interpretation arrives at the opposite conclusion. Militias were composed of common men, therefore the right extends to them. Debaters have taken the amendment and broken it down into its smallest parts. What does "well-regulated" mean? That the militia must be well trained? That it must be under the control of the state? How is "the people" used in other amendments? Does it mean the people collectively or individually?

The interpretation of the Second Amendment continues to be a topic of regular law review articles. Attorney Don B. Kates noted that the conclusions drawn by these articles has changed over the past 25 years. "Today, there is basically no dissent among law professors who have worked in this area that the Second Amendment is an individual right."

However, observed another attorney, Dennis Henigan, "Just because articles espousing it are published in law journals doesn't make it right. You don't decide a constitutional issue by counting the number of articles on it."

While the Second Amendment debate is a lively one, many people know the amendment only by its second half, "the right of the people to keep and bear arms shall not be infringed." Gun rights advocates favor those words because they seem so straightforward. But over the years, federal courts have seemed to support the collective interpretation. No gun control law has ever been overturned by a federal court on the grounds that it violated the Second Amendment.

In fact, gun rights proponents have generally moved on to other arguments to beat back gun control restrictions. They argue that the Tenth and Fourteenth Amendments contribute to an individual rights reading. The Tenth Amendment reads, "The powers not delegated to the United States by the Constitution, nor prohibited by it to the states, are reserved to the states respectively, or to the people." And the Fourteenth Amendment reads, "No state shall make or enforce any law which shall abridge the privileges or immunities of citizens of the United States; nor shall any state deprive any person of life, liberty or property, without due process of law; nor deny to any person within its jurisdiction the equal protection of the laws."

As attorney Stephen P. Halbrook said, "The Fourteenth Amendment was adopted to protect Bill of Rights freedoms (including the right to keep and bear arms) from state or local infringement."

State constitutions generally do not contain the ambiguities of the federal Constitution. For example, the Nebraska Constitution states, "All persons are by nature free and independent, and have certain inherent and inalienable rights; among these are . . . the right to keep and bear arms for security or defense of self, family, home, and others, and for lawful common defense, hunting, recreational use, and all other lawful purposes, and such rights shall not be denied or infringed by the state or any subdivision thereof."

Current events add different elements to the historical questions about the Second Amendment. Some argue that whatever the Founding Fathers believed, they could not have predicted a late twentieth-century society in which gangs and guns were so intertwined. Those who hold this position include people like Californian Deane Calhoun, director of Youth ALIVE!, which promotes a training curriculum so that young people can be involved in reducing gun violence in their own communities.

Others believe that the tyrranical government feared by the colonists could still become a reality in the United States today. Cuban-born neurosurgeon Miguel Faria, now of Atlanta, Georgia, wants to ensure that subversion of an unarmed citizenry never happens here.

Attorney Robert J. Cottrol of Washington, D.C., believes that racial oppression is rooted in society's decisions on who is allowed to own guns. He says there is little doubt that white colonists wanted to keep firearms out of the hands of Africans and Native Americans 200 years ago. And race relations in the past 200 years have not relieved all concerns. With gun regulations that rely on the state or municipality to determine who is allowed to carry guns, he argued, "we're essentially trusting our protection to the state. Before we do that, don't we have to ask how benevolent the state is? From a minority perspective, many people feel the state is unwilling to protect them."

There is, however, general agreement that society needs some regulations on who owns firearms. Federal law prohibits the sale of handguns to children, convicted felons, and those who have been declared mentally incompetent. Few argue with these laws, and people have largely accepted that there are limits to this freedom. There are many gun laws on the books in this country. Some are pro–gun control;

some are pro–gun rights. Both sides are continuing their push to enact or repeal laws they find harmful or to enact laws they believe will improve community safety.

SELF-PROTECTION

Guns can be the premiere weapons of self-protection, say gun rights activists. At the least, Americans should be allowed to choose the means of protecting themselves, their families, and their homes. But many gun control supporters won't concede that point. They argue that guns, particularly handguns, are more dangerous than helpful. The self-protection debate is an intense one within the larger gun control debate.

Lyn Bates of Massachusetts teaches self-defense with firearms through her Massachusetts-based group AWARE. Her primary audience is women. She recalls the stories of women who had taken her courses and later used guns to defend themselves. As so often happens, the mere sight of a gun will cause the attacker to break off the attack and drive away, she said. "That's what self-defense is all about. Being able to stay alive and unhurt through a situation where someone else wants you dead or injured. You have to be able to do it yourself, because attackers are smart enough to choose a time and place when you are alone. Firearms, properly used, give women a tremendous survival advantage in situations where nothing else will work reliably."

A Maryland self-defense instructor, Marty Langelan, disagrees. After years working with rape victims and women in shelters, she decided that weapons such as handguns are a significant risk to women. "If there was a weapon available during an assault—whether the attacker was a stranger or an acquaintance—the likelihood that the male would use the weapon was great, and the likelihood that the woman would be able to get to it, retain it, and use it, was small." Moreover, she argues, the incidence of injury and death increases when a weapon is involved. "In my experience with thousands of women, it's clear to me that we are safer without a gun."

Florida criminologist Gary Kleck decided to determine how often armed citizens use guns to defend themselves. In his study, researchers asked people whether they had ever confronted and threatened with a gun someone committing a crime. "If you used that definition as a minimum standard, there were about 2.5 million defensive gun uses per year. On occasion, there would actually be a shooting," he said.

Other studies seem to support the concept that armed citizens reduce crime. David B. Kopel of Colorado is the author of several studies and a book examining gun control policies and the effectiveness of "right to carry" and other gun control laws. Some of those studies conclude that while the states with right to carry laws show decreases in violent crimes, there are additional benefits. Even people who are not armed become the beneficiaries of such laws. Criminals can't tell who has a permit to carry a concealed weapon, so they might avoid confrontations with people altogether.

Not all criminologists accept the argument that criminals behave better when citizens are armed. Criminologist Philip J. Cook of North Carolina has studied whether gun availability affects crime. In a recent study, he found that gun availability had no impact on the overall robbery rate, for example, but it did influence the type of weapon. "In those areas where guns are readily available, robbers commit their crimes with guns. In Boston, for example, where there aren't many guns, not many robbers use them," he said. "The result is that Boston had a high rate of robbery but the robberies there are less deadly than in cities where guns are prevalent."

WHAT ABOUT THE RISKS?

So both sides try to weigh the risks and benefits of gun ownership. For some, the benefit of having a gun available is paramount. Risks can be minimized by careful storage and handling of a firearm. Others say the risks of certain firearms, such as handguns and assault weapons, outweigh their benefits. If handguns were not readily available in American homes, depressed teens contemplating suicide wouldn't have such deadly force available. Nor would spouses or brothers reaching for a weapon to settle an argument. And limiting the availability of guns would choke off the supply of guns on the illegal market.

How many different kinds of guns should be available to law-abiding gun owners? If rifles and shotguns, which are less likely to be involved in homicides and suicides, are effective self-protection weapons, why allow handguns? If handguns are needed, why not ban easily concealed, inexpensive handguns or assault weapons, those with a paramilitary look and feel? Should Americans have broad freedom in selecting their weapons?

Again, the gun rights advocates say yes. One person's assault weapon is another's sporting gun. One person's Saturday night special is the only form of self-protection a low-income person might be able to afford. The features that make handguns so objectionable to some—their portability and concealability—are the very features that make them desirable weapons for self-protection. Trying to classify guns by their characteristics is arguing a slippery case of semantics.

Both sides point to the Gun Control Act of 1968 as an example. The law bans the importation of guns that are not "generally recognized as particularly suitable for, or readily adaptable to, sporting purposes." The Internal Revenue Service has set up guidelines about which weapons can be imported. These originally included inexpensive, short-barreled handguns with no sporting purpose made from inferior materials. In 1989 federal legislators used the same "sporting purpose" guidelines to develop the ban on the importation of "assault weapons." That prohibition was expanded in 1994 to include nineteen named assault weapons and two guns that have specific assault weapon characteristics. The latter ban passed in part because of the testimony of victims like Stephen Sposato.

With the Saturday night specials ban, however, American manufacturers have not been prohibited from making handguns nearly identical to the ones banned from import. Gun control advocates say the bill turned out to be protectionism for American gun manufacturers.

However, gun rights advocates say the law is flawed for a different reason. They argue that guidelines based on a gun's looks, size, or price are not valid. Smaller handguns are generally less expensive, and therefore more affordable to low-income people living in high crime areas. Also, judging a gun on its barrel length or, in the case of "assault weapons," on its menacing looks, is arbitrary. Take away the choices and you take away the freedom, they say.

Sandy Chisholm's company, North American Arms (NAA), makes Saturday night specials. He argues that the guns are effective and reliable, not weapons of shoddy craftsmanship. While some gun owners may scoff at his company's palm-sized pistols and revolvers, he says their value comes from their portability. "My customers tell me that the things they carry with them every single day are their wallets, watches, and NAA mini-revolvers. That's what makes them terribly effective; they're at hand. These aren't man-stoppers because a .22 is about as small as you can get. But if someone points a gun at me—not matter what size it is—I guarantee it will change my behavior."

CREEPING REGULATION OR SENSIBLE LAWS?

Many gun companies, North American Arms included, have agreed to provide some type of gun locking device with their guns. As such, the firearms industry comes to the debate with a different perspective than the National Rifle Association and other gun rights groups. The gun manufacturers have their business interests to protect. If that means compromising on some issues—such as agreeing to make gun locks available with guns sold—that's a small price to pay to keep legislators at bay.

Critics of the gun industry say that firearms manufacturers could be doing much more to make guns safer or to render them useless in the hands of an unauthorized user. For example, Stephen P. Teret, an attorney and public health professor at Johns Hopkins University, is among those leading the push for personalized handguns. A variety of technologies exist that would accomplish the task. A microchip can be embedded in a bracelet or ring worn by the gun owner. The gun would only work if a sensor in the gun detects the radio frequency emitted by that microchip. If the gun were stolen, it would be worthless to the thief. If a despondent teenager found it, it couldn't be used in a suicide attempt. And such technology would virtually eliminate incidents in which children unintentionally shoot other children or themselves, he argued. Implementing the technology would increase gun costs by about 50 percent, he estimated.

Gun rights activists dislike such proposals. The expense could put self-protection handguns out of reach of those who need them. Furthermore, many gun owners wouldn't want the gun's utility limited to only one person. Joseph P. Tartaro, editor of *Gun Week* in Buffalo, New York, said personalizing handguns "ignores the concept that there may be more than one person in a household who has a legitimate use."

Furthermore, such proposals offend the ideology of gun rights activists. There should be no whittling away, no negotiating on what they see as the constitutionally guaranteed right to keep and bear arms.

Leave gun owners alone, they say, and go after the people who misuse them. Enforce existing laws without leniency and you'll send a message to criminals that there is a serious price to pay for breaking the laws. But in the past, there have been few disincentives for criminals. That's why the National Rifle Association's Institute for Legislative Action created CrimeStrike, its division devoted to criminal justice reform and victims' rights. Tanya Metaksa directs the division, which promotes "three strikes and you're out." "The solution is that we have to build more prisons, and hire more prosecutors and judges. That way, criminals will be given the sentences they deserve. Once caught, they'll serve time," she said.

With both sides working toward a safer community, isn't it possible to find a middle ground? When ideology plays a role, the answer often is no. To gun rights activists, giving up any freedoms is too big a compromise. Gun control supporters, they say, will always come back for more restrictions. That's how a Saturday night special ban feeds into an assault weapons ban, and an assault weapons ban leads to the prohibition of another kind of gun.

Gun control advocates say that controls that have been passed, such as the import ban on Saturday night specials, did little but serve American manufacturers' interests. They argue that unless gun controls are applied nationally, or at least regionally instead of locally, regulations can easily be skirted.

Both sides agree that the hodgepodge of laws can be confusing. As a result, many states have passed preemption laws, prohibiting municipalities from establishing their own firearms laws. Gun rights advocates say this prevents law-abiding gun owners from finding themselves in violation of the laws of a community they might just be passing through. Attorney Karen MacNutt of Boston says she has defended people caught in the web of conflicting laws. Massachusetts' Bartley-Fox Act is among the more restrictive firearms-carrying regulations in the country, imposing a mandatory jail term for anyone carrying a handgun without a license. "The bulk of those charged were out-of-state travelers who frequently didn't know the law existed or were erroneously told that their own state's license would cover them here. It doesn't. That begs the question why, when one's own police chief says the person is approved to carry a gun, should police in another jurisdiction put them in jail? People who travel interstate should be able to take with them any property which they're licensed to have," MacNutt says.

Gun control advocates say this severely limits a community's ability to solve its gun violence problems. Rural and urban areas in the same state have significantly different social environments. Good firearms policies for one area might not be good for another.

Moving firearms policies through state or national legislatures and into law is a long process. The laws that pass sometimes have little in common with the bills as introduced. And even once a law is passed, it continues to be the subject of debate as researchers and activists examine how efficient it is in deterring criminals or preventing violence.

For example, the Brady Violence Prevention Act, the law named in honor of President Reagan's press secretary, Jim Brady, passed in 1993, twelve years after the shooting took place. The law imposed a five-day waiting period before the purchase of a handgun in states where laws were less restrictive. It was designed to expire in November 1998, when a nationwide instantaneous background check system was to be ready.

On August 6, 1998, less than three months before the law was scheduled to expire, President Bill Clinton urged Congress to make the waiting period permanent. In a Rose Garden event that day, he said that while the National Instant Criminal Background Check System (NICS) will allow access to even more important records—and stop even more ineligible purchasers from buying firearms—a permanent waiting period will preserve local law enforcement's ability to defend against illegal handgun purchases.

The President also supported legislation that would require states without permit or background check systems in place to have a three-day waiting period before residents could buy a handgun. Such legislation would also require gun dealers to continue to notify local law enforcement officials of all proposed handgun purchases.

The President stated on August 6, 1998, that since the Brady Law took effect in 1994, it has prevented an estimated 242,000 felons, fugitives, and other prohibited purchasers from buying handguns. In 1997 alone, 69,000 prohibited handgun purchases were blocked as a result of Brady background checks. The President also backed expanding the Brady Law to require all firearms purchasers to undergo the NICS background check once the computerized system is in place. Brady only applied to handgun purchasers.

In addition, Clinton encouraged Congress not to undermine the Brady Law. The White House pointed to an amendment that "would prohibit the FBI from charging gun dealers a fee for background checks, even though the FBI currently charges school districts, day care providers, and many others for similar background checks. Without the resources generated by such a user fee, the FBI will either have to forego processing millions of background checks, or will have to transfer resources from other crime fighting efforts."

The same sort of extended debate followed the passage of the assault weapons law, which banned the sale of guns that have assault weapon characteristics. Since the ban became law in 1994, gun rights activists have hoped to undo it. U.S. Senator Larry Craig (R-ID) says, "Everybody has a mental image of what [assault weapons] look like, and yet the mechanism inside can be identical to a hunting rifle. While I accept society's frustrations, once you start down that slope it can get mighty slippery and overinclusive. When it comes to government and government's relationship with the citizenry, I always prefer the least amount of restriction."

Critics of the gun industry blame it for making their products increasingly dangerous. Teret said, "If you look at changes made in its products over the past 100 years, they have been to increase the lethality of guns. Guns can shoot more ammunition, and they have laser sights, and larger projectiles." Some say gun manufacturers are catering to a questionable market when they advertise fingerprint-proof gun stocks. Critics ask, who would try to hide their fingerprints on a weapon except someone with criminal intent?

As attorney general of Massachusetts, Scott Harshbarger took it upon his office to do something about unsafe handguns. Using the attorney general's consumer protection powers, he effectively banned the sale of "junk" handguns in the state. While the regulations will have to withstand a court challenge before becoming implemented, other attorneys general may well follow suit if their legality is upheld.

THE DOCTOR IS IN

Teret is among those in the public health community who have weighed in on gun control. Another public health researcher, reviled by the gun rights community and respected by the gun control advocates, is Katherine Kaufer Christoffel, a Chicago pediatrician. "My emphasis is that handguns are just too dangerous for civilian use . . . A handgun in the home turns so many ordinary situations lethal," she said. To Christoffel and others espousing this view, it doesn't make sense for people to keep handguns in a home where there are children, given what is known about the dangers they pose. "We don't do high school biology experiments with the AIDS virus. We don't sit around with nuclear reactors in our backyards. That's my focus. Handguns are just too dangerous. For long guns, I think there is a lot more room for product safety approaches," she said.

The public health researchers have harsh critics in people like Californian Don B. Kates. He contends that among public health professionals, "banning guns is a quasi-religious objective.... Their motives are for social betterment based on a quasi-religious faith that self-defense is morally wrong, and the possession of weapons for self-defense is morally wrong and they are going to prove how these evil things [guns] are socially deleterious."

Miguel Faria, who now edits a medical journal, does so in part to give voice to another view in the medical literature. He argues that most of the established medical journals do not give space to gun research that concludes that social benefits are derived from gun ownership. The fact that the bulk of the medical establishment was formally pro–gun control bothered him. As editor of the *Journal of the Medical Association of Georgia*, he characterized the literature on the subject as reminiscent of "the scholasticism of the Middle Ages when studies supported a preordained conclusion. I thought that was fraud being perpetrated on people and policy makers. I could not go along." As a result, he began printing opposing views in the journal, a move that contributed to his ouster. That didn't dissuade him, however. He soon landed the top editorial job at the newly founded *Medical Sentinel*.

Criticism from gun rights activists doesn't really bother those in the medical field researching the negative impact of gun ownership. In fact, many of them see it as a strange kind of flattery. Garen J. Wintemute seems to thrive on it. "They are a great foil. They manifest ignorance and bluster regularly. It's a pleasure to read how silly their pronouncements are. To say that doctors belong in the emergency room [not in the research arena] results from the same line of thinking that holds that women should be barefoot and pregnant."

Douglas S. Weil expects that the gun rights advocates' strategy of "broad swipes" criticisms could backfire because the public health community is responding by replicating the results and fine-tuning the studies. "We now have more work which is becoming indisputable. The studies have become more refined in response to the criticism, and the results hold up."

KIDS AND GUNS

Often, the public health debate focuses on young people. There have been alarming reports of young people bringing guns to or near schools—often with devastating results. The April 1999 shooting at a Littleton, Colorado high school is one recent and vivid example.

The Gun-Free Schools Act of 1994 calls for the one-year expulsion of any student who has brought a weapon to school. A similar sounding law, the Gun Free School Zones Act of 1990, was overturned by the U.S. Supreme Court because of what the Court saw as its shaky argument that a good education is a kind of interstate commodity. The Gun Free School Zones Act relied on the Interstate Commerce Clause of the U.S. Constitution to make it a felony to bring a gun within 1,000 feet of a school. The Interstate Commerce Clause gives congress the authority to regulate commerce among the states (article 1, section 8, clause 3). The Supreme Court ruling had no effect on the zero-tolerance policy of the Gun-Free Schools Act of 1994.

Even so, according to Handgun Control, Inc., the nation's and the states' efforts to protect children aren't particularly good. Annually, at the beginning of the school year, the organization gives letter grades to states on their legislation to protect children. The organization used five laws as criteria: whether the state allows carrying of concealed weapons and the training required for it; whether it's illegal for anyone under 18 to own a handgun; whether it's illegal to sell a handgun to someone under 18; whether adults are required to store firearms out of reach of children and if there's a penalty for leaving guns accessible; and whether the state has preemption, prohibiting localities from passing laws stricter than the state laws.

In 1998, Connecticut, Maryland, and Massachusetts received the highest grades, A−. Hawaii earned a B+, while California, Illinois, and New Jersey received a B. Delaware, Iowa, Kansas, and Nebraska made the grade of B−. Those states with Fs were Kentucky, Louisiana, Maine, Montana, and Wyoming.

However, as a nation, there are efforts under way to fight illegal gun trafficking to juveniles and youth. A demonstration program, the Youth Crime Gun Interdiction Initiative, has been expanded from its original 17 cities to a nationwide effort to identify gun trafficking patterns in communities. According to the Bureau of Alcohol, Tobacco and Firearms, the first year of the demonstration project showed the following:

- Firearms rapidly diverted from first retail sales at federally licensed gun dealers to an illegal market account for at least a quarter of the firearms that police recover from juveniles and youth.

- One out of 10 firearms recovered by police is from a juvenile (age 17 and under). When youth (ages 18–24) are included, the number changes to 4 out of 10.

- In 15 of the 17 sites, the majority or the single largest supply of the crime guns successfully traced comes from retail sources within the state. Jersey City and Washington, D.C., are the only sites where the largest single source of successfully traced crime guns is outside of their state or borders.

- Seven out of 10 crime guns recovered from adults are handguns. For juveniles and youth, the number is 8 out of 10.

- Half of all crime guns recovered by police are semiautomatic pistols, which are also the preferred weapons for juvenile and youthful offenders (60 percent).

- While thousands of different kinds of firearms are available, crime guns are concentrated among a relatively small number of makes and calibers in each city.

- Preliminary research shows that a high percentage of crime guns with obliterated serial numbers were originally purchased as part of a multiple sale by a federally licensed gun dealer and then illegally trafficked.

By being able to identify differences in adult, juvenile, and youth illegal firearms activity, law enforcement can specifically target prevention and interdiction strategies.

LAW ENFORCEMENT'S ROLE

Law enforcement professionals have a key role in shaping the gun control debate. For example, Sheriff Jay Printz of Ravalli County, Montana, found himself immersed in the gun control debate when he decided that his small department couldn't and wouldn't uphold the mandatory background check component of the Brady Law. He took his case to the U.S. Supreme Court and won.

Gun rights law enforcement officers say the rank and file of police departments across the country support a similar view. Police cannot be there to protect everyone; in fact, they generally are not even called until a crime is in progress or a dispute has reached a violent level. Well-trained, armed citizens can help keep the peace by stopping criminals or at least by protecting themselves. Law enforcement trainer Kenneth Blanchard says armed citizens also have the element of surprise on their side. Police at a crime scene could become targets; the criminal may not expect citizens to be armed. They point to polls such as those by the Southern States Police Benevolent Association, in which 65 percent of respondents agreed that "gun control laws are the least effective method of combating violent crime."

Other police say it is criminals' easy access to guns that makes law enforcement such a dangerous career. Among them is Mike Robbins, a former Chicago officer on gang detail. Robbins was shot 12 times at point-blank range—and survived. But his career as a police officer was over. He's thankful for his second chance and has devoted his career to helping other victims and working for stricter gun controls. Not knowing who is carrying guns makes everything from routine traffic stops to calls for domestic arguments a gamble, say pro-control police.

TORT REFORM

The debate over firearms has also entered the courts. When a gun malfunctions, victims often sue the gun manufacturer. But in recent years, attorneys have expanded on this concept, arguing that even handguns made as safe as they possibly can be made are still inherently dangerous. Furthermore, firearms manufacturers should know that many of their guns are being used with criminal intent.

Other consumer products can cause injury, as evidenced by accidents involving cars, baseball bats, and knives, for example. The difference is that each of these other products has some other purpose. But firearms are specifically designed to kill. And those manufacturers, distributors, and retailers who benefit from sales of guns that are particularly unsafe should pay the price for the damage caused.

Gun industry representatives and gun rights activists say this approach puts an unreasonable burden on manufacturers, distributors, and retailers, who cannot possibly know that a gun will be misused. These arguments that firearms are inherently dangerous ignore their social utility as weapons for self-protection, they say. "It's the same responsibility that auto manufacturers have regarding traffic fatalities with nondefective products. If a product is defective, then there's a liability," says attorney Richard J. Feldman, former executive director of the American Shooting Sports Council, the industry's leading trade group.

PUBLIC OPINION

The gun industry, attorneys on either side of the issue, and public health and law enforcement professionals certainly play important roles in shaping the debate. But what often drives legislation is public opinion. That's why activists on both sides of the gun control issue acknowledge the importance of grass-roots activism. Gun control is, for most people, a local issue. But once in a while, and fairly predictably after a high-profile shooting incident, the laws of a state or the entire country are called into question.

Most Americans have some stand on gun control. Often, those opinions reflect the culture in which they were raised. Rural residents, on the one hand, often believe they need to protect themselves and their neighbors because they cannot count on a small or distant police force to do it for them. In addition, target shooting and hunting are rites of passage for some rural youths.

On the other hand, urban youths rarely have that experience. Urban areas generally reflect higher crime rates and stricter gun controls. Some say those stricter laws are most unfair to the urban poor who are underserved by police and most in need of weapons of self-protection should they chose them. Others argue that the presence of guns further escalates the violence.

To determine how Americans feel about an issue, we often turn to public opinion polls. However, in gauging attitudes toward gun control, the wording and timing of opinion polls is important. Imagine a question about the ease with which handguns can be obtained being asked shortly after a paroled felon kills someone. At that time, the fear of crime and victimization would probably cause people to feel most sympathetic to those who want to select firearms as weapons of self-protection. Now imagine the same question being asked after a 14-year-old takes his father's gun and shoots five classmates and a teacher. In this case, the poll would likely reflect greater support for stricter gun controls.

In fact, polls often do reflect the uncertain relationship the country has with firearms. In October 1997, Hearst Newspapers polled more than 2,000 people nationwide. The survey found that while nearly two-thirds of Americans think the U.S. Constitution should guarantee the right to own guns, about half say handgun ownership should be controlled by the federal government.

That poll also found differing attitudes among different parts of the population. For example, African Americans were more likely to support gun control and less likely to own a handgun. And 60 percent of women favored handgun control, while 40 percent of men did.

Regional differences were also apparent. In the South, a majority said a gun in the home makes it a safer place to live, and Southerners were more likely to keep guns in several locations. In the Northeast, more than 60 percent of residents supported government control of handguns.

The Gallup Organization found that, in general, Americans do support gun laws more strict than those in effect now. The results of four polls conducted between 1990 and 1995 showed that between 62 and 78 percent of Americans would prefer stricter regulations. About one-quarter of the population felt that the laws should be kept as they are, and between 2 and 12 percent thought they should be made less strict. Very few, only 1 to 3 percent of the people polled, had no opinion on the subject.

STATISTICAL DIFFERENCES

The statistics about the annual death toll due to firearms, and to handguns in particular, probably account for much of the support for stricter gun controls. According to the National Center for Health Statistics, in 1995, for example, firearms claimed the lives of 35,957 people in the United States. Of these deaths, 18,503 were suicides, 15,835 were firearm homicides, 1,225 were unintentional shootings, and 394 were of undetermined cause. The total death toll was 21.5 percent higher than 1985 deaths attributed to firearms. Males had a firearm fatality rate (23.9 per 100,000) six times that of females, and the rate for African Americans (29.1 per 100,000) was over two times that for whites.

Much of the gun control debate centers on handguns because they account for the majority of firearm fatalities. According to the Federal Bureau of Investigation (FBI), which complies reports from law enforcement agencies nationwide, in 1995 there were 21,597 homicides in the United States—14,733 involving firearms. Handguns were used in 12,066 of these killings. From 1985 to 1995, the nation's murder rate increased 13.8 percent, the firearm murder rate increased 31.6 percent, and the handgun murder rate increased 47.9 percent.

Counting the number of fatalities each year in which a handgun was involved is relatively easy. But what do these figures mean in determining firearms policies? And do the suicide and unintentional fatality figures inflate or accurately reflect the gun violence problem?

Gun rights activists generally argue that these statistics are used to muddy the waters. They say that many of the homicide victims have violent tendencies and tempers of their own. A fight that escalates to one person shooting and killing the other reached a level of violence that could just as easily have resulted in death by some other means.

The suicides are another case altogether, they argue. Despondent people will turn to whatever means are available. Should there be no handguns, they'll use long guns. Or pills. Or drive their car at ridiculous speeds, endangering others, too. Plus, they say, using fatalities and injuries as guideposts in developing policy is flawed because it does not take into consideration the number of times handguns save lives.

But gun control activists, and many public health professionals, say that the death and injury statistics are critical to the gun control debate. They argue that the presence of a handgun, easily concealed and carried, does make it more likely that a fight will escalate to a lethal level. If those involved in the scuffle start throwing punches, there might be a broken nose, but fewer deaths or serious injuries.

And they point to studies that conclude that suicide is often an impromptu event, brought on by sudden despair. With the simple pull of a trigger, a life ends, and there isn't time for the person to reconsider or for others to save one from one's own actions. They also point out that society as a whole bears much of the financial burden for gun violence. A 1995 study showed that the average hospital cost for people admitted with firearms injuries was $52,271, while overall average hospital costs per admission were $13,794. The total annual cost of providing medical care for firearm-related injuries would have been about $4 billion that year, researchers said. Much of that is paid for either directly by public insurers or indirectly by shifting higher costs to privately insured patients.

Public health researchers are trying to refine such studies to more accurately gauge actual costs as well as lost productivity costs. However, as is true of most studies that draw conclusions on firearms-related issues, the results of these and future studies will likely be subject to debate.

There is some common ground in the gun control debate, but it

is generally only found after months or years of back-and-forth ne-
gotiation. Even then, those with strongly ideological views on either
side of the issue can probably find fault with it. With every new law
or publicized shooting, questions about this country's firearms policy
will come back into the spotlight. And the arguments for and against
the laws will be compelling and complex.

Certain checks, such as registration or licensing of guns, checking
gun purchasers' background for past criminal activity, and higher
taxes on certain guns or ammunition, have been proposed as different
methods to screen out those who might misuse a handgun. Is that
an unreasonable amount of bureaucracy for gun owners?

Ideological gun rights activists would say that any interference with
one's constitutional right is too much. Others say some limitations
are acceptable and might even contribute to a less stereotypical and
negative view of gun owners.

For the vast majority of people in this country, gun control is also
a part-time issue. We will listen and read as the essential elements
of the debate are brought forth in the national media. But for the 50
people profiled in this book, gun control is a major commitment.
They spend much of their time researching, reworking, and defending their views. Whether the reader agrees with them or not, their
commitment to the issue—and to a better society—is clear.

Madeleine (Lyn) Bates

Seed of Curiosity Took Hold with Firearms Educator, Writer

Born: 1946, Pittsburgh, PA

Education: B.S., Carnegie Mellon University; Ph.D., Harvard University

Current Positions: Manager in a high-tech company in Cambridge, MA; Vice President, AWARE; Contributing Editor, *Women & Guns*

Only when she was in her mid-30s did Lyn Bates begin to give guns serious thought. Until that point, she generally thought of guns as dangerous but had arrived at that view with little consideration. "I was too busy pursuing undergraduate and graduate degrees in computer science and computational linguistics, and getting a research career started," she said.

The moment that threw her views into question was a subtle one. "One day I learned that a colleague, a man I greatly respected, owned guns. We got into a lengthy discussion about it, and I was amazed to discover how strongly he felt about the issue. I knew he wasn't 'strange' or 'dangerous,' and I knew he was too responsible to ignore public safety for the sake of a personal whim. I couldn't reconcile what I thought I knew about guns with his attitude." That conversation didn't change her mind, but she acknowledged that there was more to the gun control issue than she had thought. A seed of curiosity was planted.

Several years later, that seed sprouted and led her to sign up for

Madeleine (Lyn) Bates. Courtesy of Lanny Photographic.

an introductory firearms course with the local police auxiliary. She informed the instructor that she didn't want to buy a gun; she just wanted to learn more about them.

"The class turned out to be fun and interesting, and so I signed up for another one. I liked the people I met at the gun club, too. They included a lawyer, a woman in real estate . . . just ordinary folk, nothing like the beer-swilling, uneducated, right wing, strange or dangerous people I had thought I might meet. By this time I was enjoying the skill of shooting, and discovered that I was rather good at it. I bought a couple of guns to use for sport, not for self-defense. And, because I've always enjoyed teaching others whatever I enjoyed learning, I started teaching shooting, too." Incidentally, she met her husband, Roger, at a shooting range.

"By this time I was participating in shooting matches of various kinds and winning occasionally. I loved the knowledge that I could shoot well under the stress of competition, particularly because I had never participated in sports in school," she said.

She also began reading more about self-defense with firearms. While she felt she was a safe and competent shooter, she wondered if she'd know how to use a gun if she were in danger. She signed up for a weeklong class at the Lethal Force Institute in New Hampshire, which provided her with new skills and answers to her questions.

While she now felt prepared to use a gun to defend her life, she also knew that most of the dangers she was likely to face in life would be situations in which it would be inappropriate to use a firearm. So she began to learn other methods of self-defense. She also met Nancy Bittle, a software engineer who was trying to launch a nonprofit organization to teach women about effective self-defense options. Bittle's own interest in firearms was sparked while she was recovering from an attack. Bates was looking for a place to teach all that she had learned. "We formed a team of dedicated, highly trained volunteers that have been the heart and soul of AWARE" (Arming Women Against Rape and Endangerment).

The organization offers a series of classes, including basic personal safety classes, introduction to firearms, basic pistol classes, and self-protection with firearms. It also offers a weapon retention class, which teaches gun owners how to prevent someone from taking their gun. "It doesn't tend to happen in real life, but it's something people are concerned about," Bates said. Women who take the classes receive training in different environments, using different skills—many of which are adapted from law enforcement. "We take the information, material and skill sets taught to police and adapt them as appropriate to civilians."

That teaching has its rewards. Her proudest moment came when one of the AWARE students came to them for help in obtaining a carry permit because her ex-husband was threatening her. "She took all the AWARE firearms courses, including Personal Protection with Firearms. When she purchased a Smith & Wesson 3913 LadySmith 9mm semiautomatic, I went to the range with her to use it for the first time. A few months later, she called to say 'You guys saved my life!' Her ex-husband had tried to force her car off the road. She had reached for her gun, and, as so often happens, the mere sight of it caused him to break off the attack and drive away," Bates said.

"That's what self-defense is all about. Being able to stay alive and unhurt through a situation where someone else wants you dead or injured. You have to be able to do it yourself, because attackers are smart enough to choose a time and place when you are alone. Firearms, properly used, give women a tremendous survival advantage in situations where nothing else will work reliably."

Because Bates has never had to defend her own life with a firearm, she wanted to personally understand the dynamics of such threatening encounters. "To that end, I started competing in tactical shooting matches, which involve very realistic, very stressful, very dynamic situations. The American Tactical Shooting Association (ATSA) sponsors an annual test of defensive, tactical firearms skills called the National Tactical Invitational—it is one of the hardest things I've ever done with a gun, but one of the most worthwhile," she said. In 1997 she was awarded the Tactical Advocate Award, given by the association to recognize achievements in teaching, writing, or educating people in the safe and effective use of firearms for self-protection.

While she sympathizes with people whose lives have been affected by gun violence or carelessness, she stressed that "it is important that social policies be thought out carefully, not enacted in hasty response to one individual's situation." She said gun control supporters take this kind of unbalanced approach to the issue. "They have lots of stories and statistics about how bad or dangerous guns can be, but they never, ever, acknowledge that guns in private hands often serve good purposes in our society, and they never, ever, want to look closely at both the good uses of guns and the bad uses of guns as part of the process of determining social policies."

That befuddles Bates because she doesn't see firearms as inherently dangerous. "People who have never been around guns much tend to think that a gun is something like a bomb—a big, dangerous thing that might go off at any moment, injuring or killing anyone around. But to me, a gun is like a fire extinguisher. It is a piece of emergency equipment to use in extremely dangerous situations. It doesn't take the place of professionals, but you can use it to keep yourself, or your family, alive until the professionals can get there to take over.

"I have a fire extinguisher in my house. That doesn't mean that I am unusually terrified of fire, nor does it mean that I eagerly expect to have a fire there. I also have guns in my house. That doesn't mean that I am excessively afraid of criminals, nor does it mean that I am looking for an opportunity to shoot someone. In both cases, it simply means that I am more prepared to deal with emergencies than the average person is."

A critical part of that preparation is safely storing firearms. "Responsible gun owners lock up their guns when not under their direct control, but many people don't realize that there are safe, effective ways of securing a defensive firearm (that is, one that is loaded) so that it can be accessed by the owner in seconds even when under stress, but not by young children. One of the ways of doing this is using a lock box, which is a very small safe with a pushbutton lock."

In 1993, when these boxes were relatively new, Bates reviewed them for an article in *Women & Guns*, a monthly publication for which she is a contributing editor. In "Keeping the Piece," she explained that she put some candy in the safes she was evaluating, and gave three young boys the opportunity to try to figure out the combination. "Then I let them use ordinary household tools (a screwdriver, for example) to try to break into the boxes, and reported on the results. It turned out to be the most popular article ever published in that magazine, and it won a prize from the Family Safety Products, Inc. writing contest to educate the pubic to the need and means of improving firearm safety in the home. One of the manufacturers wrote me that a subsequent version of their box included design improvements that were inspired by that article. The current generation of lock boxes is very good, and should be considered by every parent who wants to keep kids and a defensive gun in the same house."

ADDITIONAL READINGS

AWARE web site: http://www.aware.org

Bates, Lyn. "Concealed Carry: Purse and Fannypack Roundup." *Women & Guns*, February 1996.

———. "Critical Incident Reactions—What if I Freeze?" *Women & Guns*, May 1997.

———. "Gun Locks and Lock Boxes: What Works? What Doesn't?" *Women & Guns*, March–April 1998.

———. "Guns in Purses—Yes or No?" *Women & Guns*, June 1997.

———. "How to Get Some Courage." *Women & Guns*, July 1996.

———. "Inexpensive Targets You Can Make." *Women & Guns*, July 1996.

———. "Keeping the Piece." *Women & Guns*, June 1993.

————. "Martial Arts or Guns? Why Not Both?" *The Fisted Rose* (American Women's Self Defense Association Newsletter), January 1998.

————. "The National Tactical Test: Learning to Stay Alive." *Women & Guns*, September 1996.

————. "A Series of Moral Problems: The 1997 National Tactical Invitational." *Women & Guns*, September 1997.

————. "The 10 Dumbest Things People Say about Using Guns for Self-Defense." *Women & Guns*, March–April 1998.

————. "What Do Cops Know?" *Women & Guns*, May 1997.

————. "What Would You Do if . . . ?" *Women & Guns*, February 1996.

————. "Where Do You Aim?" *Women & Guns*, October 1996.

————. "Why Learn about Guns, if You Aren't Sure You Could Kill Someone?" *Women & Guns*, January 1996.

Eck, Beth M. "Safety Measures." *Runner's World*, February 1998.

May-Hayes, Gila. *Effective Defense*. Seattle: Firearms Academy of Seattle, 1994.

McCaughey, Martha. *Real Knockouts: The Physical Feminism of Women's Self-Defense*. New York: New York University Press, 1998.

Quigley, Paxton. *Not an Easy Target*. New York: Simon & Schuster, 1995.

Randall, Lee. "Street Smarts." *FIT Magazine*, May/June 1996.

Michael K. Beard

30 Years of Lobbying for Gun Control

Born: 1941, Huntington, WV

Education: American University, School of International Service

Current Position: President, Coalition to Stop Gun Violence

Michael K. Beard jokingly calls himself "the old man of gun control." Indeed, he has been a formal player on the stage longer than anyone else on this side of the issue.

"I got started in the issue when Robert Kennedy was killed. I had worked as a volunteer in Senator John Kennedy's office and in his campaign when he ran for president and had done some volunteer work for the Robert Kennedy campaign," he said. When Robert Ken-

Michael K. Beard.

nedy was shot in 1968, Beard was working for the United Methodist Church, which decided to start a religious coalition for gun control. Beard signed on as a staff member. Astronaut (later Senator) John Glenn was the first chairman.

"We lobbied for the 1968 Gun Control Act. It's odd, but I had never really thought of gun control as an issue. I grew up in southern Ohio. All my family were hunters. But when I started doing the research, I couldn't believe the statistics," Beard said.

It soon became apparent to Beard that the Gun Control Act of 1968 "was a bad bill. It was an important first step, but we soon came to realize it was a bill to protect America's gun manufacturers. By banning the importation of Saturday night specials [but allowing the parts to be imported and assembled in the United States] we bolstered the industry."

In 1974 Beard was working for Washington, D.C.'s nonvoting representative to Congress, Walter E. Fauntroy. "Fauntroy was a Baptist minister and he came into the office one day and said, 'I'm tired of handgun funerals. I want to ban handguns.' He asked me to help him write the speech. It was alien to my background, but he gave me three months to study it. Again, I was amazed by the statistics. I never knew how bad the problem was, especially here in D.C."

Fauntroy introduced the bill in 1974, but quickly found there was no one to lobby on its behalf. So Beard went back to the United Methodist Church, which first created an ad hoc committee, and then a formal organization, to lobby on behalf of Fauntroy's bill to ban the future manufacture, sale, and private possession of handguns. Beard, who had studied to be a diplomat, was hired as executive director of the National Coalition to Ban Handguns. The organization later changed its name to the Coalition to Stop Gun Violence.

Twenty-five years later, Beard revels in the political acceptance of those early views. "The thing I remember most about the era was being afraid to tell people what I did. We were like door to door salesmen. I would go into some town and personally visit every radio and TV station asking if they would like to have someone on the show to talk about banning handguns. We had to go begging," he said.

Even then, in the midst of doing "those horrible and unfriendly radio shows," Beard felt like he was getting in on the ground floor of something big. "This was the beginning of a social change. We weren't talking about just a political change, and social changes take a long time. For a long time, I had to keep repeating, 'Folks, there's a problem here. You may not know it, but there's a big problem.'"

On airplanes, he'd tell strangers he lobbied on behalf of the Methodist Church, simply to avoid getting into arguments. "Now I wear a lapel pin with our logo and I proudly tell people what I do," he said.

But the early days were a struggle. Gun control opponents "had a fit. They encouraged senators to challenge our nonprofit status; others challenged our mail permits. Finally, we severed our formal affiliation with the United Methodist Church because of the pressure," he said. In early direct mail campaigns, opponents sent in bricks and telephone books—for which the coalition would have to pay postage. "They tried to bankrupt us. And they tried to boycott our member organizations. We hadn't expected that. Perhaps we should have, but we were church folks."

The coalition now has 47 member organizations—national religious, medical, educational, and civic organizations. "The growth now is with the former peace groups, as gun control is becoming more of an international issue."

Over the years, the debate has changed, too, said Beard. He believes the most significant change came when public health professionals turned to the issue. "Violence is a virus that weakens the central structures that bind our society together."

Some polls also show that the number of people owning guns has dropped. "Those factors have contributed to shift the debate. It's no longer 'Can we ban handguns?' It's 'What guns are we going to ban?'"

That is not to say gun control is a foregone conclusion, Beard emphasized. "The National Rifle Association has had 120 years of an uninterrupted bully pulpit. But after 25 years of organized opposition [Handgun Control, Inc. (HCI) came into being around the same time as the Coalition], they're verging on the edge of being another American Tobacco Institute. They're not down and out, but they don't have the political or public relations clout they used to have."

Beard credited a variety of factors, such as Jim and Sarah Brady's influence on public opinion as well as their example to other victims. "Now other victims are staying with the cause and organizing."

More research on gun violence is also important. "Solid academic research is backing up what we've been saying all along. Intervention can make a difference. There's also a differentiation of guns. It's not enough to say, 'A gun was used.' We want to know what kind of guns. That's one of the contributions of the Clinton administration," said Beard, referring to the 1994 assault weapons ban which prohibited the sale of guns with certain characteristics.

Beard sees the focus of gun control shifting to prevention and battles on local levels. As such, the Coalition to Stop Gun Violence is concentrating more on grass-roots organizing and promoting community activism. "We're moving away from the legislation, leaving that more to HCI," he said.

"The principle of politics is you fight at the smallest level at which you can win. In gun control, the smallest level used to be the U.S. Congress because winning on a local or state level was out of the question. But now we're fighting at the city council level and winning."

After nearly 30 years of involvement with gun control, Beard doesn't know how much longer he's up for the fight. "I would like to be in this for the rest of my career, but I struggle because I think it might be a younger person's fight."

He maintains his enthusiasm by spending his off time on completely different projects. A member of the Screen Actors Guild and the American Federation of Radio and Television Artists, Beard is often called on to be an extra for movies and television shows. He's played a detective on the TV show *Homicide* and on *America's Most Wanted*. He has appeared in about 30 movies which were filmed in Washington, D.C. That sideline developed when he was a student in D.C. and loved opera, but couldn't afford tickets to Kennedy Center performances. He signed on as an extra and has appeared in more than two dozen operas or ballets. "No singing parts, though. I sang, once, and the director stopped the rehearsal, noting dissonance in the tenor section."

Even in silence, Beard enjoys acting. "What's important to me is that a movie or television project has a beginning, middle, and end. Even after all these years in gun control, I feel like I'm stuck in the middle. There is no end in sight. Acting provides me a sense of accomplishment of a project completed."

ADDITIONAL READINGS

Coalition to Stop Gun Violence web site: http://www.gunfree.org

Coalition to Stop Gun Violence. *NRA Report: Overrated: The NRA and the 1994 Elections.* Washington, D.C.: Coalition to Stop Gun Violence, 1995.

Coalition to Stop Gun Violence and Educational Fund to End Handgun Violence. *The Unspoken Tragedy: Firearm Suicide in the United States.* Washington, D.C.: Coalition to Stop Gun Violence and Educational Fund to End Handgun Violence, 1995.

Educational Fund to End Handgun Violence. *Kids and Guns: A National Disgrace.* Washington, D.C.: Educational Fund to End Handgun Violence, 1993.

Webster, Daniel W., Jon S. Vernick, Jens Ludwig, and Kathleen J. Lester. "Flawed Gun Policy Research Could Endanger Public Safety." *American Journal of Public Health* 87, no. 6 (June 1997).

Carl C. Bell

Psychiatrist Examines Black-on-Black Homicide

Born: 1947, Chicago, IL

Education: B.S., University of Illinois; M.D., Meharry Medical School, Nashville, TN

Current Positions: President, CEO, Community Mental Health Council, Chicago; Professor of Psychiatry and Public Health, University of Illinois at Chicago

---

Back in medical school, Carl C. Bell was taught that a good doctor will carefully treat the one patient who comes in with a rat bite. But when 50 children come in with rat bites, it's time to go after the rats.

In his career as a psychiatrist, he has found that "the rat is violence. The rat is guns." His particular interest is in black-on-black homicide and the interpersonal violence that causes the homicide rate of young African Americans to be so much higher than that of their white counterparts. "Looking at vital statistics in public health classes in medical school in 1969, I saw that the homicide rate for African Americans was six to twelve times higher than for whites," he said. That statistic stuck in his mind for years.

The issue of black-on-black homicide and violence was just beginning to emerge. He found his own niche in the area in 1976 when a four-year-old girl was assigned to his care. She had seen her mother stabbed to death by a boyfriend. "I went to the books to find out what to do and there was nothing there. I had to do child play therapy 101," he said. With her, the strategies weren't successful. The child never talked about the incident.

But this little girl wasn't alone. A few years later, after Bell had joined the Community Mental Health Council, he had seen many children like her who had witnessed violence. The council began researching how many children were exposed to violence—the real

Carl C. Bell. Courtesy of Better Image Studio.

stuff, not television violence. "We did a survey of 536 kids, and one-fourth had seen someone shot or stabbed," he said.

Astounded by the number, the council started a victims' service program to try to help victims of violence cope with the stress and trauma of the event and the criminal justice system. Through that program, they asked all of their patients if they had witnessed violence. Many had.

By this time, Bell's views about violence had changed. "There are different kinds of violence," he said. There's the psychopathic predator and there's violence that stems from interpersonal altercations. As a consultant for Chicago's public defender's office, Bell had been reviewing many murder cases. "It became clear to me that the majority of murders were in the interpersonal altercation category. These were not serial killers, not KKK murders. They were husbands and wives, boyfriends and girlfriends. Until then, I had a stereotypical impression that most murderers were predatory."

And murders are just the tip of the iceberg when it comes to violence, Bell said. He recalls the Chicago chief of police telling him that for the 950 murders that took place in the city one year, there were about 16,000 shootings or stabbings that did not result in death. Many of the shootings and stabbings were concentrated in poor African American and Latino communities, the areas served by the Community Mental Health Council's victim program.

Bell found others who were working to bring black-on-black violence to the forefront of the public policy agenda. The National Institute of Mental Health began funding some studies on the issue. Bell met Deborah Prothrow-Stith, a physician who was working on a violence prevention program at Harvard University, at a National Institute of Mental Health conference in 1984.

That same year, he was elected chairman of the National Medical Association's Section on Psychiatry. In 1986 he and Prothrow-Stith delivered the plenary session on homicide. "It hit the *New York Times'* front page. That gave me some credibility, and I started doing more studies on children. I looked at why people carry guns. It was community-based research, not necessarily scientifically controlled. So when others started doing similar studies, in a better developed format, they found the same results," he said. One of the results was that youthful exposure to violence was a serious problem and a factor in violent behavior later in life.

So how can the cycle be broken? There's no easy answer, said Bell. "One of the primary prevention solutions is to allow mothers more time at home with their children. The maternity leave in Russia is three years. Here, it's two months, if the mother is lucky, before she has to go back to work. In Russia, they understand that children need bonding time, nurturing time. We have to make an investment in our children."

Another way is to make it more difficult to obtain guns. "It doesn't make sense to me that someone can walk into a store with a credit card and walk out with just about any kind of gun they want," he said. "That's just dumb."

However, Bell recognizes the paradox of guns in the communities he serves. In studying why people carry guns, he found that many said they had been victimized before. So they're carrying guns to protect themselves because they believe police cannot or will not. "In those situations, you have to reestablish the protective shield. The vast majority of violent crimes occur after 6 P.M. The vast majority of police work from 9 to 5." Merging peak police coverage with peak hours of crime makes sense, he said. "You also have to talk to people about their fears and concerns and debrief their exposure to violence. If the incident happened at home, dogs or burglar alarms are better [than guns]."

It's not that Bell is opposed to people defending themselves. "If I'm working in the emergency room and a patient violently attacks me, I'd hit him. I don't want to die." But in most cases, conflict resolution is by far the better option.

Having said that, however, Bell acknowledges that "there are certain types of violence where conflict resolution isn't going to work. If the perpetrator is psychopathic and predatory, you're not going to be able to reason with him. I wish it were possible for us to be able to predict who the predators will be and when they'll come after us with guns. If we could predict that with 98 percent accuracy, I'd say get a gun and shoot back. But the problem is you can't predict those things because it's uncommon, despite what the gun rights people say," he said.

And that brings him to the crux of the gun control debate. Most violence is not predatory violence; it escalates from interpersonal altercations. "My experience is that when there are fights and violence, the majority is a result of interpersonal altercations. To put a gun into that equation is a serious mistake," he said. "So we have to determine what the risks and benefits are for guns in predatory violence versus interpersonal altercation violence. For me, for now, we could get higher leverage in terms of people getting hurt if guns were harder to access. There is more violence from interpersonal altercations."

"Having a gun around when someone else comes after me might be wonderful, but it's a higher risk when I'm with my wife. And because I spend more time with my wife, I won't take that risk."

It's not that Bell has any intention of harming his wife, but bringing a gun into any situation where there is a possibility of interpersonal altercation changes the dynamics. He knows of homicide detectives who don't bring their handguns home because they've investigated too many domestic homicides. People who bring guns into the home for self-defense don't do so with the intention of harming a member of the family, "but I worry about children, about suicide, about tempers flaring," he said.

As a physician, Bell knows he comes at the debate from a different perspective than criminologists do. "For those in criminal justice, their experiences center around criminals and psychopaths with guns. We are working with kids who have seen their daddies kill their mommies, in part because the gun was there. We're saying you have to get the gun out of the equation."

Getting people from different backgrounds and perspectives to talk about the issue is difficult, he said. That's what makes the gun control debate so divisive. "There are a lot of levels of gun control, ranging from background checks to prohibitions on sales across state lines to assault weapons bans to gun licensing. Even gun rights supporters wouldn't disagree with all of them, but when politics is involved, you don't give up any points. Even if they know in their hearts that it's not a good idea for a felon to be able to get a gun, they'll fight against a background check."

People on each side of the issue produce interesting and convincing evidence that leaves Bell "totally confused. All I know is it should be hard as hell for a kid, a career criminal or someone who has got a bad temper and beats his wife on regular occasions to be able to get a gun," he said.

ADDITIONAL READINGS

Bell, C. C. "Black-on-Black Homicide: The Implications for Black Community Mental Health." In *Handbook of Mental Health and Mental Illness among Black Americans*. Ed. Dorothy S. Ruiz. Westport, Conn.: Greenwood Press, 1990.

———. "Community Violence: Causes, Prevention and Intervention." *Journal of the National Medical Association* 89, no. 10 (October 1997).

———. *Getting Rid of Rats: Reflections of a Community Psychiatrist*. Chicago: Third World Press, forthcoming.

———. "A Physician's Responsibility in Preventing Violence" (editoral). *New Physician* 35, no. 7 (October 1986).

———. "Preventive Strategies for Dealing with Violence among Blacks." *Community Mental Health Journal* 23, no. 3 (Fall 1987): pp. 217–18.

———. "The Psychiatric Implications of Violence in the African-American Community." *Psychiatric Times*, May 1992.

———. "Stress-Related Disorders in African-American Children." *Journal of the National Medical Association* 89, no. 5 (May 1997).

Holinger, Paul C., Daniel Offer, James T. Barter, and Carl C. Bell. *Suicide and Homicide among Adolescents*. New York: Guilford Press, 1994.

Jenkins, E. J., and C. C. Bell. "Adolescent Violence: Can It Be Curbed?" *Adolescent Medicine: State of the Art Reviews* 3, no. 1 (February 1992).

———. "Exposure and Response to Community Violence among Children and Adolescents." In *Children in a Violent Society*. Ed. Joy D. Osofsky. New York: Guilford Press, 1997.

Kenneth V. F. Blanchard

Taking Police Training to the African American Community

Born: 1962, Suffolk, VA

Education: Federal Law Enforcement Training Center, Glynco, GA; attending University of Maryland

Current Positions: Federal Law Enforcement Instructor; Chief Executive Officer, African American Arms and Instruction; Board Member, Law Enforcement Alliance of America

Most people in this country look at police officers as protectors, helpers. But some see them as targets. Kenneth V. F. Blanchard's efforts as a law enforcement instructor go to make sure police are prepared for whatever comes their way.

Sometimes, all the preparation in the world isn't enough. That was evident on July 24, 1998, when Russell Eugene Weston, Jr., was accused of killing two U.S. Capitol police in a shootout at the Capitol in Washington, D.C.

The two officers were hailed as heroes, and their efforts were credited for saving the lives of many others. Blanchard said, "Unfortunately, there's nothing that Officers Jacob Chestnut or John Gibson could have done differently. You're always slower reacting. No matter how quickly they reacted and what they did, they were still reacting

Kenneth V. F. Blanchard. Courtesy of Jason Miccolo Johnson.

to a threat. That's a no-win situation and the best one can do in that situation is try to save your comrades."

Blanchard said in theory, a qualified armed civilian could have made a faster and more effective counterattack. "Civilians have a luxury we officers don't have and that's the element of surprise. If Weston had walked into the Capitol, and an armed civilian with the right training and in the right position had seen him pull out the gun and shoot Officer Chestnut, there's a good chance the gunman would never have gotten off another shot. The armed civilian can chose a level of involvement. He can decide to shoot, or, if he feels the situation isn't right, he can slide back out the door. That's an advantage civilians have that law enforcement officers don't."

Blanchard was busy after the Capitol shooting. His specialty, VIP protection, focuses on awareness, what he calls "the mental side of policing." Some of that includes spotting potential terrorists, but it also covers customer service attitudes. Many officers, himself included, come from military backgrounds. The kind of discipline demanded in the military doesn't generally translate well into civilian workplaces. "I was a Marine for five years, so I brought all those habits with me and I quickly learned they didn't work with civilians," he said, laughing.

Federal law enforcement trainers can work with officers from 100 different agencies. Blanchard has seen that smaller departments, strapped for cash and personnel, sometimes don't have the time or money to put into firearms training. Even he does more shooting range work on his own than in the course of duty.

To him, that supports the view that civilians can often be in a better situation than police in a public shooting. They have the element of surprise, and they're often well trained.

But civilians lack the network that law enforcement provides. And without that, they are at a disadvantage. "Law enforcement officers who are pro–gun-control are kind of hypocritical. They carry a radio with them and if they say, 'Officer needs assistance,' they get it. A civilian doesn't get that kind of response. That's why pro-gun officers are so sympathetic to armed civilians," he said.

That's how Blanchard felt, and in the early 1990s, he decided to start a small business to train "ma and pa gun owner." A newcomer to the field, he decided to go to a National Rifle Association (NRA) meeting in his neighborhood. "I had no clue what the NRA was about. I was half expecting to see a bunch of Gomers in plaid shirts, so I dressed down for the occasion, wearing jeans and cowboy boots. I was completely underdressed. Everyone there had on a business suit," he said, laughing at the recollection.

He left that meeting with "an education in politics and gun culture. I bombarded them with questions from a lifetime," he said. They patiently answered them all, and gave him the encouragement he needed to start African American Arms and Instruction.

Through his firearms training and safety instruction at African American Arms and Instruction, Blanchard has to contend with the different levels and backgrounds at play in the African American community. "We have a culture that has evolved from institutionalized slavery, and the negatives from that remain with many people. There was a time that African Americans could be put to death for even having a gun, and that mentality is ingrained with many of the grandparents. On the other end, we have veterans—who learned how to respect and use guns, and now have to quietly oppose their wives to continue with that. And there's a new group of young kids with respect for nearly nothing. To them, power looks like a stolen pistol."

What has happened is that in areas with greater restrictions on firearms, would-be legitimate gun owners are driven underground. "That means that guns that are stolen from homes might never be reported as stolen, because they weren't legal. If there were fewer restrictions, people would be more likely to report stolen guns," he said. In other words, the more hoops set up for gun owners to jump through, the less likely people are to comply.

In August 1998, Blanchard merged his company, African American Arms and Instruction, with that of a former D.C. paramedic lieutenant, Ricardo A. Royal, founder of Royal Marksmanship Instruction. The new business is called Best Shot Professional Training and Consulting Group. Blanchard continues to represent African American Arms in speaking engagements and testimony. The new company will market its training services to businesses, security professional, and new gun owners.

Speaking out for gun rights at churches and community gatherings raised Blanchard's profile. That's how he was tapped as a board member for the Law Enforcement Alliance of America (LEAA), which calls itself the nation's largest coalition of law enforcement professionals, crime victims, and citizens, with 65,000 members and supporters.

The LEAA supports a federal bill that would allow qualified current and retired law enforcement officers in good standing to carry concealed weapons anywhere in the country, exempt from state concealed carry prohibitions. "A cop may go off the clock at the end of his shift, but he never truly goes off duty. He always responds to criminal behavior whether he's wearing a badge or not," said James J. Fotis, executive director of the LEAA, in a press release posted on the organization's web site. "It is outrageous to leave our law enforcement officers and their families vulnerable to the attacks of violent and vindictive criminals whom they have previously arrested, and equally outrageous . . . to deny the American people the potentially life-saving assistance of off-duty and retired officers."

In terms of a national policy, the Law Enforcement Alliance of America would like to see a "concealed carry system that is fair and equitable. People with mental and criminal histories should be excluded from gun ownership, and we could leave it at that. America is the greatest country in the world and our freedom is what distinguishes us from the rest of the world," Blanchard said.

ADDITIONAL READINGS

Law Enforcement Alliance of America web site: http://www.leaa.org
National Rifle Association. "10 Myths of Gun Control." Washington, D.C:
    National Rifle Association, 1994.

James and Sarah Brady

Well-Known Victims Fight Back

James Scott Brady

Born: 1940, Centralia, IL

Education: B.S., University of Illinois

Current Positions: Member, Board of Trustees, Center to Prevent
    Handgun Violence. Former Press Secretary to President Ronald Reagan

Sarah Kemp Brady

Born: 1942, Kirksville, MO

Education: B.A., College of William and Mary

Current Position: Chair, Handgun Control, Inc., and Center to
    Prevent Handgun Violence

Theirs is perhaps the best known story in the gun control debate. Jim Brady, the affable press secretary to President Ronald Reagan, was shot in the head during an assassination attempt on the President in 1981. Sarah Brady stepped into the glare of the spotlight to cam-

Sarah Brady. Courtesy of Murray Bognovitz.

paign for stricter access to handguns. One of the results: the Brady Law, the enactment of a national five-day waiting period and background check before an individual can buy a handgun.

But that was far from the role Sarah Brady imagined for herself in early 1981. The two had been married about eight years and had a two-year-old son, Scott. Jim Brady had just been appointed to his dream assignment as press secretary to the President. Known as "the Bear," he was earning the respect of the Washington press corps for his honesty and sense of humor in a demanding job.

On March 31, 1981, Jim Brady accompanied the President to an event at the Washington Hilton Hotel. After the event, surrounded by Secret Service agents and police officers on security detail, Jim approached the crowd of reporters standing behind a roped-off area. He was hit by the first of six bullets fired by John W. Hinckley, Jr., a disturbed 25-year-old who apparently thought assassinating the President would gain him the respect and love of actress Jodie Foster.

Hinckley's bullets did their damage. The President was hit in the ribs and seriously injured by a bullet that ricocheted off the car; Washington, D.C., police officer Thomas Delahanty and Secret Service agent Timothy J. McCarthy were also seriously wounded. But Brady suffered the most serious life-threatening injury. Before the afternoon was over, word spread that Brady had died.

The quick actions of the trauma team at George Washington Hospital are detailed in a book by Mollie Dickinson, *Thumbs Up: The Life and Courageous Comeback of White House Press Secretary Jim Brady*. She also tells about his repeated surgeries, the long road to recovery, "the physical terrorists," as Brady called the physical therapists who worked him through painful exercises, and the setbacks along the way.

For Sarah Brady, her interest in gun control preceded the shooting. The daughter of an FBI agent, she learned respect for guns early on. "I never saw my father's service revolver. He always had locked it up as soon as he came home," she said.

She also worked on the issue between 1970 and 1972, when she was an administrative aide in the office of U.S. Representative Mike McKevitt (R-CO), a former district attorney from Denver. "He was extremely interested in the Saturday night special ban. Part of the 1968 Gun Control Act banned the importation of Saturday night specials, but it failed to ban the importation of the parts. So the parts could be shipped into the U.S. and assembled and sold here. It was one of those guns that Hinckley used to shoot Jim," she said.

She also had firsthand knowledge of the way handguns can be used to devastating end, even when purchased for good. A co-worker in McKevitt's office was shot and killed with her own handgun by her boyfriend. The irony is that the boyfriend bought her the gun for self-protection, Brady said.

Even after her husband's shooting, Sarah Brady didn't immediately add her voice to the cry for handgun control. In the fall of 1982, she was contacted by Peter Hannaford, a longtime associate of President Reagan. "He wanted to know if I was interested in doing a political spot for Proposition 15 [requiring registration of existing handguns and a freeze on the sale of new handguns] in California. I really wanted to do it, but I was a little dubious because Jim still worked for President Reagan and California was his home state. I wasn't a Californian, so I finally decided not to. I felt bad that I didn't."

In the summer of 1984, she and her son were visiting friends in Centralia, Illinois, when five-year-old Scott picked up what looked like a toy gun lying on the seat in a friend's truck. It was a loaded Saturday night special. "I was so angry," she said.

That anger carried over to the next day, when back in Virginia she was watching television and saw a news report that the National Rifle Association was trying to repeal aspects of the Gun Control Act of 1968 by passing the McClure-Volkmer bill or the Firearm Owners' Protection Act.

"I was doing the dinner dishes and when I heard that, I got livid. It was 7:30 at night and I picked up the phone and called the NRA office. Who knows who answered the phone," she said, laughing. "I said, 'I'm Sarah Brady and you may not know who I am, but I am furious at what you're doing and I'm going to make it my business to put you out of business.' The next day, I called Handgun Control, Inc., and asked how I could help."

And help she did. Her testimony before Congress and her lobbying, especially with Republicans, contributed to the passage of the Brady Law. "The day the Brady Law was signed was an absolutely wonderful day. But probably the best day of all was the first time the bill passed Congress, three years before it was signed into law. President George Bush didn't sign it, and that was a huge disappointment, but we had gotten it that far and at that point, we knew it would happen. Attitudes had begun to change; Congress was listening."

Along the way, Jim Brady joined his wife in his public espousal of stricter handgun control laws. Just before a book party in Baltimore for Mollie Dickinson's biography of Jim, a reporter asked him what he thought of Maryland's newly passed Saturday night special ban. "Jim gave them a thumbs up sign and said, 'Thumbs up for Maryland.' It wasn't planned," she said. Now Jim Brady serves as a member of the board of trustees of the Center to Prevent Handgun Violence. "Jim's been traveling all the time. He does more than I do now. It's great for the movement and great for him, too, because he loves it. It's doing the kinds of things he did before he was hurt."

State and federal legislators have heard often from Sarah and Jim Brady. "Jim and I together were able to bring the whole issue to the attention of the American people," she said, quickly adding that it takes the effort of many people to pass such legislation. "We defeated almost all of McClure-Volkmer, we got a ban on machine guns, plastic guns [not toys], cop-killer bullets, and many significant acts in state legislatures."

Brady credits those on both sides of the political aisle. She praises President Bill Clinton, a Democrat, for his work on seeing the Brady Law become a reality. In fact, the Bradys addressed the crowd at the 1996 Democratic National Convention and were greeted with a thunderous standing ovation. But she also credits Jim Brady's former boss, President Ronald Reagan, a Republican. Both Bradys are lifelong Republicans and it bothers her that the issue is sometimes seen as a political one. "It shouldn't be Republican versus Democratic. We've worked hard to make it as nonpartisan as we can. An awful lot of wonderful Republicans, like Ronald Reagan and Jim, helped ensure the passage of the Brady Law," she said.

In retrospect, she wishes she had lobbied President Reagan for stricter handgun controls. "But at the time, I hesitated. I thought it would be taking advantage of Jim's position. I was new to the movement and decided to make my case to the public." But then she saw a transcript of a press conference President Reagan held in Canada, during which he said he was very much in favor of background checks and waiting periods.

"It was toward the end of his tenure, but I wrote him a note right away. And he called me back that night and told me of his support. He noted how the NRA always claimed him as a member, but he said the organization gave him the membership and that he had never joined. Later, when the Brady bill was on the floor [being debated in Congress], he came out publicly and made a speech about it. He did the same for the assault weapons ban, so he provided a cover for a lot of Republicans."

Brady is pleased with the effect of the law that carries her husband's name. "It's done exactly what it's supposed to do—stop the over the counter sales. It was never meant to be a panacea," she said.

As such, "there is so much more to be done," she added. "We need to stop secondary sales. We need to make sure there is no access to weapons for children or fugitives or felons. We need to concentrate on child safety issues. We need to begin to treat guns as any other consumer product. We should pursue the idea of personalized guns, which can only be fired by a designated owner of the handgun, and make it mandatory, at the very least, that all guns have a safety and load indicators" [so that a user can know for certain if there are bullets in the gun].

Her outspoken comments haven't curried her any favor with the National Rifle Association, but she doesn't care. "I don't care what they think of me, but I'd be very upset if people I respected highly didn't like me," she said, laughing. She was quick to add that many NRA members supported Brady, pointing out that her beef is with the national board of the organization. "Overall, it has been our goal to make this a national debate that is not going to go away."

She finds strength from her own experience and from that of others. "I can't play Pollyanna. Jim's been through numerous dangerous and life-threatening situations as a result of the injury. For our son, growing up, this was extremely difficult. But there are hundreds of thousands of others that are in the same boat we're in. We may be more visible, but we're not the only ones. The more I travel and meet victims and families of victims, the more drive I have to keep working at it."

ADDITIONAL READINGS

Brady, Sarah. ". . . And the Case Against Them . . . The Head of Handgun Control Says Weapons Are Killing the Future." *Time*, January 29, 1990.

Center to Prevent Handgun Violence. "Latest Crime Statistics Refute the Gun Lobby: More Guns Do Not Make Us Safer" (press release). Center to Prevent Handgun Violence, January 18, 1999.

Dickinson, Mollie. *Thumbs Up: The Life and Courageous Comeback of White House Press Secretary Jim Brady.* New York: William Morrow, 1987.

Handgun Control, Inc., web site: http://www.handguncontrol.org

Deane Calhoun

Training Young People to Get Involved in Violence Prevention

Born: 1944, Swarthmore, PA

Education: College of Wooster (OH); University of Wisconsin (M.A., Urban Affairs)

Current Position: Executive Director of Youth ALIVE!

Well-publicized shootings often spur people into action. But for many people, that action is short-lived. Deane Calhoun saw that theory play out in Oakland, California, in the mid-1980s. Following two shootings in junior high schools, a commission was set up to look at gun issues in the city. Calhoun remembers that 75 people attended the first meeting. A few meetings later, only a handful of people remained.

Around the same time, Calhoun attended a meeting at which a paraplegic patient—a young gunshot victim—spoke. He went around to Detroit schools, talking about what can happen to kids who get mixed up with guns. He felt that during his talks, many kids heard for the first time a message about negative consequences instead of glory resulting from guns. That confirmed what Deane already believed: kids will listen to kids.

It was the beginning of Teens on Target, a program to train youth to prevent violence. At the time, Calhoun worked for the Trauma Foundation, focusing on unintentional injuries and possible solutions. "In the mid-1980s, I saw that more kids were dying from intentional injuries—specifically gun violence—than from what people thought kids were dying of—car crashes," she recalled. That represented the beginning of the shift in the public health community to also include intentional firearms injuries in their reporting.

For Calhoun, it was a perfect blending of her primary interests— young people and health. "I saw gun violence as something that not only kills people, but something that generates a fear that separates

Deane Calhoun.

people from each other. It causes racial separation—separating everyone else from young men of color. And it also separates young people
from each other."

Kids were telling her that no new friendships could bloom in this
kind of environment. "They thought they could stay safe by looking
straight ahead and not talking to anyone they didn't know. If it were
the same for me and I were afraid of middle-aged women, it would
make me crazy. That's the kind of fear that divides, isolates, and
paralyzes communities. It's pernicious and devastating," she said.

What bothered her most was that the gun industry was profiting
from this fear. "Every time there was a shooting, ironically, more
guns were sold. The gun industry reaped the profits of their un-
limited, unregulated ability to saturate the environment with four
million new guns a year. It was that combination—the means of destruction made so readily available and the resulting carnage and fear
which continues today—plus my passion for kids that made me fixate
on this issue. I felt that we could do something together. We could

provide policy makers the reason and passion to get over their own fear of the gun lobby."

Teens on Target is now a program of Youth ALIVE!, a nonprofit violence prevention organization with programs in Oakland and Los Angeles. The Teens on Target curriculum has reached 15,000 young people in those communities, and the model has been presented at local, state, and national conferences. It has received awards and recognition from U.S. Attorney General Janet Reno and President Bill Clinton.

Young people are completely involved in developing the program and curriculum, which combines research from the fields of criminal justice and health with youth experience to develop strategies for prevention. Young people are trained to be peer educators, leaders in their community, and advocates for violence prevention. The first group of students was recruited through a media teacher in the Oakland Unified School District. "At that first meeting, I brought 17 pages of public health facts and told the young people to select those facts that they felt were most important," Calhoun said. The statistics were mostly from national and state reporting agencies; the students wanted local statistics. They began calling police departments and hospitals to gather local numbers.

Even getting state numbers wasn't always easy. At the time Calhoun was working for the Trauma Foundation, the state health department "buried gun data" under homicides or suicides, not specifying what weapon was involved in the death. There was little information on gun injuries that didn't result in death. "I worked closely with two public hospitals to determine how many kids were getting injured and [with] the coroner's office to determine who was dying from gunshots," she said.

"It's not an anger management or behavior modification program," Calhoun explained. "We're training kids to be messengers in making their communities healthier and safer places to live. The focus is on how and why guns are getting into the environment and made so accessible to young people. The kids work with law enforcement, schools, local politicians, and community leaders to get them involved in solving this problem."

One problem area the young people have regularly identified is the zoning regulations which allow for easy access to gun dealers. "Why is it that these kids have to get on the bus to go buy school supplies, but can walk around the corner to get a gun?" she asked.

Another program of Youth ALIVE! is Caught in the Crossfire.

Through a trauma surgeon, Calhoun met Sherman Spears, who was shot and became paraplegic when he was 17. "Sherman goes to the hospital when people are shot and, together with a medical social services worker, tries to talk the recovering youths into a positive lifestyle and the victim's families and friends out of retaliation," Calhoun explained. The program has expanded, and Sherman also visits suspension sites—special schools for students expelled from the regular public schools. "He emphasizes that this is the last opportunity for these students to make a positive choice."

Calhoun's interest goes beyond young people. The gun industry's appeal to women enraged her. "The industry was facing a flat sales line, so in the mid-1980s they came up with this campaign of stranger danger to scare women into believing they were at risk from strangers when they went out by themselves. The impression made by the campaign was simply that alone and without a gun, you were in danger. It was a seductive and false campaign. Ultimately, it was a hate campaign against women since you're more likely to be shot with a gun if you have one. Also, women are more likely to be injured by someone they know," she said.

That prompted her to help write the grant proposal that ultimately funded the statewide Women Against Gun Violence Campaign. About 40 of the major women's organizations in the state signed on, pledging their involvement on policy and legislative levels. Because it was such a labor-intensive project to keep viable on the state level, Women Against Gun Violence decided to focus its resources just in Los Angeles.

Calhoun has collaborated with the East Bay Corridor Partnership, a coalition of 21 cities and two counties working to reduce crime and violence along state Route 80. "We wanted to pass local legislation that reduced death and injuries from guns, reduced access to guns, was likely to be passed, and could educate people about the gun violence problem," she said of the collaboration's four goals. As a result, the communities began passing Saturday night special bans, mandatory trigger lock requirements, limited bans on residential gun dealers, and a gross receipts tax that increased retailers' overall taxes if firearms were any part of their trade.

Over 40 ordinances were passed in the East Bay area. "More than half of California's residents are protected from the sale of Saturday night specials in their communities. We hope that this contributed to the pressure for statewide legislation," she said.

How successful have these types of violence prevention programs been? "We haven't figured out a way to isolate the impact of one prevention measure, but the kids say that if there are fewer guns, there will be fewer gun deaths," Calhoun said. "The best prevention study I've ever seen examined the effects of a mandatory motorcycle helmet law. There you could look at the rate of injuries and death before and after the law." But with violence prevention programs, "there are parallel activities going on. Different people can claim the success—and they should. But there's a common sense feeling that these programs work because we're addressing risk factors in the environment. In the city of Oakland, there were 115 gun dealers. Now there are 6. There formerly was a lack of positive peer role models; now there are role models and alternatives to destructive behavior. The gun death rate for young people in Oakland has dropped substantially. That's a success."

There's also the anecdotal evidence of young people who have gone through the Teens on Target program who say they don't use violence to resolve their problems any more and that they have talked their friends out of violent behavior. They are also now part of a network of people who can help them change their environment. There are those who heard Sherman Spears speak who said he convinced them not to retaliate after a gang shooting because retaliation would only lead to more violence for them and their friends. Yet proving the effectiveness of a prevention program is difficult. "It's hard to count what didn't happen. The prevention field grapples with this," Calhoun said.

ADDITIONAL READINGS

Fenley, MaryAnne, and Mark Rosenberg. *Violence in America*. New York: Oxford University Press, 1991.

Violence Prevention: A Vision of Hope. A final report of Attorney General Daniel E. Lungren's Policy Council on Violence Prevention. Sacramento: State of California, 1995.

Women Against Gun Violence. *Get Organized, Get Active*. Oakland, Calif.: Youth ALIVE!, 1997.

———. *How to Answer Pro-Gun Arguments*. Oakland, Calif.: Youth ALIVE!, 1997.

———. *How to Find Out about Gun Violence in Your Community*. Oakland, Calif.: Youth ALIVE!, 1997.

———. *How to Reduce Gun Sales in Your Community*. Oakland, Calif.: Youth ALIVE!, 1997.

————. *How to Talk to Kids about Guns*. Oakland, Calif.: Youth ALIVE!, 1997.

————. *I Never Thought My Child Could Get Shot*. Oakland, Calif.: Youth ALIVE!, 1997.

————. *Taking Action on Preventing Gun Violence in Your Community: The Teens on Target Training Curriculum*. Oakland, Calif.: Youth ALIVE!, 1997.

————. *Teens on Target*. Oakland, Calif.: Youth ALIVE!, 1997.

Matthew C. C. (Sandy) Chisholm III

Gun Company Makes "Saturday Night Specials" . . . Proudly

Born: 1954, Philadelphia, PA

Education: B.S., University of Florida; M.B.A., University of Western Ontario

Current Positions: President and Owner, North American Arms; Member of the Board, American Firearms Council

Sometimes Sandy Chisholm sits at the North American Arms booth at gun shows and chats with people as they file by. Almost always, someone will stop, take a look at one of his company's palm-sized revolvers, and make some critical remark about its size. "He might say, 'I only pack a .45.' My response is, 'Where is it?' and the answer is almost always 'I don't have it with me,' or 'At home.' "

That's when Chisholm, the president and owner of a gun manufacturing company known for its mini-revolvers and pistols, drives home his point. "It's no damn good to have a big gun if it's not with you when you need it. My customers tell me that the things they carry with them every single day are their wallets, watches, and NAA mini-revolvers. That's what makes them terribly effective; they're at hand. These aren't man-stoppers because a .22 is about as small as you can get. But if someone points a gun at me—no matter what size it is—I guarantee it will change my behavior. Nine times out of

Matthew C. C. (Sandy) Chisholm III.

ten, when a weapon is brandished, that's all that needs to happen," he said.

North American Arms makes small pistols and revolvers. In fact, if it weren't a U.S.-based company, he couldn't import the handguns. But the Saturday night special ban, a part of the Gun Control Act of 1968, which prohibits the import of such small handguns, doesn't apply to U.S. manufacturers.

Pistols and revolvers have separate criteria tests in which a gun is assigned points based on its overall length, construction, weight, caliber, and safety features. Only those guns which meet a specified number of points can be imported. U.S. manufacturers are not held to these restrictions.

" 'Saturday night specials' is a pejorative term typically used to describe guns which, in addition to their small size, are often made of lesser-grade metals and which frequently operate unreliably. In comparison, the materials, workmanship, and reliability of North American Arms products compare favorably to the highest quality firearms presently manufactured," contends Chisholm.

When the Gun Control Act of 1968 was passed, Sandy Chisholm wasn't all that interested in the policies being created. His experience with firearms had been limited to his college days, when he bought a gun "on a whim" and occasionally took it to a rural dump to plink at tin cans.

Beyond that, he gave little thought to firearms regulations. Then in the early 1990s he was working for Teleflex, a large publicly traded company that acquired Talley Manufacturing. Talley was an engineering and manufacturing firm that made aerospace defense products. It was also the parent company of a small firearms manufacturing company, North American Arms. Teleflex wanted Talley's aerospace component, but had no interest in firearms manufacturing. Chisholm was assigned to sell off the North American Arms division.

Two years later, there were still no buyers. But the more Chisholm learned about the company, the more potential he saw. "The light bulb went on and I decided to buy it myself. Its attraction was simply that it was a manageably sized business staffed with excellent people, and I saw it as a career opportunity."

He was most impressed with the little company's staying power. "It was the red-headed stepchild [of Talley]. It received little time or attention and few resources. Even so, it continued to exist, and I thought that someone with time, interest, money and enthusiasm could offer this business some support and give it a new lease on life."

That someone was Chisholm himself, and his hunch turned out to be true. He attributes the company's success as much to luck as to his leadership. "Within 60 days of my becoming owner, the market became very robust. That was driven by several factors. For one thing, the assault weapons ban and magazine capacity restrictions were hot-button issues. The biggest driver in this market is the threat that there will be additional restrictions on firearms ownership. There are some people who will leap and make purchases anticipating these restrictions," he said.

On this ground, Chisholm might benefit—but maybe not. "It is my sense that Saturday night specials have become the next identifiable class of firearms—after so-called assault weapons—considered most threatening or most distasteful. That makes it the group of weapons that is most likely to be the target of legislative threats," he said. On this issue, gun makers like North American Arms have the NRA on their side. Affordability and small size are desired characteristics of personal protection firearms, and Chisholm and the NRA are in complete agreement on the value of their availability. "Personal protection is a legitimate use of firearms. Additionally, it has been demonstrated to my satisfaction that firearms are very viable personal protection weapons. The legitimacy of concealed carry is probably no better illustrated than by the relatively recent spate of states passing or expanding concealed carry laws. That suggests that state legislatures have been satisfied by the argument that enabling citizens to carry guns has a demonstrable effect on reducing violent crime."

These are not target-grade sporting guns. North American Arms markets its guns for one reason: personal protection. "Our bread and butter of the product line is a family of small .22-caliber stainless steel single action revolvers. They're inexpensive primarily because they're so small. But we recently introduced a similarly small .32-caliber pistol with a retail price of $425. That's very much in the high end of the general population of pocket-sized handguns."

The small size is particularly attractive to the company's target markets. These include law enforcement officers wanting a small backup firearm, and hikers or outdoorsmen who can fill the gun with buckshot and use it against snakes, for example. Because of their unique styling, collectors are keen on them. But the largest market for the company is women. "From a woman's perspective, the guns' diminutive size makes them less intimidating. They're certainly more portable and easier to use than big caliber, big framed guns."

Those features that make the gun so attractive to women also potentially make it more dangerous to households with children, say critics. Chisholm doesn't agree. "The safe handling and storage of a firearm is absolutely a matter of personal responsibility." However, the company does provide a lockable "gun rug" or zippered pouch with each gun. It's been doing that for 10 years. The guns are so small that a trigger lock won't fit. So putting the gun in its pouch, closing the zipper, and locking it shut is one way a gun can't be too easily accessed.

North American Arms was one of the first gun manufacturers to sign on to provide some type of gun locks with their firearms. Manufacturers followed suit because it was the pragmatic thing to do, he said. "It was a major concern with the [Clinton] administration. So most of the industry responded, 'We recognize and will address that concern. You don't have to go through the machinations of legislating us.' It made more sense, we felt, to do it voluntarily than to see what would happen with legislation. It was absolutely the right strategy from our point of view, but the National Rifle Association found it objectionable."

That move exemplifies the difference between the gun industry as represented by the American Shooting Sports Council (see profile of Richard J. Feldman) and the National Rifle Association, which works to protect gun rights on an ideological basis. "For a long time, the industry didn't have any politically oriented trade association at all and through our inaction, we depended on the efforts of the NRA. We don't represent the same constituencies at all although we do share similar beliefs. They represent retail—our customers; we represent the industry. Aside from the different agendas, our [lobbying] styles are dramatically different. I think by virtue of that, we are enjoying recognition and credibility in the political process and have been increasingly effective since we entered the debate."

While the two don't walk in lockstep, the gun industry can benefit from the lobbying activities of the NRA. Certainly, the NRA can be counted on to oppose any legislative restrictions on Saturday night specials, for example.

While Chisholm is concerned that his company's guns can be misused with devastating consequences, he is buoyed by the frequent reports of cases in which one of his guns was used to deter a crime. He points to the "Because I Was Armed" column in the July 1998 issue of *American Guardian*, one of the NRA's publications. The column told the story of a man who was assaulted by two attackers early one morning walking to the medical clinic where he worked. Trained in martial arts, the man tried to defend himself, but was outnumbered and knocked down. He was also unable to reach his primary weapon, holstered beneath the two coats he was wearing. But he could reach his North American Arms .22 Magnum mini-revolver, which he carried in an outer coat pocket, and wounded one of the attackers.

Chisholm also hears from customers directly, like the Louisville, Kentucky, man who injured a robber fleeing a bank. "Our commitment is to make sure that these are the finest small reliable effective personal protection devices," Chisholm said.

Even after acquiring a gun manufacturing company, Chisholm admits he would rather be golfing. His sporting interests remain on the links, not at the range. In fact, he said, he remains "a poor marksman." Those might not be the expected credentials of the head of a gun manufacturing company, but Chisholm has completely grown into the part.

ADDITIONAL READINGS

McElrath, Daniel. "Because I Was Armed." *American Guardian*, July 1998.
North American Arms web site: http://www.naaminis.com
Tartaro, Joseph P. "Yes, Barbara, There Are 'Junk Guns,' but Size, Price and Caliber Are No Yardsticks." *Gun News Digest*, Fall 1997.

Katherine Kaufer Christoffel

Pediatrician Devotes Research to Childhood Gun-Related Injuries

Born: 1948, New York, NY

Education: B.A., Radcliffe College; M.D., Tufts University; M.P.H., Northwestern University School of Medicine

Current Positions: Medical Director, Handgun Epidemic Lowering Plan; Director, Statistical Science and Epidemiology Program, Children's Memorial Institute for Education and Research, Chicago; Pediatrician

Katherine Kaufer Christoffel went into pediatrics because she thought it was "an optimistic field." But it also had some disturbing

Katherine Kaufer Christoffel.

elements. "I came out of my residency with a clinical interest in child abuse and battered child syndrome. My earliest publications were on that."

While studying for her master's degree in public health at Northwestern University Medical School, she began to look at other leading causes of childhood death and injury. Motor vehicle crash injuries topped the list, and policies on reducing passenger injuries were being developed. "Pedestrian injuries was an area where much new work could be done, as was violence. The number of cases of reported child abuse was increasing, but we didn't know whether that was because there were more incidents or better reporting. By studying deaths, we thought we might be able to skirt that confounding methodological problem," she said. In truth, it didn't really help, because someone still had the difficult task of determining whether a death was child-abuse related.

But the direction of her study secured her a grant from the U.S. Department of Health and Human Services to look at Chicago homicides of victims under age 15. "What emerged was a bimodal pattern. For young children, the [leading] cause was child abuse, but after age 11, it was guns," she said.

At the same time, the hospital pulled together a multidisciplinary injury team which examined recent cases. "One of the first ones was an 18-month-old with a BB in the brain. I didn't know anything about BB guns. I thought they were toys and I was quite indignant. How could a toy cause such an injury?" She called the Consumer Product Safety Commission and found out that BB guns are not toys. They and firearms were—and are—not regulated by that agency, which oversees essentially all other consumer products.

By the early to mid-1980s, there was an increasing number of deaths related to powder gun injuries. "I started receiving telephone queries, and began to write and speak about them. It was a great way to learn, so I accepted the challenge," she said. She was appointed to the American Academy of Pediatrics (AAP) Committee on Injury and Poison Prevention. She led the work to refine the AAP's policy on guns, and by 1992 the AAP came out with two strong policy statements on private gun ownership. "There are inevitable stages of development for children and adolescents. If the children are around guns during some of these stages, there will be great danger. There is no way to eliminate that fact. To protect children from guns, you have to get the firearms out of their environments."

The policy called for many changes, including a ban on handguns. The AAP policy statement wasn't the first to call for this action; the American Public Health Association had adopted a similar policy years earlier. But the AAP statement coincided with what turned out to be the modern peak of gun deaths, and the interest of other medical groups was sparked.

The ire of a few vocal pediatricians who were handgun rights supporters was also piqued, so the academy decided to include questions about the policy in one of its regular member surveys to better assess member opinion on the policy statements. Using a rotating sample, so the same people aren't questioned regularly, the academy surveys its members on attitudes toward various issues. "In 1997 the support [for the firearms policy] was tremendous for even the strongest position," Christoffel reported.

Christoffel wanted to take advantage of other medical professionals' interest in the topic. With funding from the Joyce Foundation, she established the Handgun Epidemic Lowering Plan (HELP) in 1993; it had 120 medical and allied organizations in its international membership in early 1998. Christoffel serves as its medical director.

"I've been traveling all over the country and have had a chance to collaborate with colleagues in various fields to further develop this work. When we first got into this, viewing gun injuries as a public health problem was a bit on the quirky side, but now it is pretty well accepted," she said. HELP is the only such public health network in the world.

There isn't a consensus on exactly how gun injuries can best be prevented, even within HELP, she noted. Indeed, Christoffel's opinions are more ardently pro-regulation than those of some of her colleagues. "My emphasis is that handguns are just too dangerous for civilian use. Stranger danger does not show up very often, but the family is at home every day. A handgun in the home turns so many ordinary situations lethal. When people see guns this way, most won't want them around. I predict consensus on this point eventually."

To Christoffel, it doesn't make sense for people to keep handguns in a home where there are children, given what is known about the dangers they pose. "We don't do high school biology experiments with the AIDS virus. We don't sit around with nuclear reactors in our backyards. That's my focus. Handguns are just too dangerous to keep around. For long guns, I think there is a lot more room for product safety approaches," she said.

Her views make her a target of gun rights supporters, but that doesn't bother her. "It's actually a funny kind of compliment. If I weren't a problem for them, they wouldn't bother attacking my work. In some ways, it feels like a measure of my effectiveness. The colleagues who support my work feel that a large part of my contribution is that I state things clearly. I present the argument for handgun regulation step by step, so the conclusions speak for themselves. That's a problem for the people on the other side."

Still, she notes that working on both the science and the advocacy sides is difficult. "Most of my colleagues select one role or the other, and as a result, they're not quite as threatening. If they focus on research, they're not as attractive as targets of policy debates for the gun rights side. If they only focus on advocacy, as Sarah Brady does, their political role is more straightforward. Science-based advocacy bridges these roles, and it is harder to buttonhole." However, it is not new.

"Public health has advanced, in part, by those on the science side guiding the application of knowledge on the policy side," she said. However, gun control opponents have made it harder in this area by limiting federal funding on firearms issues. "This level of policy involvement in research is extraordinary."

She sees similarities to public health work on guns in other major public health interventions, such as those to reduce cigarette smoking and motor vehicle injuries. "For these, the application of public health approaches marked the beginning of dramatic declines in risk. The effects on deaths have been most visible a generation later. Today, it looks like the effect may be faster for guns," she said.

Even so, being on the front line is tough. "The days I get hate mail . . . who needs it? I don't do this as a form of self-destruction. But on other days, when I talk to people who encourage me or we have an opportunity to make a difference in how some people think about this issue, or how they deal with their own guns, I'm buoyed. No one said it would be easy or fun, but it's still a wonderful opportunity."

Now that the effort is being spread among more pediatricians, Christoffel feels she can begin to broaden her career work again. In March 1998 the academy trained about 100 pediatricians to be leaders in their areas on gun injury prevention. "That means there will be 100 of us, instead of 1 or 2. I don't plan to leave this area after I've put so much into it," she said. But she's also ready to go back to research and other work.

Despite criticism and a seemingly unending number of children injured by guns, she still feels her original optimism about pediatrics. "My career has given me an extraordinary opportunity to make a difference for children . . . and their children."

ADDITIONAL READINGS

American Academy of Pediatrics. "Firearms and Adolescents" (policy statement). *Pediatrics* 89 (April 1992).

———. "Injuries Related to 'Toy' Firearms" (policy statement). *Pediatrics*

79 (March 1987). [Both of the above are available on the American Academy of Pediatrics web site: http://www.aap.org]

Christoffel, Katherine K., "American as Apple Pie: Guns in the Lives of U.S. Children and Youth." *Pediatrician* 12 (1985).

———. "Firearm Injuries Affecting U.S. Children and Adolescents." In *Children in a Violent Society*, ed. Joy D. Osofsky and Peter Scharf. New York: Guilford Press, 1997.

———. "Handguns and the Environments of Children." *Children's Environments* 12 (1995): 39–48.

———. "Homicide in Childhood—A Public Health Problem in Need of Attention." *American Journal of Public Health* 74 (1984).

———. "Violent Death and Injury in U.S. Children and Adolescents." *American Journal of Diseases of Children* 144 (1990).

Christoffel, Katherine K., and T. H. Christoffel. "Handguns as a Pediatric Problem." *Pediatric Emergency Care* 2 (1986).

———. "Handguns: Risks vs. Benefits." *Pediatrics* 77 (1986).

Christoffel, Katherine K., and K. Liu. "Homicide Death Rates in Childhood in 23 Developed Countries: U.S. Rates Atypically High." *The International Journal* 7 (1983).

Christoffel, Katherine K., D. Marcus, S. Sagerman, and S. Bennett. "Adolescent Suicide and Suicide Attempts: A Population Study." *Pediatric Emergency Care* 4 (1988).

Christoffel, Katherine K., S. Sagerman, R. Tanz, and Y. Hahn. "Childhood Injuries Caused by Nonpowder Firearms." *American Journal of Diseases of Children* 138 (1984).

Naureckas, Sara M., and Katherine K. Christoffel. "Pulling the Rigger: If Mom Can, the Kids Can Too." *Archives of Pediatric and Adolescent Medicine* 149 (1995).

Powell, Elizabeth C., Karen M. Sheehan, and Katherine K. Christoffel. "Firearm Violence among Youth: Public Health Strategies for Prevention." *Annals of Emergency Medicine* 28 (August 1996).

Senturia, Y. D., Katherine K. Christoffel, and M. Donovan. "Children's Household Exposure to Guns: A Pediatric Practice-Based Survey." *Pediatrics* 93 (1994).

Somerville, Janice. "Gun Conrol as Immunization: Pediatrician Says Prevention Is Best Way to Fight Epidemic of Violence." *American Medical News* (January 3, 1994): 7.

———. "Toward Reducing Pediatric Injuries from Firearms: Charting a Legislative and Regulatory Course." *Pediatrics* 88 (1991).

Tanz, R., Katherine K. Christoffel, and S. Sagerman. "Are Toy Guns Too Dangerous?" *Pediatrics* 74 (1985).

Philip J. Cook

Criminologist Believes Gun Availability Affects Homicide Rate

Born: 1946, Buffalo, NY

Education: University of Michigan; Ph.D., University of California, Berkeley

Current Position: Director, Terry Sanford Institute of Public Policy, Duke University

---

Philip J. Cook put himself into robbers' shoes—figuratively speaking. After working on his doctoral dissertation on parolee recidivism, he began consulting for the U.S. Department of Justice when he moved to Duke. "At that point, the data from the national crime survey was just becoming available. We had a nationally representative sample of the population talking about their experiences with crime, providing details not available through the Federal Bureau of Investigation's Uniform Crime Report or from police reports."

Working on the victimization survey, Cook analyzed the crime of robbery, including holdups. "From the robber's point of view, several inputs were required. One was having a weapon. Another was having an accomplice or two, and the third was having a victim. I found that the choices the robbers were making could be understood from that perspective," he said.

A robber's two main concerns are control and compliance. "The gun is more effective in accomplishing that than other weapons. It turned out that those who were more likely to use guns were less likely to use accomplices. They were also more likely to rob commercial places. The findings showed that robberies are more likely to be successful if they used a gun and the average loot was higher. In other words, there is a real payoff to using a gun," he said.

He also found a dichotomy in resulting injuries. In those cases where a robber used a gun, there was less chance of a physical attack, and victims were more likely to be compliant. Therefore, victims

Philip J. Cook. Courtesy of Jim Wallace, Duke University Photography.

were less likely to be injured. However, they were also more likely to be killed.

Cook wasn't the only one studying criminals and guns. At the time, James D. Wright (see profile) and Peter Rossi were working on a project for the National Institute of Justice. Their resulting report, *Weapons, Crime and Violence in America*, was published in 1981 and was embraced by gun rights advocates as proof that gun controls would have little impact on criminals.

Cook noted that its two main themes have been distilled to bumper-sticker philosophies: "If guns are outlawed, only outlaws will have guns" and "Guns don't kill people; people kill people." "I think Wright and Rossi did a lot of good things, but I didn't agree with their conclusions," said Cook. "The evidence shows that the type of weapons matters a great deal in robberies, but what Wright and Rossi were saying was that there are other explanations, not that the weapon was an independent causal factor. Wright and Rossi went on to say that we shouldn't have a handgun-only gun control policy because then criminals will switch to rifles and shotguns, which are more deadly. Yet they also say that handguns are not more deadly than knives. That's internally inconsistent."

He also disagrees with the conclusion that the availability of guns has no influence on whether someone will commit a crime with a gun. Wright, Rossi, and other gun rights advocates assume that violent people tend to be determined and persistent and will use whatever means are necessary to complete their crime. "It doesn't fit the evidence. It doesn't fit my image of a 15-year-old punk kid who isn't persistent, determined, or smart about how they approach their lives or crimes. If you impose even small barriers, you may be able to divert them," he said.

Cook set out to test the theory that gun availability influences crime. He conducted a study of the 50 largest cities in the United States. He compared the percentage of homicides and suicides with guns and the prevalence of gun ownership. "If you look at cities in the Northeast, where there are low gun ownership rates, you'll find a relatively low percentage of homicides and suicides involve guns. In the Phoenix area, where there are high rates of gun ownership, there are high percentages of homicides and suicides with guns," he said.

He took it to the level of robberies and found that gun availability had no impact on the overall robbery rate, but did influence the choice of weapon. "In those areas where guns are readily available, robbers commit their crimes with guns. In Boston, for example, where there aren't many guns, not many robbers use them," he said. "The result is that Boston had a high rate of robbery, but the robberies there are less deadly than in cities where guns are prevalent."

That has led him to devise several policy recommendations. In "Regulating Gun Markets," Cook noted that people accept the commonsense view that if guns were not available to an angry person or a suicidal kid, that homicide or suicide might not occur. "But people despair about reducing gun availability as the statistics show that 40 percent of households have guns. If there are 200 million guns in circulation, trying to dry up the gun supply is a huge task," he said.

Cook, the economist, looks at it a different way. "Step back and talk about it with a little common sense. There are as many cameras as guns in circulation, but people don't talk about cameras as though they were free. People own these guns. They don't give them away on the street corners."

The best evidence that guns are not that readily available is the fact that a majority of robbers use other weapons—knives and fists—despite the evident advantage that a gun provides in controlling the victim.

In the study, Cook and his colleagues looked at how youths gain access to guns and how guns move from the legal economy to the illicit economy. The first finding was discovered even before they formally conducted the experiment. "There were gaping holes in the [enforcement] efforts. Police weren't paying attention as to whether transactions were being made to kids. Gun shows were allowed to go forward," he explained.

"Since then, police departments have become more aggressive in pursuing gun markets similar to the way they pursue drug markets. They're going after the scofflaw dealer. The Bureau of Alcohol, Tobacco and Firearms has greatly increased its efforts and the number of dealers is much lower," he said.

It's no mere coincidence that the homicide rate is going down at the same time the number of gun dealers is going down and that regulatory and police efforts to keep guns off the street are going up, he said.

His main focus now is on estimating the cost of gun misuse. "It's an effort to find out how much gun assaults and suicides and accidents are costing the public at large. We'll include the medical care costs, but also the costs of lost productivity and other kinds of costs. We'll spend two years trying to improve the current estimates."

That includes determining the total cost and who is responsible for paying for it. He and his colleagues will try to establish how the total will be divided by the public, and how much is shared through insurance, Medicaid, hospital charity work, and lost tax revenues. "I think it's easy for people to discount criminal violence by saying, 'It's not my problem. It's not near my family.' But you're paying for it. It's increasing your insurance premium and your tax bill," Cook said.

These kinds of cost analyses have encountered criticism from those who say that the estimates are overblown. Many victims are poor and unskilled, and researchers are assigning values of lost productivity that they never would have realized, critics say. Cook acknowledges that has been a factor in earlier studies. "One way in which our study is going to be better is we'll factor in how much education the victim has had and whether they're employed. Our lost productivity estimates may be smaller than that in other studies. But we're stuck with the same medical costs," he said, noting that those are not open to interpretation.

With his latest work, Cook bridges the area between criminology and public health. "The public health approach has some aspects appealing to criminologists. They have urged us to get more and better data," he said. As such, he's convinced criminologists and public health professionals will continue to work together with a public policy perspective to produce reasonable approaches to guns and violent crime.

ADDITIONAL READINGS

Cook, Philip J. "The Role of Firearms in Violent Crimes: An Interpretive Review of the Literature with Some New Findings and Suggestions for Further Research." *Criminal Violence* 236 (1982).

Cook, Philip J., and Thomas B. Cole. "Strategic Thinking about Gun Markets and Violence" (editorial). *Journal of the American Medical Association* 275, no. 22 (June 12, 1996).

Cook, Philip J., and John Laub. "The Unprecedented Epidemic in Youth Violence." In *Crime and Justice*, ed. Mark H. Moore and Michael Tonry. Chicago: University of Chicago Press, 1998.

Cook, Philip J., and Jens Ludwig. "Guns in America: Results of a Comprehensive National Survey on Firearms Ownership and Use." Washington, D.C.: Police Foundation, 1996.

Cook, Philip J., Jens Ludwig, and David Hemenway. "The Gun Debate's New Mythical Number: How Many Defensive Uses per Year?" *Journal of Policy Analysis and Management* 16, no. 3 (1997).

Cook, Philip J., Stephanie Molliconi, and Thomas B. Cole. "Regulating Gun Markets." *Journal of Criminal Law and Criminology* 86 (Fall 1995): 59–92.

Cook, Philip J., and Mark H. Moore. "Gun Control." In *Crime*, ed. James Q. Wilson and Joan Petersilia. San Francisco: ICS Press, 1995.

Teret, Stephen P., Daniel W. Webster, Jon S. Vernick, Tom W. Smith, Deborah Leff, Garen J. Wintemute, Philip J. Cook, Darnell F. Hawkins, Arthur L. Kellermann, Susan B. Sorenson, and Susan De-Francesco. "Support for New Policies to Regulate Firearms: Results of Two National Surveys." *New England Journal of Medicine* 399, no. 12 (September 17, 1998).

Robert J. Cottrol

Gun Control: Public Safety or Power to the Oppressors?

Born: 1949, New York, NY

Education: A.B. and Ph.D., Yale University; J.D., Georgetown Law School

Current Position: Professor of Law and History and Harold Paul Green Research Professor of Law, George Washington University

---

From the time he was a young boy, Robert J. Cottrol thought about guns and the power they might grant to the oppressed. It's not that he considered himself a gun rights advocate. He grew up in New York City, a place decidedly not a part of the American gun culture. As a child neither his family nor any of the families that he knew had firearms. Still, he formed some early impressions on the subject, impressions that would influence his later thinking as an adult and as a scholar.

When Cottrol was around 10 years old, two of the last of the murders officially recognized as lynchings, those of Emmet Till and Mack Charles Parker, took place in Mississippi—with the connivance of local officials. "This anti-black violence and the knowledge that this violence had the support of local officials made a strong impression on me," he said.

At roughly the same time, he saw the 1959 movie *The Diary of Anne Frank*, which told the story of Anne Frank, a Jewish girl, and her family and their efforts to hide from Nazi authorities in the German-occupied Netherlands of World War II. The Frank family was captured by the Nazis just two months before the country was liberated. At about age 12, Cottrol read an essay in which the author wondered what would have happened had the Frank family had a gun. "Years later, in the early 1990s, I visited the house and saw the attic where

Robert J. Cottrol. Courtesy of Stan Barouh.

the family had hid. It was tremendously difficult to climb the stairs; the steps were almost vertical and the passage was very narrow. It would have been very difficult for anyone to have stormed their attic hideout under fire. Had they managed to shoot the initial group that came after them, perhaps they might have been able to get away," he said.

Also in his preteen years, Cottrol read a book by Robert Williams, *Negroes with Guns*. Williams had been an NAACP organizer in Greensboro, North Carolina, in the late 1950s. He was threatened by the Ku Klux Klan. Rather than allow the Klan to halt his civil rights activities, Williams formed a self-defense group among NAACP members. They armed themselves with army surplus rifles, then sold through the National Rifle Association. The Klan became highly reluctant to tangle with Williams and the members of his NAACP chapter. The lesson was not lost on Cottrol as he entered his teen years.

Gun control would become a national issue in 1963 after the assassination of President John F. Kennedy. Cottrol, then in junior high, remembers disagreeing with teachers and fellow students who advocated stricter gun control in the wake of that national tragedy. He remembers arguing against strict licensing requirements on the grounds that if he were a resident of Mississippi, he wouldn't want his ability to get a gun for self-defense to depend on the fairness of a Mississippi sheriff.

"Fairly early in life I had formed these views, but I didn't think too much about the subject. When I went to Yale, my major intellectual interest was the history of race relations," he said. As a graduate student there, he wrote a study of the black community in antebellum Providence, Rhode Island. It was later published as a book, *The Afro-Yankees: Providence's Black Community in the Antebellum Era*. The book, a broad examination of the political, social, and economic life of African Americans in this period of New England's history, had one segment that would be relevant to Cottrol's later work on race and arms in America. Black men in Providence had gained the right to vote in the 1840s. That right was frequently under attack by hostile whites. When black men went to the polls, they carried muskets to ensure that they were not attacked while exercising their right.

In law school, Cottrol broadened his research into examination of legal history issues. He was particularly interested in questions of constitutional law and the issue of original intent. That's when he decided to look more closely at the Second Amendment. "It had long been an interest of mine and I was fascinated by the way it intersected with the history of American race relations."

While a student at the Georgetown University Law Center, Cottrol began writing on the legal history of American race relations. One of his earliest writings, on the history of racial classifications laws, led to a long-term collaboration with Raymond T. Diamond, then an attorney with the Federal Trade Commission and now a professor of law at Tulane University.

Later, after both became members of law school faculties, Cottrol and Diamond co-authored their first major piece on race and the right to arms, "The Second Amendment: Toward an Afro-Americanist Reconsideration." Their research led them to the conclusion that the history of race relations in America helped modify the traditional English right to arms in significant ways. While the English right to arms, as codified in the English Bill of Rights of 1689, was limited by class and religious restrictions, the American right was more ro-bust—at least for the white population. That broader right came about, in part, because a universally armed and deputized white pop-ulation was seen as necessary in order to control the black and Indian populations, he explained. In many locations the law sought to keep the African American and Indian populations disarmed to ensure their subjugation. The authors argue that one reason for the passage of the Fourteenth Amendment was to prevent southern states from disarming the newly freed black population after the Civil War.

They also argue that the right to bear arms was particularly im-portant for southern blacks after Reconstruction and well into the twentieth century. Lynching and other forms of anti-black violence were commonplace, he said. "Local law enforcement did little to stop it and the federal government had totally abandoned its responsibility to protect the lives and safety of black people. What little relief ex-isted from this grim reality occurred when southern blacks defended themselves." He noted that this pattern continued well into the 1960s.

The Cottrol-Diamond article also indicates that the concern with race, oppression, and arms is not simply an issue of the nation's re-mote past. "It was our view that many well meaning people, partic-ularly liberals, were simply assuming that people and especially poor people in communities plagued by high crime would be better off with strict gun control without subjecting their views to hard ques-tioning," Cottrol said. "If we have strict gun control (or more accu-rately a prohibition on the ownership of guns for self-defense) we are essentially trusting our lives, and especially the lives of the most disenfranchised among us, to the benevolence of the state. Is that wise? How benevolent, how competent, is the state? How much con-cern has it shown for minority lives in the past, or even today?"

For example, Cottrol rankles at the efforts to ban guns in public housing. "It's unconscionable. We force people who live in public housing, who receive inadequate police protection, to give up the means of self-defense. Housing projects are places where police often will not venture unless they have extensive backup. The people who live in public housing and other people in inner city neighborhoods are often as much oppressed by the violence caused by black gangs as their grandparents were by the Klan in the rural South. In too many communities the law has made matters worse by disarming the victims while leaving the victimizers armed."

Cottrol doesn't gloss over the terrible toll that gun violence takes on young black men. "The numbers are absolutely horrible. One of the problems is that we have a micro culture of criminal violence within the underclass subculture. We are talking about a small number committing an inordinate number of homicides."

"But I'm not sure that gun control will make a difference; indeed, I believe its only effect will be counterproductive. Some of the arguments advanced on the pro-control side are simply too emotional and too illogical. We frequently hear that a particular gun must be banned because it (allegedly) is the weapon of choice of drug pushers. We need to ask an elementary question: If we can't keep drugs out of the hands of drug pushers, what makes us think a simple statute is going to keep a gun out of the hands of drug pushers? We know that prohibitions bring forth black markets. Disarming criminals through a general prohibition isn't going to occur. What we may do, and what has happened in a number of jurisdictions, is that we do manage to coerce substantial numbers of peaceable, law-abiding citizens into foregoing the means of self-defense, giving a tremendous advantage to the criminals who prey on them," he said.

Cottrol believes the distinction between gun control and gun prohibitions is an important one that often gets lost in the debate. "Screening measures designed to insure that those with suspect backgrounds—such as criminal behavior, histories of violence, and mental instability—don't get firearms are important. That is very different from the notion that we should constantly search around for whole categories of firearms used overwhelmingly by law-abiding citizens to prohibit." Cottrol also cited what he sees as the failure of the courts to enforce the Second Amendment as a major reason why it is so difficult to get agreement on proper screening measures. "It is the fear that screening measures are simply a way station on the road to prohibition that has led to efforts by the NRA and others to block the passage of legislation ostensibly designed to strengthen screening measures. If the courts would protect the individual's right to arms we would no more have a mass movement attempting to block screening measures than we have a mass movement challenging the existence of parade permits."

"The gun control movement spends too much effort trying to bring about prohibitions and not enough trying to make common cause with gun owners, including the NRA, in trying to strengthen screening measures," said Cottrol. "Let's look at two issues. We have heard a lot of noise concerning so-called assault rifles for the last decade. The federal government and about five states have passed assault weapon legislation. If we take a look at this legislation we can see that it is an incredible fraud. First, rifles of all sorts, including the so-called assault rifles, are a minor factor in gun crime. Second, assault weapons legislation usually defines a rifle as an assault weapon based on cosmetic features that are criminologically trivial. Take two nearly identical rifles. One might be classified as an illegal assault rifle only because it has a bayonet lug. Is there really a problem with drive-by bayonettings in late twentieth century America, or are we being treated to industrial strength political grandstanding?"

Cottrol suggests that it would be "more productive to plug up the holes in our procedures for screening who should or should not be eligible to purchase firearms. Federal law currently prohibits purchase of firearms by people who have adult felony convictions or misde-meanor convictions for domestic violence. We need to also prevent the purchase of firearms by those convicted of violent felonies before they were adults or by those who have long histories of violent be-havior even if that behavior only resulted in misdemeanor convic-tions." Cottrol indicated that he believed the development of proper screening measures would require working with gun owners and the NRA and not demonizing them, as the gun control movement often does.

This form of "political demagoguery on the gun issue has hurt our ability to search for rational solutions. Unfortunately this is true in other areas that touch on the issue of crime, such as the death pen-alty. We are frightened by crime and rightfully so, and we are thus willing customers for feel-good politicians promising relief."

"But we should remember," he concluded, "that civil rights should not be surrendered lightly and that for minorities who have historically not been able to rely on police protection . . . the right to arms can mean the right to self-defense and indeed, for many, the difference between life and death."

ADDITIONAL READINGS

Cottrol, Robert J. *The Afro-Yankees: Providence's Black Community in the Ante-bellum Era*. Westport, Conn.: Greenwood Press, 1982.
———. "The Second Amendment." In *The Oxford Companion to the Supreme Court of the United States*, ed. Kermit Hall et al. New York: Oxford University Press, 1992.

————, ed. *Gun Control and the Constitution: Sources and Explorations on the Second Amendment*. New York: Garland, 1994.

Cottrol, Robert J., and Raymond T. Diamond. "The Fifth Auxiliary Right." *Yale Law Journal* 104 (1995).

————. "Public Safety and the Right to Keep and Bear Arms." In *The Bill of Rights in Modern America: After 200 Years*. Bloomington: Indiana University Press, 1993.

————. "The Second Amendment: Toward an Afro-Americanist Reconsideration." *Georgetown Law Journal* 809, no. 2 (December 1991): 309–361

National Rifle Association. *Laws Designed to Disarm Slaves, Freedmen, and African-Americans*. http://www.nra.org/crimestrike/csrace.html

Preston King Covey

Guns: First a Physical Outlet, Then a Cause for Outrage

Born: 1942, Minneapolis, MN

Education: B.A. and Ph.D., Stanford University

Current Position: Director, Center for the Advancement of Applied Ethics, Carnegie Mellon University, Pittsburgh, PA

Firearms returned to Preston King Covey some of what polio had taken from him. The disease, which killed many youngsters, left Covey, then 11, without the use of his right arm. But one afternoon, he pulled his shotgun out of the closet and fired a few rounds. "This was something I could do that two-handed people could do," he said.

By the time he was 15, he had collected about 15 guns. "All I asked for for birthdays and Christmas were particular guns. I probably would have been as much of a gun nut as anyone growing up in that culture," he said of growing up in rural Minnesota. "But the intensity of my enthusiasm was increased because I was one-handed."

Then decades later, post-polio syndrome set in, leaving Covey exhausted as his muscles deteriorated. He gave up running, tennis, and racquetball. But he once again found pleasure and sport in shooting.

His personal enjoyment was soon matched by a disgust for the

Preston King Covey.

arguments put forth in favor of gun control. He found himself moving
from a position of moderation to one of contempt for gun controls
based on emotion and semantics. But that progression took years.

For the first decade after he began collecting guns, the politics
behind them meant little. He displayed his gun collection on living
room walls wherever he lived—a mistake that cost him his entire
long gun collection when his house was burgled.

His few remaining handguns were stolen in another burglary in
1978, when he had moved to Pittsburgh. The burglars even found
the "hidden" loaded handgun in his dresser drawer. "That burglary
hit the paper and named me. When I reported to work, my colleagues
said, 'Wow, you had guns?' "

Until that moment, no one had expressed surprise or concern over
his guns. "It occurred to me there was a change in the culture," he
said.

Many of the guns in Covey's collection had increased in value, and he received a significant settlement from the insurance company. A new assistant professor with a mortgage, Covey used the money to pay bills rather than to replace the guns. He had gotten married and had a baby. There were other things to think about.

Then in August 1988, his house was burgled again. "It was no big deal; they took a little 10-inch TV from the kitchen. But five days later, we were burgled again and they took the VCR and broke some stuff," he said. "The burglars hit every house in our cul de sac, frightening the entire neighborhood."

When the police arrived, Covey's wife asked what they should do. The police suggested getting a dog, but Covey had recently put an old dog to sleep and didn't want to start over with another. His wife then suggested he sleep on the couch that night. "I was having the same thought, but realized it was a dumb idea. What was I supposed to do? Wave my limp arm at the burglar and say, 'I'm an ethics professor and please leave us alone?'"

Instead, he decided to get a gun. While the 48-hour waiting period prohibited him from getting the gun right away, he arranged with a friend to borrow a handgun until he could purchase his own.

The sense of security of having a gun in the home was matched by the pleasure of a physical outlet and hobby, one he could handle despite the post-polio syndrome.

His wife at the time, Kate Maloy, wasn't thrilled with the introduction of a gun into the house with a toddler. A magazine writer and editor, she wrote an article entitled "Gun Shy?" as a way to work through her resistance. "At that time, her point was: I shall not be an armed citizen, but I must live in an armed household. Later on, instead of just accommodating me, she would actually take up the gun. She was a Quaker with the conviction that she would rather die than take a life herself. But I told her it wasn't just her anymore. She was a mother now. When it comes down to the gravest extreme, are you going to stand on philosophy or something else? Why do you have a fire extinguisher even though you don't expect your house to burn down?" Covey arranged for Lyn Bates (see profile) to give his wife private lessons. The couple was divorced in 1996, but Covey gave Kate a Valentine's Day gift, a Ruger handgun and gun vault.

Covey started thinking about guns on a broader scale when he encountered questions and skepticism from his friends and colleagues. Their impressions of him as a mild-mannered philosophy professor didn't match his enthusiasm for guns, he said. They started questioning him on registration and licensing issues, and he pronounced himself in favor of those, in part because that moderate view assuaged his interrogators.

In fact, when the assault weapons debate first surfaced, he remembers thinking, Who needs one? Nobody I know. "But responding to people's reactions got me thinking. My intelligence got the better of me and I started to do research. I wanted better answers than reflexive ones. I did what I have always taught my students to do: analyze."

What he found, he said, was that he had been lied to by the media and taken in by simple-minded arguments. "I became enraged and became a rabid pro–gun rights advocate. I wasn't just angry at the media and at all the people who purveyed falsehoods or misrepresentations. At the heart of it, I was really pissed at myself. I was ashamed that I had come so far so ignorant. I decided to adopt this as my main research focus and pursue it as long as it takes."

He initially didn't think that process would take very long, but has found out differently. "My son is 12 now and I'm thinking about the society he'll have to negotiate when I'm not there to protect him. I want to try to offer some perspective. I think we're heading in the wrong direction," he said.

Specifically, the nation's gun control efforts are misdirected, he said. "Regulation of a right in a true sense first acknowledges there is a right, such as the right to free speech. Everyone recognizes that these rights must be regulated, but that doesn't mean regulating them increasingly out of existence. In gun control, the regulation is a strategy for the elimination of a fundamental right."

Covey has taken his arguments before the Pennsylvania General Assembly, testifying on an assault weapons ban. He rankled at the term, insisting instead that these types of weapons be called "combat weapons." "To be sure, these guns are designed for combat.... Law-abiding citizens, as well as our police, have use for these guns for defensive combat, in the exercise of the most fundamental of human and moral rights: the right to self-defense, including the right to resort to deadly force in the defense of the innocent, albeit only in the gravest extreme and as a last resort. By the same token, the martial arts are not called 'assault arts.' "

"Calling any firearm an 'assault weapon' obscures—intentionally obscures—this fundamental moral distinction between assault and defense. Feckless name-calling will not suffice to justify banning anything. Moral illiteracy is no basis for public policy," he continued.

He acknowledged that the intensity of the debate makes it difficult to reach mutual understanding or respect. He sees that in himself, too. "Deep down and viscerally I am pro–gun rights."

To balance his advocacy, Covey sought out additional firearms training and then decided to become a firearms instructor himself. "I wanted gun owners to be responsible. So that became my second focus of applied research. To make it useful, I decided to go as far as needed to train law enforcement and thereby be connected with the important ethical and legal issues on the use of deadly force. Self-defense is the essence of why we care about firearms," he said.

He is a member of the International Association of Law Enforcement Firearms Instructors and the American Society of Law Enforcement Trainers as well as a staff instructor for the Lethal Force Institute and Defensive Training International, Inc. Covey also serves as a fully sworn special deputy sheriff in the Allegheny County Sheriff's Reserve.

To him, such continuing education is natural. "I do not just seek training for the sake of being responsible myself. I make it a collateral career of mine as an educator," he said.

"As an antidote to my own bias and advocacy, I have assiduously studied, and teach a very popular university course in, conflict and dispute resolution—in which I deal in a rigorously evenhanded way with the cultural/political divisiveness of the gun control controversy. I work strenuously to provide a well-researched and balanced perspective despite my own visceral pro–gun rights bias, no more or less of a conscientious effort than I ask of my students and colleagues."

ADDITIONAL READINGS

Covey, Preston K. "Gun Control." In *The Encyclopedia of Applied Ethics*. San Diego: Academic Press, 1997.

———. "Principled Firearms Policy: Ethics, Logic, and Conflict Resolution." Testimony before the Pennsylvania General Assembly's Select Committee to Investigate the Use of Automatic and Semiautomatic Firearms, Harrisburg, September 20, 1994.

———. "The 'Sporting Purpose' Issue in Gun-Control Policy." *Journal on Firearms and Public Policy* 6 (Fall 1994).

———. "What Kind of Person Needs an 'Assault Weapon?' " *The Innovator* (Indiana University), March 1993.

Covey, Preston K., with Lance Swell. *Gun Control: For and Against.* New York: Roman & Littlefield, 1999.

Covey, Preston K., ed., with Emanuel Kapelsohn. *Standards and Practices Reference Guide for Law Enforcement Firearms Instructors.* Laconia, NH: International Association of Law Enforcement Firearms Instructors, 1995.

Maloy, Kate. "Gun Shy?" *New Woman*, February 1990.

Larry Craig

Senator Wants Congress to Stop Blaming Guns

Born: 1945, Council, ID

Education: University of Idaho

Current Positions: U.S. Senator (R-ID); Board of Directors, National Rifle Association

When gun rights supporters need a friend on Capitol Hill, they turn to Republican Senator Larry Craig of Idaho. Craig, who was elected to the Senate in 1990, has served on the 76-member board of directors of the National Rifle Association since 1983 and is one of the strongest defenders of gun rights at the federal level. Working with other gun rights legislators, he has successfully turned back attempts by gun control supporters to add restrictions to gun ownership and use.

When asked to name his biggest contribution to the debate, Craig doesn't describe a particular legislative battle. Instead, he points to his efforts to give other legislators a new way of looking at this thorny topic.

"There are issues that a lot of my colleagues prefer not to talk about and probably in many instances, guns would fit into that category," he said. "It's kind of like, 'Gee, I hope that issue doesn't come up.' What I have tried to do over the years is provide my colleagues with good, sound information and ways of dealing with it."

Larry Craig.

For example, when Senator Barbara Boxer of California proposed legislation in 1998 requiring trigger locks on all handguns sold in the United States, Craig proposed instead to require dealers to offer trigger locks for sale and to provide money to law enforcement for gun safety training. The Senate tabled Boxer's amendment and passed Craig's by a 72 to 28 vote.

Craig also worked that year with fellow Republican Senator Bob Smith of New Hampshire on legislation to prevent the Federal Bureau of Investigation (FBI) from charging gun purchasers a fee to support the National Instant Check System (NICS), which is designed to keep felons from buying guns. Gun rights supporters said the fee would be like a tax on law-abiding gun purchasers.

However, in a White House briefing, President Clinton encouraged Congress to reject this effort, noting that "the FBI currently charges school districts, day care providers, and many others for similar background checks. Without the resources generated by such a user fee, the FBI will either have to forego processing millions of background checks, or will have to transfer resources from other crime fighting efforts." Craig rejects the user fee argument by pointing out that, unlike background checks for employment, the NICS check on gun purchasers has always been touted as a crime-fighting tool; therefore, it is well within the FBI's mission and a service to the public at large. Furthermore, he notes that Congress has already invested hundreds of millions of dollars in NICS and fully expected to provide any further funding necessary for its operations through the normal appropriations process. The FBI never put in a request.

Smith's amendment also prevented the government from collecting information on people whose gun purchases had been approved.

Craig said gun rights legislators often find themselves playing defense. "Given the current attack that Second Amendment rights are under, it's probably the best we can do."

But not all of the legislation Craig has supported has been defensive. He also won Senate approval for expanding the Youth Crime Gun Interdiction Initiative, a federal program designed to keep illegal supplies of firearms out of the hands of young people. That program, which is run by the Bureau of Alcohol, Tobacco and Firearms (ATF), was started as a demonstration in 17 cities around the country but will now be expanded nationwide. By collecting data on guns used in crimes, ATF and local law enforcement officials can target what kinds of guns are being used in crime, and what kinds of guns are specifically being used by juveniles and youth (18- to 24-year-olds). In a report issued at the end of the first year of the demonstration project, ATF reported early findings, such as that at least one-quarter of the firearms that police recover from juveniles and youth have been rapidly diverted from a first retail sale to an illegal market. In other words, crime guns are often getting out onto the street fast. The study also found that 8 out of 10 crime guns recovered from juveniles and youth are handguns; 60 percent are semi-automatic pistols. By expanding the program nationwide, it will be easier for ATF and local law enforcement officials to correctly identify specific patterns of illegal gun trafficking in communities and act accordingly.

In 1998 Craig also fought off an attempt by Senator Richard Durbin of Illinois to make gun owners criminally liable if their weapons are stolen by juveniles and then misused. "It's amazing how easy it is to talk about the issue if you know how," he said. "You can make the kind of sound logic and sense that anybody defending the constitutional rights of American citizens ought to make." Craig also won passage of a proposal to get tougher on those who use weapons in crimes. His amendment to the Youth Crime Gun Interdiction Initiative expands and enhances the program by requiring prosecutors to focus on the prosecution of gun crimes, using Project Exile in Richmond, Virginia, as an example. Federal and state prosecutors there worked to bring accused felons to trial in federal rather than state courts, which would subject them to tougher penalties.

Craig says that kind of approach is critical to winning the debate over firearms in this country. When legislation targets the criminal use of a firearm instead of the weapon itself, it defuses the arguments of gun control supporters. "The standard liberal argument historically has been that guns are evil objects. My argument was quite the opposite. The gun, when used by an evil person," can inflict criminal injury. It's the person who is evil, not the firearm. "I always chuckle on the [Senate] floor and say, 'You don't go out and arrest guns, you arrest people.' " That is how gun rights supporters should frame the issue. "Once you effectively counter the [liberal] argument, the gun control advocate really loses his base."

Plus, he said, legislation that goes after crime gives gun control legislators something they can support. "I think you have to give the urban legislator more opportunity to be for something rather than against something when it comes to firearms."

One of the biggest challenges to reframing the debate has been the mainstream media, Craig said. "It's very tough to overcome." Gun control supporters "have had such support from the press over the years." He cited instances in recent years of shootings at schools, saying that the first impulse from media sources "is to take away guns from society, instead of trying to understand what causes people to take actions of that nature." When a student in Oregon opened fire in school on his classmates in May 1998, Craig says, media reports initially overlooked the heroic actions of students who knocked him down and prevented more injury. Those boys were NRA members with weapons training. "Those young men knew what to do."

That type of media coverage is extremely frustrating to gun rights advocates. In fact, the National Rifle Association sought to quantify the media's pro-control bias through an analysis of one year's worth of television network firearms stories (excluding those on assault weapons). The analysis was done by the Media Research Center.

"Overall, 62 percent of the stories devoted substantially more time to pro– than anti–gun control arguments; talking heads who endorsed gun control outnumbered opponents by nearly 2-to-1; in stories concerning the Brady bill, the bias against gun control opponents was even greater, a ratio of 3 to 1," the study found. The National Rifle Association Institute for Legislative Action said the research "confirms what most gun owners already knew all too well—when it comes to the national media reporting the gun issue, objectivity is lost as emotion replaces fact."

Craig was born on a ranch in Idaho that his grandfather started in 1899. "From my earliest memories, there were firearms in our house," he said. They were mostly long guns used for hunting, though there were a few pistols around for shooting varmints. "I know when my Daddy rode for cattle he always packed one."

"I clearly understood the issue of the Constitution and gun rights, all rights within the Constitution, from a fairly early age," Craig said. "I won't tell you that my family talked often about the Constitution, but there was probably a reference to, 'This gun is a right that no one can take away from us.'"

Craig learned more about the issue as a student at the University of Idaho, where he was elected student body president. After graduating in 1969, he returned to the family ranch. He was elected to the Idaho State Senate in 1974 and served three terms there before winning election in 1980 to Congress as Idaho's First District representative. He held that office for 10 years before being elected to the Senate. He and his wife, Suzanne, have two sons, Mike and Jay, and a daughter, Shae.

Craig has held leadership posts in the Senate. He was elected by his fellow Republicans as chairman of the Republican Policy Committee and has served as chairman of the Steering Committee, a legislative action group for Senate conservatives. He has been a strong supporter of the proposed balanced budget amendment, private property rights, and limited taxation. He also serves on the powerful Senate Appropriations Committee.

Cultural differences play a role in the gun control debate, he said. In Idaho, "the second thing you put in your pickup is a gun rack. I do believe there is a different understanding of the use of firearms with those folks who come from the West, or from a background where their families have been active in hunting. And certainly westerners would argue [the issue] from the standpoint of personal safety, because the West was the last part of the United States where firearms were considered an important part of your make up."

A major defeat for gun rights supporters was the 1994 ban on assault weapons, the Violent Crime Control and Law Enforcement Act. The bill banned the future manufacture, transfer, and possession of 19 named semiautomatic weapons and 2 guns that have specific assault weapon characteristics. Craig considers it a bad law because it gives the federal government authority to define what is and isn't an assault weapon. That's not easy to do, because a few cosmetic changes to a firearm can make it look like an assault weapon, he said. "Everybody has a mental image of what [assault weapons] look like, and yet the mechanism inside can be identical to a hunting rifle. While I accept society's frustrations, once you start down that slope it can get mighty slippery and overinclusive. When it comes to government and government's relationship with the citizenry, I always prefer the least amount of restriction."

Craig's membership on the NRA board has proved an asset among most Idaho voters, though it comes up every election year, he said. In the 1996 race, his opponent challenged him to resign from the board, and Craig refused. When he joined the board "I viewed it as an important job to do, because by then my belief in our constitutional rights was well-established," he said. Every year in the Senate, he swears an oath to protect the U.S. Constitution and views his NRA membership as an extension of that effort.

With a seat in the Senate, Craig is in a good spot to try and reshape federal gun laws to fit his views. But the country already has the perfect gun law, he said. "It's called the Second Amendment. Does that fit modern-day society? It does with proper education and understanding and with swift enforcement of the laws."

ADDITIONAL READINGS

National Rifle Association web site: http://www.nra.org
Senate Bill S816 (bill was not passed). Washington, D.C. 1997.
Senator Larry Craig web site: http://www.senate.gov/~craig
Youth Crime Gun Interdiction Initiative web site: http://www.atf.treas.gov/
      core/firearms/ycgii/ycgii.htm

Miguel A. Faria, Jr.

Presenting Opposing Views in Medical Literature

Born: 1952, Sancti Spiritus, Cuba

Education: University of South Carolina, Columbia; M.D., Medical University of South Carolina, Charleston; Neurosurgery Residency: Emory University, Atlanta, GA

Current Positions: Neurosurgery Consultant; Editor, *Medical Sentinel*

Miguel A. Faria, Jr., had a busy neurosurgery practice, but he always made the time to review medical journals. He saw increasingly more written about guns and violence and saw that "only one side of the debate was being promulgated."

In 1993 he was asked to become editor of the *Journal of the Medical Association of Georgia*. "It was a sleepy little journal at the time. One of the jokes was if you wanted to keep something secret, publish it in this journal," he said. That soon changed.

As editor, he received information from the American Medical Association [AMA] on the association's positions on guns, violence, and domestic violence. "The slant was always toward gun prohibition and there was no other side to it. I decided I would try to obtain authors and investigators interested on the other side. First I published a few editorials, and then a few issues portraying the other side of gun control," he said.

That culminated in the March 1994 issue, with its cover story by Edgar A. Suter, "Guns in the Medical Literature—A Failure of Peer Review." The articles therein questioned the methods and conclusions of medical literature on guns and violence.

In his editor's introduction to that issue, Faria wrote that it was important to hear other views on the gun control debate because health care policy was being determined on the basis of currently published medical literature. "As it turns out, both the impact of gun

Miguel A. Faria, Jr. Courtesy of Bard Wrisley.

ownership by law-abiding citizens (for self-protection) and its purportedly adverse relationship to the American health care system take a diametrically opposed perspective when analyzed critically from what one hears and reads from the biased media coverage and distorted television sensationalism."

"I realized I was the first editor of a major medical journal to ever have published any article or editorial that demonstrated the benefits of gun ownership by law-abiding citizens," he said. "It was extremely controversial and received attention by national media."

So controversial, in fact, that Faria believes it cost him his job as editor in 1995. But he saw no alternative, he said. "As I delved more deeply, I realized the public health establishment, the Centers for Disease Control and Prevention (CDC) and more specifically the National Center for Injury Prevention and Control (NCIPC), was essentially doing results-oriented research. They had a preordained view that guns do not belong in hands of ordinary citizens. Their studies always found that gun availability was the number one factor for domestic and street violence, but they always refused to consider the beneficial aspects of guns in the hands of law-abiding ordinary citizens. And they wouldn't publish scholarly articles that did not come to that conclusion."

So Faria decided to make the journal the "conveyor of medical literature not being published elsewhere." The bulk of the medical literature on guns was reminiscent of "the scholasticism of the Middle Ages when studies supported a preordained conclusion. I thought that was fraud being perpetrated on people and policy makers. I could not go along," he said.

"Not just the public health establishment, but the AMA had joined the fray and was decidedly for gun control. Because I was involved in organized medicine and an AMA member, I was in the midst of it. In a free society, we need the free exchange of ideas. I determined that even if my professional livelihood was threatened, I would still do what was right."

The history of his native land contributed to his views. In 1966 Faria emigrated from Cuba. Throughout most of the 1950s, Fulgencio Batista was Cuba's president and dictator. Cuban citizens were allowed to keep, but had to register, their firearms. When Batista's government was overthrown by Fidel Castro in 1959, Castro had the Cuban secret service obtain those records and confiscate all privately held firearms. "That's one of the reasons it's still a Stalinist-style, communist dictatorship," he said.

An unarmed citizenry cannot protect itself, he said. A 1994 revolt in the malecon of Havana, in which protesters were literally armed with sticks and stones, ended when the Communist Blas Roca Brigade came in with their guns, killing many. "Tyranny is all too vivid in my mind. When science is subjugated to the state, the results have been as perverse as they have been disastrous. I don't want science and medicine to be subverted by the state in this country which I love. It's very dangerous to play politics with science," he said.

Faria sees his role in the gun control debate as being the one to publish the contrarian view in the medical literature. "Doctors have a lot of influence on their patients. People don't go to see their constitutional lawyer or their criminologist, but they do go see their doctor. If doctors are only seeing literature that amounts to gun control, that's scary," he said.

He's found a way to continue doing that. After he lost his job editing in 1995, the Association of American Physicians and Surgeons (AAPS) asked him to develop and edit their new journal, *Medical Sentinel*. "We continue to publish articles critical of the perversion or distortion of the scientific method. It's one of our missions to try to make sure that science and the scientific method are not being subverted by politicians for political purposes," he said.

"I'm proud to have been the editor who for the first time in the medical literature showed both sides of the gun control debate and arrived at the conclusion that guns in the hands of ordinary, law-abiding citizens can be extremely beneficial to society. There are benefits in terms of reduction of health care costs, by preventing injuries and death and protecting lives and property. It continues to be a contribution because *Medical Sentinel* has taken that role, along with defending the practice of private medicine according to the oath and tradition of Hippocrates."

ADDITIONAL READINGS

Faria, Miguel A. *Medical Warrior—Fighting Corporate Socialized Medicine*. Macon, Ga.: Hacienda Publishing, 1997.
———. "On the Journal's New Look and the Right to Self-Protection." *Journal of the Medical Association of Georgia* 83 (March 1994).
———. *Vandals at the Gates of Medicine*. Macon, Ga.: Hacienda Publishing, 1995.
Hacienda Publishing web site: http://www.haciendapub.com
Medical Sentinel web site: http://www.haciendapub.medsent.html

Richard J. Feldman

It's about Business, Not Ideology

Born: 1952, Brooklyn, NY

Education: B.A., Union College; J.D., Vermont Law School

Current Positions: former Executive Director, American Shooting
Sports Council; past President, American Firearms Council

While Richard J. Feldman is a true believer in gun rights, he's also
a pragmatist in representing the firearms industry. It's a business, and
thousands of people make their living manufacturing, distributing,
and selling guns. That's the focus for those inside the industry in
fighting gun control battles.

"If an organization's prime motivation is simply to defend Second
Amendment issues, in order to be true to that ideology it forces you
to fight everything counter to that. From a philosophical view, that's
fine, but we live in a real world," he said, and business can't function
from the same point of view.

"In business, you're involved in the sale of a product for profit. In
an ideologically based organization, if an obstacle shouldn't be there,
you fight until it's removed. As a business entity, we confront that
obstacle differently. We take one step right, one step forward and
one step left. We don't expend the energy it would take to remove
that obstacle."

Case in point: the Brady Act, which required states without comparable laws to abide by a five-day waiting period before the sale of
a handgun could be completed. "I understand how a gun owner feels
about the waiting period provision. I own 120 guns and I'm at a total
loss as to why I'd have to wait five days to buy my 121st gun," he
said.

But Feldman realizes that the waiting period, especially for first-
time gun owners, allows local police to do a background check. "We
don't want criminals to get guns. I'm more than willing to undergo

Richard J. Feldman.

a background check to make sure I'm not a felon. It's an interference, but it's a reasonable and limited one. It takes five minutes and I walk out with my gun. From where we sit, that's a good thing. We enthusiastically support and endorse mandatory background checks," he said.

Dealers, he said, do not innocently want to transfer firearms to felons or other prohibited people. And they have no way of determining if their customers have a criminal background without that check. "Even if we think philosophically that a background check is not exactly right, we've been able to direct this to a livable compromise."

Feldman hasn't always taken such a middle of the road approach.

In 1985 he had been a lobbyist with the National Rifle Association for less than four months when Bernhard Goetz shot four men on a New York City subway who Goetz said were threatening him and asking for money. "What a wonderful opportunity this created for us to get involved in New York City in supporting citizens' rights to defend themselves. The [NRA's] Institute for Legislative Action people looked at me like I was crazy. What they didn't grasp was that I was from New York City and I'm not intimidated by the capital of anti-gun sentiment," he said. In fact, Feldman moved quickly. Within days he had created some ads, gained the endorsement of some women's groups and the Congress of Racial Equality, and held a press conference in Manhattan on January 10, 1985. It was a huge media event, "because it was a great issue and the timing was perfect. We positioned ourselves on the side of the good guy," he said. "Everyone in New York felt for Bernie Goetz. I never said that what he did was right, but I used the case as a springboard to say that armed citizens have the ability to defend themselves." He still remembers the line of his that was most quoted or used on television coverage of the event: "The government which cannot protect its citizens has no right to deny them the means to protect themselves."

Goetz, who was alternately portrayed as vigilante or hero, was eventually convicted on a gun-carrying charge, and not on more serious charges of assault. However, a Bronx civil jury ordered that Goetz pay $43 million in punitive and compensatory damages to Darrell Cabey, who was left with permanent brain damage and paralysis.

The press event helped cement Feldman's place in the gun rights movement. Up until then, some found his allegiances suspect. He had worked with and for several gun control proponents. Indeed, "if you asked me 25 years ago, I would have said I was for gun control."

He grew up on Long Island, he's Jewish, his father was a psychiatrist, his mother a social worker. "My demographics suggest I should be the executive director of Handgun Control, Inc.," he said, laughing. He learned to fire a gun when he went to camp as a child. He learned how to shoot a handgun when he was a police officer in Cambridge, Massachusetts.

"I can probably point to the day when my rational understanding of the language of gun politics came face to face with the realities of life," he said. He went to investigate a robbery scene. The victim, a Portuguese immigrant, said it was the third robbery he'd had in two months. Feldman told him he should get a gun, and he said he had tried, but was denied. "I thought, 'He's got a criminal record.' So I went back to the station and had someone run his background. It came back clean." He asked his lieutenant why this man would have been denied a gun permit.

"He said the chief didn't believe anyone should be able to get a license unless they've been around. I asked what that meant and he said, 'If we know who you are.' I didn't need to ask. I knew that meant if you're a member of the social or political elite. But if you're an ordinary taxpayer, we have this discretionary authority and we'll use it against you. We're OK and you're not. That was the day I realized I hadn't thought out the gun control issue in real life."

A few months later, Feldman left the force and started law school in Vermont. That state's laws are often viewed by gun rights advocates as a model. Anyone who is not prohibited by federal law from owning a gun may lawfully carry concealed firearms. "The state trusted me. The same government that wants me to trust it, trusts me. As a Jeffersonian Libertarian, that reinforced my sense of righteousness."

He and his law school buddies regularly enjoyed target shooting near the campus of the rural law school. After law school, he worked in telecommunications law for President Ronald Reagan's administration. In the summer of 1984, the NRA job opened up.

He stayed at the NRA for three years and then went to work for the Sporting Goods Manufacturers Association doing tort reform. Soon after the gun industry formed the American Sports Shooting Council (ASSC), he was hired as its executive director from 1991 to 1999.

He believes the gun industry holds no particular responsibility for the gun violence in this country. "It's the same responsibility that auto manufacturers have regarding traffic fatalities with nondefective products. If a product is defective, then there's a liability," he said.

But the industry is misunderstood, he said. Unlike car manufacturers who know exactly where their cars are being shipped, gun manufacturers work with a small number of distributors. Those distributors then ship to licensed dealers. Those dealers then sell guns to the public. Those layers of distributorships mean that gun manufacturers don't have any idea where their guns are going.

That leads to another example of how the gun industry moves along a path separate from the NRA. The Bureau of Alcohol, Tobacco and Firearms is the federal agency charged with overseeing firearm sales. "Six years ago, I thought of the ATF as evil, working to harass gun dealers. I had never met with them until around 1994 and we started having discussions. They were tentative at first but once we started communicating, they started calling us for our opinion on prospective regulations," he said.

One of those was how to more easily trace firearms used in crimes. It used to be that if a police department wanted to run a trace on a firearm, it would contact the ATF with the make, model, and serial number of the gun. The ATF would contact the manufacturer, which would pull its charts to find out who the distributor was. The distributor would then determine which dealer it was sold to. And the dealer would have to review its transfer forms to see who bought the gun. "If the process started on a Friday night, it could easily be the following Wednesday before it was determined who the dealer was," Feldman said.

So the ASSC and ATF worked on developing a computerized system to trace much of this information on line. "Now if the tracing request comes in on a Friday night, an agent can be in Joe's gun shop by 10 A.M. Saturday morning," he said.

Computerized records of gun transfers make many gun rights advocates justifiably nervous, he acknowledged, "but we built a lot of firewalls and we did it without legislation and without regulation because it makes sense. The manual process of tracing guns is slow and expensive for the gun industry. This is good for law enforcement and it's good for the industry."

In other words, it was a good business move. And for Feldman and the groups he represented, that's what it's all about.

ADDITIONAL READINGS

American Shooting Sports Council web site: http://www.assc.org
Feldman, Richard J. "40 Years of Gun Control." *Guns & Ammo*, September 1998.
———. "Pro-Safety or Anti-Gun?" *Guns & Ammo*, September 1997.

Alan M. Gottlieb

"It Takes More than One Organization to Have a 'Pro-Gun' Movement"

Born: 1947, Los Angeles, CA

Education: University of Tennessee

Current Positions: Executive Vice President and Founder, Second Amendment Foundation; Chair, Citizens Committee for the Right to Keep and Bear Arms; Publisher

---

Alan M. Gottlieb wears the name like a badge of honor: gun nut. It's part of his e-mail alias, in fact. While he sees humor in the term, he finds little to amuse him in what he sees as an attack on Americans' most fundamental right. That's why he founded and continues to run the Second Amendment Foundation.

"I believe the need for the Second Amendment Foundation is great. First off, it is unwise for gun owners to put all their eggs in one basket," he said, referring to the National Rifle Association. "While the NRA does a great job defending gun rights they do not have a monopoly on all the best ways to do it." Gottlieb is a life member of the National Rifle Association.

By founding another gun rights organization, Gottlieb made what he sees as one of his biggest and most important contributions—creating a gun rights movement. "You can't have a movement with only one organization. Another major contribution I have made is to help create a grassroots army from the bottom up so that no one organization can any longer control the playing field for the gun rights movement. The net effect has been the creation of a real movement similar to that of the civil rights movement of the 1960s," he said. Gottlieb is also chairman of the Citizens Committee for the Right to Keep and Bear Arms, which claims 650,000 members and supporters.

Gottlieb sees his knack in being able to figure out "where the anti-gun movement will make its next moves and preempt the attack

Alan M. Gottlieb.

before it happens. I have gotten great satisfaction out of seeing that the gun rights movement is positioned in a way that it can be ahead of the curve in the gun control debate," Gottlieb said.

An early example is the defunding of the U.S. Conference of Mayors' gun control project. At an annual meeting in Tucson, Arizona, he got the mayors to pass a resolution in favor of banning Saturday night specials. "The anti-gun movement immediately announced this as a victory. But the real effect was to kill the funding of about one million dollars from a private foundation for the gun control project because the foundation would only support the banning of all handguns," Gottlieb recalled.

More recently, he was involved in the strategy used to defeat the 1997 Washington State gun control ballot measure. After reviewing polling data commissioned by Washington Ceasefire that showed 68 percent of the voters supporting the measure, "I developed a game plan to strip away supporters by using issues important to them that conflicted with the reasons why they supported the measure. The result was an astounding 71 percent to 29 percent defeat for the measure on Election Day, the biggest ballot box gun rights victory in history," he said.

While he believes his organization and the Citizens Committee for the Right to Keep and Bear Arms, of which he is chairman, have had a significant impact in molding the gun control debate, it has been a source of frustration to be in the shadow of the National Rifle Association. "It seems like every major victory we have, both the media and the anti-gun groups credit the NRA . . . or attack them," overlooking the role the smaller organizations played.

But as a result, Gottlieb can also have a little more fun with the media and the public than the NRA can. For those who would label him a loose cannon anyway, he might as well play the part. For example, he can issue press releases that reflect his sense of irony. On April 1, 1996, he sent out a press release entitled "Gun Lobby Endorses Clinton." In it, he wrote:

> President Clinton received another re-election boost today from an unlikely source—the gun lobby. The Citizens Committee for the Right to Keep and Bear Arms has announced that they will back his effort to retain the White House for four more years.
>
> "President Clinton has done more for gun owners than any previous administration," proclaimed [Gottlieb]. "Thanks to President Clinton, we now have a pro-gun Congress and our members are more energized than ever before."
>
> In addition to a friendly Congress, Clinton is responsible for record gun sales and huge profits for gun manufacturers, distributors and dealers. Without the specter of massive unconstitutional government intrusion raised by the passage of the Brady Bill and the "Assault Weapons" Ban, several manufacturers and scores of gun dealers might have been put out of business.

On May 10, 1998, he issued another press release slamming the voluntary gun turn-in program held by "the rabid gun control group, Ceasefire Oregon" (in the gun turn-in program, gun owners can trade in their unwanted firearms for $50 gift certificates):

"While we have no objection to a citizen voluntarily choosing to surrender an unwanted firearm, these people should understand that most firearms are worth far more than the flat $50 being offered," noted [Gottlieb]. "Before rushing down to surrender a potentially very valuable firearm, we strongly suggest that the owner stop at a local gun shop to have the firearm properly appraised. The gun store may even be willing to buy it from you for substantially more money."

Gottlieb took it a step further in the press release, suggesting that those who "don't care about the value of your guns . . . should donate them to us. We can give them to people who can't afford to purchase a gun for self-protection."

These examples are "proof that while the NRA is a 'big army,' we are like the Marines. We hit the beach first," he said.

Gottlieb faces another frustration in "the lack of objectivity of the national media. While anti-gunners' claims get accepted as fact at face value, the pro-gun side is forced to prove every statement we make and when the media prints our position, it always says the gun lobby 'claims.' "

He has tried to counter some of that by writing prodigiously himself. He is a member of the Outdoor Writers Association of America, and his articles have appeared in the Seattle *Times*, Manchester *Union Leader*, San Francisco *Examiner*, *Washington Post*, *Guns* magazine, *Guns & Ammo* magazine, *Gun Week*, Orlando *Sentinel*, Cincinnati *Inquirer*, Chicago *Tribune*, and *USA Today*. Articles about him have appeared in numerous other publications, and he has appeared on more than 2,500 television and radio talk shows. His work in defense of gun rights has won him the Cicero Award from the National Association of Federally Licensed Firearms Dealers and the Golden Eagle Award from the American Federation of Police in 1990.

In 1985 Gottlieb became publisher of *Gun Week*, the only national weekly newspaper for shooters, hunters, and gun enthusiasts. He now is also publisher of *Gun News Digest*.

He has recently become president of three radio stations: KBNP in Portland, Oregon, KSBN in Spokane, Washington, and KZTY in Las Vegas, Nevada. He is also chairman of the Talk America Radio Network, syndicating 24-hour programming to more than 450 affiliates coast to coast.

He is also president of the WorldWeb News Network, which has 96 affiliated radio stations. And he is president of Merril Associates, a nationally recognized direct response advertising agency specializing in direct mail, television and print ads, fund-raising, and public relations.

ADDITIONAL READINGS

Gottlieb, Alan M. *The Gun Grabbers*. Bellevue, Wash.: Merril Press, 1985.

———. *The Gun Rights Fact Book*. Bellevue, Wash.: Merril Press, 1997.

———. "Gun Ownership: A Constitutional Right." *Northern Kentucky Law Review* 10 (1982).

———. *Gun Owners Political Action Manual*. Ottawa, Ill.: Gun Hill, 1976.

———. *Politically Correct Guns*. Bellevue, Wash.: Merril Press, 1996.

———. *The Rights of Gun Owners*. Bellevue, Wash.: Merril Press, 1995.

Gottlieb, Alan M., and David Kopel. *Things You Can Do to Defend Your Gun Rights*. Bellevue, Wash.: Merril Press, 1997.

Second Amendment Foundation web site: http://www.saf.org

Daniel Gross

Channeling Anger into Formation of National Gun Control Group

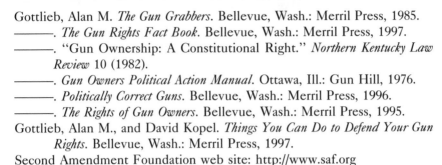

Born: 1967, Philadelphia, PA

Education: B.A., Tulane University

Current Position: Co-Executive Director, PAX

It was a lazy Sunday afternoon, February 23, 1997. Daniel Gross was relaxing at home, watching the Knicks game on TV. The game was interrupted by a news bulletin: someone had gone on a shooting rampage at the Empire State Building. Two people were dead; one was gravely injured.

Later, news reports would piece together the story of Palestinian Ali Abu Kamal, the lone gunman. He had arrived in New York in late December 1996. A few weeks later he traveled to Florida, moving into a hotel there. After 20 days, Kamal applied for a state identification card using his passport and another immigration paper as identification. Later that day, he used his new state-issued card to buy a .38 caliber Beretta handgun. His police background check

Daniel Gross.

turned up clean, and after a three-day waiting period he returned to the shop to pick up his new gun. News reports said Kamal went to Florida to evade New York's stricter gun laws.

Back in New York that Sunday afternoon, Kamal stormed onto the observation deck of the Empire State Building and started yelling and shooting. Horrified onlookers dove for cover and later described the scene as chaotic. Before Kamal shot himself, he killed Christoffer Burmeister, a young Danish guitar virtuoso and lead guitarist in the alternative rock band the Bushpilots. Seriously injured, with a bullet through his brain, was 27-year-old Matt Gross, leader of the same band.

But, back home, Dan Gross knew none of those details. The TV station picked up the Knicks game again. "I remember being upset that the Lakers tied the game up and it was going to go into overtime," Gross said. "That was my last moment of sanity."

Because then the phone rang. Gross heard his father on the other end saying something terrible had happened. "As soon as he said it, I put two and two together," Gross said. "Matt's been shot and Chris is dead," his father continued. Then Gross heard his father say, "Matt's going to be all right." His father disputes ever having said that.

Whether real or conjured in his own mind, Gross clung to those words as he went to the hospital. It was incomprehensible to him that he could lose his brother. "We were extremely close. I describe us as two halves of the same heart. Matt was the musician with a keen business sense; I was the businessman with an artistic flair," he said.

At the hospital, the scene was chaotic. New York City Mayor Rudolph Guiliani was there. Social workers swarmed around the family as they entered. Gross said he was in denial about Matt's condition until a young surgeon, a friend of Matt's, came over, looked him straight in the eye, and said, "Your brother might die tonight."

If that was to be the case, the family desperately wanted to see Matt alive one last time. The hospital bent its policies to allow them to watch as Matt was wheeled from the operating room, after eight hours of surgery, to the post-op area. Gathered behind a glass partition, family members yelled their encouragement as the gurney passed. "C'mon, Matt. Go, Matt!" Later on, in the recovery area, Gross held his brother's hand. "It was so cold. I'll never forget that."

Matt underwent another five hours of surgery the next day to relieve the swelling in his brain. For the next week, he lay in a coma. During that time, dozens of friends and family members kept a constant vigil at Matt's bedside. Music filled the room—Bushpilots, Van Morrison, classical, and other rock music. The hospital was flooded with calls from well-wishers everywhere.

During his vigil, Gross had plenty of time to reflect on the week leading up to the shooting. It had been a protracted 30th birthday celebration for him, and his memories were both silly and sublime.

On Thursday night, the Bushpilots played a small gig—and allowed him to sing along, dressed as Elvis. "I had rented the costume. The band was playing the riffs to 'Burning Love,' and Matt introduced me, saying, 'I've waited my whole life to see this.'" While he was singing, Dan looked to his left and saw Matt. He looked to his right and saw Chris. "Chris was an amazingly talented guitar player. And he had a smile that proceeded him into a room. As a rock guitar player, he didn't smile. He just found his zone and played. But that night, I looked at him and he had an ear-to-ear grin. Later that night, I told my girlfriend the thing I would never forget about the night was Chris's smile."

He never saw Chris again.

On Saturday night—the night before the shooting—friends and family gathered for a party. The whole Gross family posed for a family photo. It was an emotional moment for Gross to see his divorced parents putting aside their differences to celebrate the moment with him. Overcome by his feelings, he had to leave the room; Matt picked up the cue and followed him. "We had a special moment then," he said. Gross treasures a photo that was taken later that night of him and his brother hamming it up for the camera, kissing each other on the lips in a moment of spontaneous affection.

It was difficult to reconcile those recent images with the vision of his brother in a coma. But Matt defied the odds and survived. Two months later, as they were celebrating Matt's 28th birthday in the hospital, one of the attending physicians remembered seeing the family cheering Matt on that first night. "I thought, 'Those poor people. This guy's not going to wake up,'" he told Gross.

In fact, Matt exceeded all expectations for his recovery. Less than one year after the shooting, he was again fully mobile and able to speak. But damage to the brain is not so easily repaired. "Your brother took a bullet through his mainframe" is how one nurse described it to him. "When you talk to him, you can see how much rehabilitation he still needs," Gross said.

Dan Gross has sought his own kind of rehabilitation. Until late 1997 one of the youngest-ever partners in the New York advertising agency J. Walter Thompson, Gross quit his job to co-found PAX ("peace" in Latin), which he hopes will become a national movement to demand social and political change.

Immediately after the shooting, "it became apparent to me that in some way I was going to need to dedicate myself to making sure other people don't go through the living hell we've been through,'' Gross said. He met with Handgun Control, Inc., representatives, and while he speaks whenever they request him to, he decided that lobbying wasn't enough. "You're never going to out-lobby the National Rifle Association. The closer I got to this issue, the more I realized how absolutely insane the situation is. The will and welfare of the people is being so blatantly controlled by a lobbying group that represents only a small segment of the population. It's embarrassing as an American and it's heartbreaking as a victim.''

Gross said he is particularly frustrated by the argument that had others at the Empire State Building that day had a gun, Ali Abu Kamal could have been stopped sooner. "In this specific instance, there is no doubt to anyone who was there that if anyone else had a gun, it would have resulted in more injury and death. The scene was already mass chaos. More people would have been shot," he said.

That argument points to a larger issue, Gross added. "Guns do not protect us. That's a myth perpetuated by the NRA. In fact, guns put us more at risk. A gun in the home is 43 times more likely to be used in the death of the owner or another person in the household than in the death of an intruder. A household with a gun in it is five times more likely to have a suicide and three times more likely to have a homicide." He acknowledged occasions where a person uses a gun in self-defense, but added, "Those are the exceptions. And the NRA uses those to its advantage.''

Gross will rely on his media savvy to promote PAX's agenda. "PAX is a communication-oriented organization designed to deal with the issue of gun violence from a mass media perspective. The fact is, the overwhelming majority of Americans already support commonsense measures to prevent tragedies like my brother's, and the hundreds of others like it that occur in this country every day. There are organizations like Handgun Control, Inc., that are dealing with the issue very well from a legislative and lobbying perspective; however, no organization has stepped forward to rally that support into an effective national movement. That's why PAX was created. PAX's mission is to instigate a powerful national anti–gun violence movement through an innovative and aggressive mass communications strategy. PAX believes that for real change to occur, a powerful national movement must be formed—a movement based on common sense and the common good that unites all of us in this country in passionate rejection of gun violence,'' Gross said.

Gross and his partner Talmage Cooley have devised a three-pronged approach for PAX. They take their lessons from other influential causes. The first strategy is "to create an unrelenting presence in the national consciousness. We'll do that through traditional means such as TV, print, and radio advertising and through nontraditional means. Looks at AIDS and the red ribbon. Or a rallying cry like 'Friends don't let friends drive drunk.' " PAX was working with a clothing manufacturer to get its logo on the back of a line of leather jackets. The group plans huge concerts, like those that made Amnesty International's goals well known. "I want to create the perception that this is one of the defining issues of our time," he said.

Gross has the background to make that work. "In advertising, I helped build brands. As far as I'm concerned, there's no brand more important to build than a vision of America free of gun violence."

The second component of PAX is to create a sophisticated grass-roots Internet network where various groups operating autonomously can collect and share strategies.

Finally, PAX wants to make it easy to get involved. "That can be as simple as voting correctly on the issue or speaking out intelligently at a cocktail party. We provide those resources on the Internet site. By typing in your zip code, you can find out who your representatives are, how they've voted on gun control issues, and you'll also be able to find out what grass-roots efforts are going on around you."

His motivation to start PAX and work to prevent similar tragedies has kept his rage at bay. As far as gunman Ali Abu Kamal goes, "I will think of him with utmost contempt and as the personification of evil, heartbreak, disaster, and tragedy. But I do not feel rage. There are too many rational commonsense things that can be done to waste my time with rage. That's an emotion that tends to come up when there are no alternatives. I have alternatives. I want to make sure that others don't get the chance to do what he did. As long as I have this opportunity, my family and I may be spared the rage," Gross said.

ADDITIONAL READINGS

Bruni, Frank. "Brother of Shooting Victim Backs Stiff Gun Controls." *New York Times*, April 14, 1997.

———. "Calls for Stricter Gun Control Laws Increase in Aftermath of Shooting." *New York Times*, February 26, 1997.

———. "Man Shot on Empire State Walks Back Toward Life." *New York Times*, April 26, 1997.

———. "Rock Band's Promise Was Bright Until Gunman Shattered Their Hope." *New York Times*, February 25, 1997.

———. "A World Remade by Empire State Gunfire." *New York Times*, May 18, 1998.

PAX web site: http://www.paxusa.org

Van Gelder, Lawrence. "For Victim of Attack, a Memorial Full of Music." *New York Times*, March 1, 1997.

———. "Man Who Was Shot atop Empire State Building Goes Home." *New York Times*, May 24, 1997.

Stephen P. Halbrook

Defending Gun Rights, All the Way to the Supreme Court

Born: 1947, Greenwood, MS

Education: B.S. and Ph.D., Florida State University; J.D., Georgetown University Law Center

Current Positions: Attorney; Author

Not many attorneys in this country get to argue a case before the U.S. Supreme Court. And only half of those win. Stephen P. Halbrook is among the latter elite group. Halbrook is considered the premiere litigator in the country for gun rights. He is regularly called on by the National Rifle Association and gun manufacturers to represent them.

Halbrook served as lead counsel in *Printz v. United States*, representing local sheriffs who argued that the federal government's mandate to conduct background checks on purchasers of handguns was unconstitutional (see profile of Jay Printz). The highest court in the nation agreed in 1997 and struck down that component of the Brady Act. As long as the Brady Act would stay on the books, through November 1998, gun dealers would still have to forward their pa-

Stephen P. Halbrook.

perwork to the chief local law enforcement officer, but that officer could not be forced to conduct a background check.

In arguing *Printz* and in his writings, Halbrook looks beyond the Second Amendment. He has focused on the Tenth and Fourteenth Amendments to the U.S. Constitution. Those amendments read:

> The powers not delegated to the United States by the Constitution, nor prohibited by it to the States, are reserved to the States respectively, or to the people. (U.S. Constitution, Amendment 10)

> No state shall make or enforce any law which shall abridge the privileges or immunities of citizens of United States; nor shall any state deprive any person of life, liberty or property, without due process of law; nor deny to any person within its jurisdiction the equal protection

of the laws. (U.S. Constitution, Amendment 14, section 1)

Halbrook explained: "The Tenth Amendment affirms that the federal government has limited, enumerated powers and that the powers not delegated to it are reserved to the states respectively, or to the people. Its purpose is to maintain individual liberty by decentralizing centers of power and allowing community participation. It is equally important that states and localities not violate fundamental freedoms, and the Fourteenth Amendment was adopted to protect Bill of Rights freedoms (including the right to keep and bear arms) from state or local infringement."

"Prohibitions on firearms ownership by law-abiding citizens often violate other parts of the Bill of Rights. Several laws have been declared unconstitutional for being vague, which violates the due process right to notice of what is illegal," he said.

What Halbrook has found, in arguing against gun control on the basis of the Tenth Amendment, is a way to circumvent the debate on whether the Second Amendment provides an individual right to keep and bear arms or a collective militia right, such as for the National Guard. Halbrook firmly believes it's the former. "The 'collective' rights view of the Second Amendment argues that 'the people' in the Second Amendment (unlike the First and Fourth) means the state militia or National Guard. Ex-Chief Justice Burger argued this position in a fittingly superficial publication: *Parade* magazine. The argument was invented in the twentieth century and is contrary to the weight of scholarship."

However, his arguments are more expedient. Second Amendment arguments haven't been very successful in federal courts in overturning gun control laws. Halbrook, in an interview with *Legal Times*, noted, "When you have a law that you don't like, you're going to attack it with whatever works in the courts."

That's because he has seen how laws can get twisted. His decision to specialize in firearms law cases came early in his legal career, when he was the court appointed defender for a man charged with transferring pipe bombs. "It turned out that the federal gun police [Bureau of Alcohol, Tobacco and Firearms or BATF] was paying a drug dealer to entrap drug users to commit unrelated firearms offenses so that BATF could get credit for making arrests. The BATF informant offered drugs to the addict in exchange for finding someone to make pipe bombs. The government instigated crimes that never would have been committed in order to make arrests," he said.

Halbrook also defends gun manufacturers in tort liability cases. In tort law, in which a person gains the right to sue for damages, it is being argued that manufacturers should be held responsible for injuries and deaths caused by the consumer products they create. Applying that theory to guns, said Halbrook, means that as soon as a handgun is sold "it would be said to be transformed into an unreasonably dangerous, and hence defective, product." It wouldn't matter whether the gun was used recklessly or had been stolen. The blame is traced back to and placed on the manufacturer and everyone who transferred the gun. "The purpose of existing tort law is to enable members of the general public to enjoy the use of safe and reliable handguns, not to deprive them of that use," he wrote in *Hamline Law Review*. In that article, he compared those who believe that guns are unreasonably dangerous products to Luddites, a group of British workmen who, fearing progress, attempted to prevent the use of labor-saving machinery by destroying it.

While Halbrook takes his work seriously, he also enjoys the humor that arises. Perhaps that's why the lightest moments of arguing *Printz* before the Supreme Court still stand out in Halbrook's memory. "A Handgun Control brief filed in *Printz* asserted that '27 percent of armed felons claimed to have bought their buns at retain outlets.'"

Attorney General Janet Reno sent out a letter to the law enforcement community explaining the Court's decision. The typo that tickled Halbrook stated that the law enforcement officer had five "dismays" rather than "days" to respond.

Even Halbrook didn't escape blunder-free. During oral arguments, he stated that on average there are one and a half deputies on patrol at any given time. Chief Justice William Rehnquist stopped him. "You're not trying to tell us that one and a half deputies could be on duty, are you?"

His personal interest in guns goes back to his days as a boy at summer camp in the Tennessee mountains. "I was taught how to shoot safely and won the .22 caliber rifle sharpshooter medal. Plenty of youngsters hunted with shotguns in those days, but there were no schoolyard shootings—nor were there video games glorifying the fun of killing sprees. I cannot understand why intolerant people seek to criminalize wholesome and victimless activities like the shooting sports. Imprisoning someone because her target rifle has a bayonet stud—no one has been killed with a bayonet in the U.S. since the Civil War—recalls the Inquisition," he said.

By the time he entered college in the mid-1960s, Halbrook said, the Second Amendment was being "ridiculed by smug social engineers who knew what was best for the people. In my Ph.D. program, I discovered that Aristotle and the great political philosophers held an armed citizenry to be necessary for balance in a commonwealth."

Yet study on the Second Amendment was limited. In fact, he said the right to bear arms received not a single mention in his law school classes, including his constitutional law classes. "This has dramatically changed. The Second Amendment today holds a respectable place in scholarship, and most academics agree that it guarantees an individual right of the peaceable citizen to keep and bear firearms. As Yale law professor Akhil Amar puts it, the cartridge box is just as much a cornerstone of democracy as the ballot box and the jury box."

Halbrook continues competitive shooting and is regarded as a superior marksman. He also competes in about three triathlons each year. "It doesn't get any better than a one mile ocean swim, a 24 mile bike ride on country roads, and a 10K run," he said. He's been a marathon runner since 1984 and noted that running 26 miles "gives you lots of time to think—you can write a book in your mind and take a good look at your personal life all in one race."

Or prepare your arguments for another Supreme Court case.

ADDITIONAL READINGS

Cohen, Julie. "Tenth Amendment's Hired Gun: NRA Advocate Litigates Against Federal Power." *Legal Times*, June 19, 1995.

Halbrook, Stephen P. "Bill of Rights Redivivus: Amendment II." *The Champion* (National Association of Criminal Defense Lawyers) 17 (January/February 1993).

———. "Congress Interprets the Second Amendment: Declarations by a Co-Equal Branch on the Individual Right to Keep and Bear Arms." *Tennessee Law Review* 62 (Spring 1995).

———. "Encroachments of the Crown on the Liberty of the Subject: Pre-Revolutionary Origins of the Second Amendment." *University of Dayton Law Review* 15 (Fall 1989).

———. *Firearms Law Deskbook: Federal and State Criminal Practice.* New York: Clark Boardman Callaghan, 1995. Supplements, 1996, 1997.

———. *Freedmen, the Fourteenth Amendment, and the Right to Bear Arms, 1866–1876.* Westport, Conn.: Praeger, 1998.

———. "Guns, Criminality and Federalism: Supreme Court Curbs Congressional Power; Reins in Courts of Appeals." *The Champion* 20 (June 1996).

———. "The Jurisprudence of the Second and Fourteenth Amendments." *George Mason University Law Review* 4 (Spring 1981).

———. "The Original Understanding of the Second Amendment." In *The Bill of Rights: Original Meaning and Current Understanding*, ed. E. Hickok. Charlottesville: University Press of Virginia, 1991. Pp. 117–129.

———. "Personal Security, Personal Liberty, and 'The Constitutional Right to Bear Arms': Visions of the Framers of the Fourteenth Amendment." *Seton Hall Constitutional Law Journal* 5 (1995): 341–434.

———. "Rationing Firearms Purchases and the Right to Keep Arms: Reflections on the Bills of Rights of Virginia, West Virginia, and the United States." *West Virginia Law Review* 96 (1993): 1–83.

———. "The Right of the People or the Power of the State: Bearing Arms, Arming Militias, and the Second Amendment." *Valparaiso University Law Review* 26 (Fall 1991).

———. "The Right to Bear Arms in the First State Bills of Rights: Pennsylvania, North Carolina, Vermont and Massachusetts." *Vermont Law Review* 10 (1985): 255–320.

———. *A Right to Bear Arms: State and Federal Bills of Rights and Constitutional Guarantees*. Westport, Conn.: Greenwood Press, 1989.

———. "Second-Class Citizenship and the Second Amendment in the District of Columbia." *George Mason University Civil Rights Law Journal* 5 (1995): 105–178.

———. *Target Switzerland: Swiss Armed Neutrality in World War II*. New York: Sarpedon, 1998.

———. *That Every Man Be Armed: The Evolution of a Constitutional Right*. Albuquerque: University of New Mexico Press, 1984.

———. "To Keep and Bear Their Private Arms: The Adoption of the Second Amendment, 1789–1791." *Northern Kentucky Law Review* 10 (1982): 13–39.

———. "Tort Liability for the Manufacture, Sale and Ownership of Handguns?" *Hamline University Law Review* 6 (1983).

———. "What the Framers Intended: A Linguistic Analysis of the Right to 'Bear Arms.' " *Law and Contemporary Problems* 49 (1986).

Halbrook, Stephen P., with Richard Gardiner. "NRA and Law Enforcement Opposition to the Brady Act: From Congress to the Courts." *St. John's Journal of Legal Commentary* 10 (Fall 1994).

Halbrook, Stephen P., with Michael K. McCabe, eds. *Defectless Firearms Litigation*. Washington, D.C.: NRA-ILA, 1984.

Hunter, Gorden. "Gun Ruling Gives Davidians Firepower." *Legal Times*, February 5, 1996.

Marion P. Hammer

From Local Activism to NRA's Top Spot

Born: 1939, Columbia, SC

Education: attended Georgia State College, Atlanta

Current Positions: Executive Director, Unified Sportsmen of Florida, and board member and Past President, National Rifle Association

---

Marion P. Hammer was raised on a farm by her grandparents. "My grandfather taught me to shoot a .22 rifle just before I was six years old. I went hunting with him and guns were a natural part of my life," she said.

Those early lessons in handling and respect for firearms have stayed with her throughout her life. She married a gun owner, and the couple found enjoyment in hunting and competitive shooting. These were very natural progressions and personal choices, she said. Issues of gun rights and criminal violence didn't figure much in her thinking.

Then came the 1968 assassinations of civil rights activist Martin Luther King, Jr., and presidential hopeful Robert F. Kennedy, which resulted in the Gun Control Act of 1968. "I was offended that my government would attempt to take away my rights because of the egregious violent actions of a handful of criminals. Of course, we were all saddened by the tragedies leading up to Gun Control Act, but the attempt was like a bucket of cold water in my face. I didn't intend to sit by and allow my government to take my rights without a fight," she said.

So she took up the cause, speaking out, becoming a part of grass-roots efforts wherever she was living. By 1974 she and her family had moved to Florida, where the Unified Sportsmen of Florida (USF) was chartered in 1976 as a voice for gun rights. "When USF was formed, there was an intense push in Florida to totally close down

Marion P. Hammer.

individual firearms rights. We were seeing every kind of gun control you could imagine. I became involved as a member of USF, attended organizational meetings and became secretary/treasurer for one year before I was hired as executive director to set up an office in Tallahassee," she said. That was in 1978, and she's held the position ever since.

Among the shining moments of her tenure was the state's passage of a right to carry law in 1987—the one that spawned a nationwide trend in right to carry legislation. Hammer explained the background of the law. "In 1892, Florida put a law on the books that required a license to carry a concealed firearm. Until that time, people were allowed to carry and were not prosecuted unless the sheriff didn't like you and wanted to lock you up. Many court cases arose in the early 1900s, alleging that gun control was not only discriminatory, it was discretionary. The licensing requirement was a tool that sheriffs had for punishing people they didn't like."

Depending on where you lived in the state, the process for obtaining a permit to carry varied. In some areas, the process involved a modest fee and background check. In others, the application fee cost hundreds of dollars and wasn't refundable—and very few permits were granted, she said. "The situation in the state was one of geography and politics. If you lived in the wrong place and had politicians who didn't like guns, you weren't going to be able to exercise your right to carry."

The right to carry law that passed in 1987 set uniform standards statewide. It established a division of licensing under the secretary of state as the issuing authority. The legislation was "shall issue," meaning that the licensing authority was required to issue a license unless the applicant had been convicted of a felony, was an alcohol or drug abuser, or had been adjudicated mentally ill.

It wasn't an easy process to pass the bill into law. The year before, the state legislature passed it, but Democratic Governor Bob Graham vetoed it. The following year, when Republican Governor Bob Martinez was in office, he signed the bill the day it passed.

The results have been tremendous, Hammer said. "It's worked even better than we thought it would. All you have to do is look at the statistics. Since the law went into effect and people began to be licensed, the murder rate has dropped dramatically in this state."

In fact, it has made criminals in the state rethink their strategies, she noted. Juveniles interviewed in a detention center said they would avoid anybody they feared had a gun because they didn't want to be shot. "That's the reason they had begun to target tourists coming out of the airport. They knew tourists wouldn't have guns. But they didn't know about residents because all law-abiding citizens could get one," she said. "Criminals will leave you alone if they think you're armed. That's one of the primary reasons for being armed. You don't want to use it, but you should be prepared to protect yourself if necessary."

Besides the decline in murders, Hammer finds another success in the right to carry law. The law's opponents fretted that an increase in the number of guns readily accessible would result in higher numbers of homicides, suicides, and accidents. "Because of the statistical tracking required by the law, we've been able to prove that licensed holders are not a problem. That's one of the reasons other states have used Florida as a model. The data is the only way you can dispel these emotional claims about Florida becoming another OK Corral and these predictions of blood in the streets," she said.

Hammer is as critical of those who abuse guns as she is of those who try to pass blanket controls that aim to affect criminals and law abiding citizens alike. "We have been doing all we can to ensure that the rights of law-abiding citizens are not diminished while the rights of criminals are stripped away. I've always believed that when you abuse a right by your action, you give up that right," she said. She points to those laws which prohibit possession by minors and by anyone convicted of serious crimes. "Those are what we call gun controls because they attempt to keep guns out of the hands of criminals and youngsters not properly trained and supervised. Those laws work if they are enforced. But some politicians seem to fall into the habit of adding layers while failing to enforce existing laws."

Hammer's role in Florida activism got her noticed on a national level. She joined the board of directors of the National Rifle Association in 1983. In 1992 she was asked to run for the office of second vice president. She had declined the offer in earlier years because she wasn't ready to commit the time and take attention away from her work in Florida. This time, she held a family meeting. Her children, all adults by then, acknowledged that her time with them and their children would be lessened, but they were willing to make that sacrifice. "It wasn't easy. The time I spend with them gives me great joy," she said.

She was unanimously elected and reelected the following year. By 1994 she was tapped as first vice president, and was reelected to that position in 1995. "Our president died unexpectedly of a heart attack in 1995 and I was thrust into the position and into the limelight," Hammer recalled. She finished out his term as president and was elected to the position in 1996 and 1997. The NRA presidency is limited to two consecutive one-year terms. She was followed in 1998 by actor Charlton Heston.

Hammer was the first woman to hold the top position, something she finds unique and ordinary at the same time. "It was only unique because I was the first president. The first woman was elected to the NRA's board of directors 50 years ago. Women have always played a role with the National Rifle Association. That never had come across to the general public. The stereotype is that NRA members are tough guys with five o'clock shadows and stogies hanging out of their mouths. That image is not now and has never been accurate," she said. Once described by a legislator as being a "good old boy in a skirt," Hammer noted, "That's how little some people know about this organization. It's not an organization of 'good old boys,' but of people who believe in education and safety and care about our rights to pass along to future generations."

With the lead role behind her, she can spend more time focusing on NRA issues and projects that are most important to her. A member of the board of trustees of the NRA Foundation, she can see that endowments established for the youth programs under her presidency are continued. "In the summer of 1997, after years of talking about building a National Firearms Museum, the plans were finalized. The museum opened in June 1998," she said.

The museum occupies 15,000 square feet on the first floor of NRA's headquarters in Fairfax, Virginia. "There are more firearms on display there than in the Smithsonian," she said. Seeing that project through, from fund-raising to ribbon-cutting, has been one of her joys.

That's also true of the Eddie the Eagle program, Hammer's brainchild for gun safety education for young children. "I'm called the creator, mother, founder . . . and ramrod," she added, laughing. But she doesn't joke about the program itself. "I believe we needed it because there was no program to teach preschool through sixth grade children that guns are not toys and that they shouldn't play with them or touch them. The challenge was to find a program that the little ones could understand and relate to and would still be meaningful to older youngsters. It has been a source of great pride to me that in 10 years this program has been taught to more than 10 million youngsters." Among its awards, the program netted Hammer a Citation for Outstanding Community Service from the National Safety Council in October 1993. She also received the Golden Achievement Award from the National School Public Relations Association in April 1994. The emphasis on education is the legacy she would like to claim for herself and the National Rifle Association in general.

ADDITIONAL READINGS

Eddie the Eagle web site: http://www.nra.org/eddie/eddiemain.html

Lindstrom, Andy. "Marion Hammer on the Firing Line." *Tallahassee*, March/
    April 1996.

National Firearms Museum web site: http://www.nra.org/museum/mus-
    new.html

National Rifle Association web site: http://www.nra.org

Schneider, Jim. "Marion Hammer: Old Friend of the NMLRA at Top of
    NRA." *Muzzle Blasts: Official Publication of the National Muzzle Loading
    Rifle Association*, March 1998.

Scott Harshbarger

Using the Power of the Attorney General's Office to Regulate Junk Handguns

Born: 1941, New Haven, CT

Education: B.A., Harvard University, 1964; Harvard Law School, 1968

Current Position: Former Attorney General, Commonwealth of Massachusetts

Don't tell Scott Harshbarger he's not tough on crime and criminals. That charge is often thrown at gun control supporters, but Harshbarger, the former attorney general of Massachusetts and a former district attorney, said it can't stick to him. "As a criminal prosecutor, I have taken a very aggressive position on juvenile and serious offenders, particularly in gun crimes," he said.

In Massachusetts, "we have put more serious felons in jail. We've worked hard at getting at gun trafficking through tracing weapons. But we still see weapons crimes occur that we could have prevented," he said. As attorney general, he asked everyone in his office to give violence prevention and crime control their attention. "An obvious element was to support the assault weapons ban, which also had the support of law enforcement in this state."

Scott Harshbarger. Courtesy of Marilyn Humphries.

Independent of the state legislature, the attorney general's office has broad consumer protection powers—and Harshbarger used them. He created regulations effectively banning "junk handguns" from being sold in the state.

"We used the consumer protection powers that we have. If there is any product from which we need such protection, it's handguns. We have consumer protections on everything from baby rattles to toothpaste. Handguns shouldn't be the exception."

The goal of the regulations isn't to ban handguns, he said. In fact, his staff worked for two years discussing standards with Massachusetts-based gun manufacturer Smith & Wesson. "There's nothing in our regulation that would preclude them from making good quality handguns. Our regulations are aimed only at handgun manufacturers which make defective products. We won't allow them to be sold in our state."

His motivation was simple. "Handguns are a major threat to our public health, especially that of our children. Since we have the power, we thought these were common steps to make handguns safer and prevent tragedies among our children. Gun control alone isn't the answer to gun violence, but it is part of the solution."

The regulations were challenged by the gun lobby, yet Harshbarger is confident of prevailing. "This long established power of the attorney general has been upheld numerous times. I don't intend to allow the gun lobby to change that," he said. Harshbarger sees parallels between this fight and the one waged by him and 41 other attorneys general in the mid-1990s with the tobacco companies, another industry with a powerful lobby.

Many other state attorneys general have shown interest in Harshbarger's action "but face stiff resistance," he said. He expects that will subside as the regulations are upheld and are shown to be effective. "The fight is going to have to come from the states. Sadly, Congress is the home court of large interests, like tobacco and the NRA. But the attorney general's power is a tremendous opportunity. The vast majority of the people in the state support our efforts to ban assault weapons and make handguns safer. We need to listen to the people, not to the special interests."

He finds irony in the gun lobby's challenge, because their usual argument is that firearms policies should be dealt with at the state level. "The only time they say the matter should be dealt with federally is if an attorney general does something," he said, laughing. "They have tremendous lobbying power and influence, but one thing they lack is common sense."

Harshbarger was born in 1941 and was a three-sport athlete in high school in central Pennsylvania. He was a star halfback for Harvard University's football team and completed his undergraduate degree there in 1964. After graduation, he spent a year volunteering at an urban ministry in East Harlem in New York City.

"What I experienced there crystallized everything for me," he recalled. "I saw how a group of caring and committed citizens could come together as a community to improve their quality of life, despite the overwhelming forces arrayed against them. I decided that the best way I could serve others and make a difference was through the law."

At Harvard Law School he served as president of the Harvard Voluntary Defenders, and graduated in 1968. He later served as deputy chief counsel for the Massachusetts Defenders Committee, the state's public defenders agency. In 1975 he was named chief of the state's Public Protection Bureau, where he championed consumer protection, environmental protection, public charities, and civil rights issues.

He served eight years as district attorney in Middlesex County before being elected attorney general in 1990. In his first term in that office, Harshbarger worked on combating urban and school violence; advocating criminal justice reform; pursuing health care reform, fair lending, and domestic violence initiatives; and prosecuting white-collar crime and public corruption.

He deployed dozens of prosecutors to district courts around the state, where they won hundreds of convictions against violent criminals. Working with district attorneys and mayors, he created and expanded the Safe Neighborhood Initiative, a community policing and prosecution model for improving the quality of life in urban neighborhoods.

He also expanded an award-winning student mediation program to reduce violence in urban middle and high schools. He sponsored and won passage of a law against stalking in 1992, and won passage of a victim's compensation law in 1994. He also played a lead role in passage of court reform legislation and a truth in sentencing law. He secured the longest state prison term ever for an environmental crime and won more than $5 million in restitution for consumers. He proposed and implemented the guidelines for hospitals to protect community health care and won a historic agreement to reform mortgage lending practices.

Harshbarger was overwhelmingly reelected in 1994. In his second term, he worked on an array of quality of life issues, including tobacco litigation, handgun safety, gambling, and health care fraud. He was one of the first attorneys general in the nation to sue the tobacco industry to recover health care costs borne by taxpayers.

He served on the White House Conference on Aging; the Advisory Council on Violence Against Women that was jointly sponsored by the U.S. Departments of Justice and Health and Human Services, and the National Research Council's Committee on the Assessment of Family Violence Interventions. He was elected in 1996 to a one-year term as president of the National Association of Attorneys General, and made protection of the elderly his national priority.

He is married to Judith Stephenson, who has worked as an assistant district attorney in Middlesex and Norfolk counties. He has two sons, Michael, 34, and Benjamin, 30, and three stepdaughters, Tenley, 28, Cameron, 23, and Ann, 21. A diehard Elvis Presley fan, Harshbarger also enjoys mystery novels, running, and fast-pitch softball.

Harshbarger, who ran for governor in 1998, said his work on handguns as attorney general was generally a help. "Running for governor, I can't run away from my principles or my record. I will always stand up for the people and against the special interests. People may or may not agree with me, but they respect that this is a serious problem that needs to be addressed."

His work on gun safety has never been a matter of political posturing, he said. "I'm a parent of five now-grown children, but it's something I thought about often while they were growing up. As a parent and a former coach, I worked with many young people before becoming a prosecutor. In that role, I had to deal with tragedies at the end of the line—whether it was gun violence, drunk driving, or drug abuse. I saw the value in prevention, at getting at the cause."

His efforts at banning assault weapons and making handguns safer are a natural evolution of this prevention effort. He said he's saddened by those stories in which young people are unintentionally killed or injured by friends while playing with guns. "Every time I see the parent of a 12-year-old boy who went to play at a friend's house on Christmas Eve and never came home, it reinforces my will. Those parents who are willing to take their tragedies public are the great heroes of the gun control movement."

Those stories, he said, are the ones that will help reduce the influence of the gun lobby and turn attention to prevention. As attorney general, when he realized he had the regulatory power to do likewise, "I knew I had better seize the opportunity."

ADDITIONAL READINGS

Ayers, B. Drummond, Jr. "California Advances Ban on Cheap Handguns." *New York Times*, June 5, 1997.

Commonwealth of Massachusetts Regulations, 940 CMR 16.00: Handgun Sales. Published in the state Register.

Massachusetts Gun Control Act of 1998. Available online at www.state.ma.
    us.eops.
Salant, Jonathan D. "Harshbarger Urges National Gun Laws." *The Standard-
    Times*, New Bedford, Massachusetts, October 9, 1997.

Richard and Holley Galland Haymaker

Exchange Student's Shooting Prompts Gun Control Efforts

Richard Haymaker

Born: 1940, San Francisco, CA

Education: B.A., Carleton College; Ph.D., University of California
    at Berkeley

Current Position: Physics Professor, Louisiana State University.
    Past President, Louisiana Ceasefire

Holley Galland Haymaker

Born: 1944, Goshen, NY

Education: B.A., Smith College; M.D., Tulane University; M.A.,
    Columbia Teachers College

Current Position: Associate Professor of Clinical Family Practice,
    Louisiana State University Medical School

It was a simple mistake, really. Just two boys on their way to a party,
knocking on the door of the wrong house. But it triggered a violent
act, one that took the life of a 16-year-old boy and threw Richard
and Holley Galland Haymaker of Louisiana deep into the debate
over guns.

The Haymakers had a contented life in Baton Rouge. Both were
at Louisiana State University, where she taught medicine and he was
a professor of physics. On an evening in October 1992, the couple's
son, Webb, headed out to a Halloween party with his friend, Japanese
exchange student Yoshihiro Hattori. Yoshi, as he was known to

Richard Haymaker. Courtesy of Sarah Fujiwara.

friends, was an exuberant and outgoing teen who had been living with the Haymakers for two months.

But that night the boys mistakenly went to the wrong house in a Baton Rouge community called Central. In their Halloween costumes—Yoshi was dressed as John Travolta in the movie *Saturday Night Fever*—the boys apparently startled the couple inside the house. In a few horrifying seconds, the man of the house, 30-year-old Rodney Peairs, shot and killed Yoshi outside the home with a .44 Magnum.

The horror the Haymakers felt over Yoshi's death transformed

Holley Galland Haymaker. Courtesy of Sarah Fujiwara.

them into crusaders against the easy availability of guns and the American attitude toward firearms as a means of self-defense.

"Yoshi died at the hands of an armed citizen in a country that is still in its infancy in facing the consequences of unrestricted gun possession," Richard Haymaker said. "And thus he died as an ambassador to America in a peculiarly American way."

The Haymakers began a public awareness initiative that brought together hundreds of local, statewide, and national organizations on the issue. They worked closely with the Washington, D.C.–based Coalition to Stop Gun Violence, which later took over the Ceasefire Action Network that the Haymakers had helped develop.

They also gathered 150,000 signatures on a petition asking for tougher restrictions on the "easy availability of guns in this country" and presented them to President Bill Clinton in a meeting at the White House in 1993. The Haymakers were joined at that meeting by Yoshi's parents, Masa and Mieko Hattori, who helped organize a petition drive that had gathered 1.5 million signatures in Japan.

In 1996 the Haymakers formed Louisiana Ceasefire, a nonprofit organization based in Baton Rouge that lobbies for "responsible gun laws" at all government levels. "It has been given to us to speak," Holley Haymaker said. "We must. We must."

Much of what the Haymakers have done has been with the support and cooperation of the Hattoris. The huge public response in Japan to media accounts of Yoshi's death convinced the Hattoris to begin their own petition drive and public awareness campaign. Coming from a country where firearms possession is banned, the Hattoris and other Japanese couldn't understand the American view toward guns.

"The thing we really must despise, more than the criminal, is the American law that permits people to own guns," they said in a statement at Yoshi's funeral.

Details of what happened the night that Yoshi died came out in media accounts and testimony at Rodney Peairs' manslaughter trial. The boys left the house in the family's red Volvo with instructions on how to get to the party, to which other exchange students had also been invited. They had only the street address for the house where the party was being held. But somehow the directions got mixed up and the boys mistakenly wound up at a house five doors down from the party.

They rang the front doorbell. The sound of a door opening came from the carport around the corner. It was Bonnie Peairs, who had heard the bell ring. Still thinking the party was inside, the boys came around the corner of the house toward her. Startled to see the boys, she slammed the door.

The boys didn't understand. They turned to go back to their car. Then they heard the side door open again. At the sound, Yoshi turned back toward the house and Webb followed him. Looking past Yoshi, Webb saw a man standing in the doorway holding a large handgun with both hands.

Yoshi moved toward the man, smiling and laughing. "We're here for the party," he said. His arms were shoulder high and bent at the elbows. In his left hand, Yoshi held a small camera.

The horror unfolded in seconds. The man shouted, "FREEZE!" Webb, who had seen the gun, called "Come back!" to Yoshi. But he kept moving forward. Webb said later that Yoshi may have seen the weapon and thought it was a Halloween prank. The man shot Yoshi in the chest with a bullet from a .44 Magnum. It tore through his body, spinning the boy around and knocking him down.

The man with the gun was Rodney Peairs, a meat cutter at a local Winn Dixie grocery store. After the shooting, he went inside his house and closed the door behind him. Webb ran next door to get help, and then knelt at Yoshi's side and tried to stop the blood oozing from his friend's chest while he waited for help.

The Haymakers were on their way home from a movie when Holley's beeper went off with an unfamiliar number. She called from a pay phone.

"There's been a terrible accident," a deputy sheriff told her. "Webb is all right. But his friend has been injured. We'd like you to come up here to the sheriff's substation."

"I think we should meet you at the hospital," Holley said.

"That won't be necessary," the deputy said.

"You mean he's dead?" Holley asked.

"Yes," the deputy said. "I'm sorry."

Yoshi's parents arrived two days after the shooting at New Orleans International Airport amid a crush of reporters. When Mieko Hattori came through the gate, she walked up to Holley Haymaker and the two women embraced.

"I'm so sorry," Holley told her. "He was a wonderful boy."

Mieko Hattori's first words touched the Haymakers. Even amid her grief over Yoshi's death, she asked, "How is Webb?"

The next day, the Haymakers brought the Hattoris to their home, and slowly the two families began to forge a bond. At a memorial service that night at the Unitarian Church of Baton Rouge, friends of Yoshi comforted the Hattoris. The Hattoris, too, tried to tell the crowd that they were grateful for what Yoshi had gained during his stay in the United States.

"Now that we are in the land of Louisiana ourselves, we are . . . aware how rewarding Yoshi's experience has been, owing greatly to your friendship and the support you offered him," they said. "We are especially grateful to the Haymakers, who accepted Yoshi as a real member of their family."

"Last but not least, we cannot help but wonder why . . . guns are so easily accessible in this society. Without them, Mr. Peairs would not have been put in the position he is in right now."

During interviews with investigators after the shooting, Peairs described what he remembered: "My wife went to the door, and uh, I don't know whether she opened the door or she went to lock the door, but she hollered at me to go get the gun. So I ran. I didn't ask questions. I reached in the top of my closet and pulled down my suitcase that I keep my gun in. And I opened it up, pulled it out and started for the front of the house. . . . I didn't see anything at first, but then I saw something moving behind my pickup truck, to the right I mean, and a few seconds or split seconds later here comes this guy. . . . He appeared to have a white suit and he was waving something in his hand, and was saying something or appeared to be laughing, but he saw me standing there with the gun. And I had it pointed not at him but towards him and I told him to freeze. And he continued forward, seemed to speed up a little bit. And, and, uh, I guess I must have shot him." Peairs said that after the shooting, "I just remember saying, 'Why didn't he stop, I told him to stop.' "

During the 1993 manslaughter trial of Rodney Peairs, his defense lawyer was able to convince a jury that Peairs was defending his home when he pulled the trigger, despite testimony that Yoshi had done nothing more threatening than walk toward Peairs.

Louisiana is one of many states that has a "Shoot the Burglar" legal doctrine among its case law. The law states that any homeowner can claim self-defense if he is inside his dwelling and shoots an intruder. During the trial, the prosecution focused its attention on what Peairs did before pulling the trigger—that he asked no questions, that by coming outside he actually drew the two boys back toward his house. The defense instead focused on the fear that Peairs felt, and pointed out that he had called out a warning to a stranger standing in his carport, an area he considered part of his house.

In an essay in the *New York Times* two weeks after the shooting, the Haymakers wrote, "Had Mr. Peairs not been armed, he might have acted on the human instinct to exchange words, to ask questions. But the gun perverted that instinct, substituting its voice for the human one. . . . We must put behind us the imperatives of an unpoliced frontier, of an era when a homeowner couldn't lock his door and dial 911, as Mr. Peairs might have done."

After Peairs was acquitted, the Hattoris sued him and won a limited payment from his homeowner's insurance company, said Richard

Haymaker, which helped to start Yoshi's Gift, a funding source for other grassroots efforts supporting gun control.

The Haymakers have been able to advance their cause. Through their petition drive and work with the Coalition to Stop Gun Violence, and later through their organization Louisiana Ceasefire, the couple expanded the network of people and organizations working together on gun control efforts. Louisiana Ceasefire has backed federal legislation requiring child safety locks on handguns and fought the governor and the National Rifle Association over a law allowing the carrying of concealed handguns.

"We do not have a particular legislative agenda right now," Holley Haymaker said. "Our agenda is to be a voice. We are hearing more and more voices speaking out. We will be more effective by joining our voices." Richard Haymaker has donated some of his papers to a special collection of the Louisiana State University library.

"We are part of a story, quite a story," Holley Haymaker said. "Look at the elements—children, Halloween, violence, Wild West gun attitude, dueling lawyers, southern justice, racism, international interest, exchange students, vocal Japanese reaction, sympathetic parents, two petitions to the President, a visit to the White House at a time of international negotiations. . . . All this and the story still makes no sense. We need to move forward. That will happen. This problem is not going away. The stories keep happening."

ADDITIONAL READINGS

Behrens, David. "For the Love of Yoshi." *Newsday*, November 26, 1993.

Ceasefire Action Network Newsletter, http://www.gunfree.org.ceasefir.htm

Crone, Moira. "Beloved Son: Another Life Cut Short by a Handgun." *Family Circle*, September 21, 1993.

Haymaker, Holley, and Richard Haymaker. "Another Magnum, Another Victim." *New York Times*, October 31, 1992, op-ed page.

Dennis Henigan

Attorney Takes on Firearms Industry in Court

Born: 1951, Washington, DC

Education: B.A., Oberlin College; J.D., University of Virginia Law School

Current Positions: Director, Legal Action Project, Center to Prevent Handgun Violence; General Counsel, Handgun Control, Inc.

Dennis Henigan is one pro–gun control attorney who doesn't mince words. "Fundamentally irrational" is how he describes the anti–gun control arguments. As general counsel for Handgun Control, Inc., one would expect Henigan to be partisan in his comments. But it's not just a mantle he began wearing with the job, he said. It's a position he had always held.

As a private law practice attorney with the corporate firm Foley & Lardner, Henigan did pro bono work for a progressive bar association and other public interest groups. When the Center to Prevent Handgun Violence decided to begin its Legal Action Project in 1989, it was the perfect opportunity for someone looking to run his own public interest law program.

In addition, it was with a group whose opinion he shared. "This was an issue where I didn't feel my own personal beliefs would be compromised. I'd be comfortable articulating the various positions of the gun control movement. It was difficult for me to see any gray areas. The case for reasonable gun controls is so overwhelming. The challenge is in creating the national will to act, to overcome the financial and political power of an irrational minority," he said.

His first six months on board were spent studying the issues and case law involving gun manufacturers, dealers, and owners. He looked at constitutional issues relating to guns and gun violence. That led to a prioritized agenda. "Our first goal was to make the gun

Dennis Henigan. Courtesy of Dunn Photographic Associates, Inc.

industry more accountable for irresponsible conduct leading to gun violence. The second was helping to protect all reasonable gun laws against legal attack by the gun lobby. And the third was trying to strengthen current federal regulation of guns by the [federal] Bureau of Alcohol, Tobacco and Firearms and other agencies. The fourth approach would be to educate the public about the legal issues bearing on the gun violence problem," he said.

That gun control opponents have been able to shape much of the debate on the Second Amendment baffles him, he said. He argues that the U.S. Constitution in no way guarantees an individual right to keep and bear arms, a view that is supported in court. "This [individual rights] position is not taken seriously because it should not be taken seriously. Just because articles espousing it are published in law journals doesn't make it right. You don't decide a constitutional issue by counting the number of articles on it. The courts have been aware of these pro-gun arguments and continue to find them unpersuasive."

As far as the other goals go, Henigan feels progress is continually being made. "The gun industry has benefited from a rather unique immunity. That starts with the exclusion of guns from basic consumer protections," he said, noting that firearms are specifically excluded from jurisdiction by the Consumer Product Safety Commission. "What that means is, unlike other industries that have to meet basic consumer product safety standards, the gun industry only has to be concerned about regulation of its product through the tort system, through civil liability."

However, courts have not generally held the industry responsible for making and selling products "that have no legitimate societal use and are at high risk for being used in criminal activity." He cites Saturday night specials, assault weapons, high capacity magazines, and "cop-killer bullets" as examples of firearms and parts of interest primarily to criminals.

"This will continue to happen unless the courts begin to hold the industry responsible for the inevitable result. For example, Intratec sells an assault pistol [the TEC-9] with a standard 32-round ammunition magazine, barrel shroud to protect hands from burn during rapid fire, combat sling and military accouterments to make it efficient for battlefield use. It's designed to kill a lot of people quickly. No one seriously claims it has a sporting use. It's a terrible choice for civilian self-defense. The emphasis isn't accuracy but firepower," he said. The manufacturer has been selling it for years to the general public. But Henigan said those most interested in its features—such as its fingerprint-resistant finish—are those intending violent criminal use.

The TEC-9 was used in a San Francisco massacre (see profile of Stephen Sposato), and Henigan brought a lawsuit against Intratec because of that. "We achieved an early victory when we survived a motion to dismiss. Most of the cases asserting liability for criminal use of guns have been dismissed at the pleading stage. Our case was allowed to go forward into full-scale fact discovery, which provided us an extraordinary inside view of the workings and decision making process inside the assault weapon industry," he said. The case is now on appeal after a summary judgment dismissal.

Another area of the industry's accountability centers on the design of firearms. "We believe this is an industry that generally devotes its research and development to making products more lethal and more concealable, not into making the product safer," he said.

So far, lawsuits brought against manufacturers haven't resulted in firearms redesign. Henigan said the industry claims its responsibility is to make guns sufficiently safe for the trained user, but it is "well aware that guns fall into the hands of untrained users, particularly kids who don't know the basics of working guns and kill themselves, other kids, and adults." A predictable pattern is that two youngsters or teens will find a loaded handgun. They take out the ammunition magazine and think they have unloaded the gun. They are unaware that a round may remain in the chamber ready to be fired.

That's exactly the scenario of the *Dix v. Beretta* case, in which 15-year-old Kenzo Dix was unintentionally shot by a 14-year-old friend. The case asserts that any handgun sold for civilian self-defense is defective if it doesn't incorporate technology to personalize it. Some of that technology is relatively high-tech, involving radio frequencies and receptors without which the gun won't operate. But the goal could be achieved through simple mechanical systems, such as a combination trigger lock built into the pistol grip.

"We believe it's shameful that the industry has not marketed guns that are personalized. It's as absurd as if the auto industry marketed automobiles without a unique key. Imagine if you could just get in a car and push a button. That would be completely irresponsible," he said.

While Henigan believes the firearms industry hasn't stepped up to its responsibility to prevent tragedies, he doesn't lay all the blame at its doorstep. "We're not denying the user has a responsibility, but the law contemplates multiple parties bearing responsibility to prevent tragedy. We'll sue both the negligent gun owner and the gun manufacturer. That's what we did in *Dix*. We brought suit against the gun owners [the shooter's father and stepmother] who left the gun accessible to Dix's best friend, who fatally wounded his buddy," he said.

ADDITIONAL READINGS

Dix v. Beretta U.S.A. Corp., Clarence Soe, Nancy Okano and Michael Soe, Alameda County Superior Court, Case No. 750681–9.

Ehrman, Keith A., and Dennis A. Henigan. "The Second Amendment in the Twentieth Century: Have You Seen Your Militia Lately?" *University of Dayton Law Review* 15 (1989).

Handgun Control, Inc., web site: http://www.handguncontrol.org

Henigan, Dennis A. "Arms, Anarchy, and the Second Amendment." *Valparaiso University Law Review* 26 (1991).

———. "The Right to Be Armed: A Constitutional Illusion." *San Francisco Barrister*, December 1989.

———. "Victims' Litigation Targets Gun Violence." *Trial*, February 1995.

Henigan, Dennis A., E. Bruce Nicholson, and David Hemenway. "In Conversation with the Editors of Aletheia Press." In *Guns and the Constitution: The Myth of Second Amendment Protection for Firearms in America.* Northampton, Mass.: Aletheia Press, 1995.

Stephen Sposato et al. v. Intratec Firearms, U.S.A. Magazines, Inc., Hell-Fire Systems, Inc. and AAL-Jays Super Pawn (In Re 101 California Street Litigation), San Francisco County Superior Court, Case No. 960937.

Joshua M. Horwitz

Product Liability and Education Efforts Twin Goals for This Attorney

---

Born: 1963, Boston, MA

Education: B.A., University of Michigan; J.D., George Washington University

Current Positions: President and Executive Director, Educational Fund to End Handgun Violence; Legal Counsel, Coalition to Stop Gun Violence

---

After law school, Joshua M. Horwitz felt torn. He had joined a private law firm, but did not like the focus on billable hours. He was interested in public interest law and had spent a few summers working in a civil rights law firm. He enjoyed the work, but following that opportunity meant moving to Mississippi. Having recently moved to Washington, D.C., he was reluctant to leave. "Being in Washington makes you want to stay there," he said.

So when the Educational Fund to End Handgun Violence was looking for an attorney to run its Firearms Litigation Clearinghouse, Horwitz found the opportunity "extremely appealing. One of the associates where I had been working had taken her own life with a handgun. I felt it was an appropriate place for me to work," he said.

While Horwitz shared the basic philosophy of the organizations he was joining, he hadn't really studied the issue. "What I wasn't aware of at the time was how the Second Amendment had been misinterpreted, how the gun lobby at that point still had control of a lot of the regulatory process, and how it had stymied basic industry regulations. I had always shared a desire to stem the killings of people by handguns, but I didn't understand the reckless grip or intrinsic systemic problems that the gun lobby had managed to perpetuate," he said.

Horwitz feels there have been significant changes in the past decade. "When I started [in 1989] we were the only ones doing litigation [against gun manufacturers]. Ultimately, that will be one of the most important tools we have. Just like in the tobacco industry, instead of using this as an ancillary strategy, it may become the lead strategy," he predicted. Horwitz doesn't litigate these cases himself, leaving that up to the attorneys who are more familiar with their local and state rules. "My role is more catalytic; I work to bring the right people together," he said.

While Horwitz still assists attorneys suing gun manufacturers, he has broadened his interests in the last several years. "When I started, there were very few positive public education campaigns. What few there were, were based on the 'scared straight' model. But the more scared young people got, the more they wanted to carry firearms," he said.

In 1995 the Educational Fund began its focus on positive youth development and empowerment. The Hands Without Guns program (see profiles of Jo Ann Karn and Michael Robbins) is the brainchild of Horwitz and 2pm: *poesica per musica*, a small communications firm.

The program is in effect in several communities, including Boston, Massachusetts, Washington, D.C., Chicago, Illinois, and Holland, Michigan. Its purpose is twofold: to change youth attitudes about gun ownership and to change the debate from its current "crime control versus gun control" focus to youth empowerment and development, he said. "The issues are fundamental. If you don't want youth to use guns, adults in the community have to provide alternatives. The message has to be that there are a lot of other things you can do without a gun in your hand. We need to help provide those opportunities and we need to include the youth in building those."

The Educational Fund helps get the Hands Without Guns program off the ground by building a coalition to run it in the community. In Washington, D.C., for example, the campaign has created television spots as well as radio and bus advertising and conducted events such as a community arts festival and assemblies in schools. They've had toy gun turn-ins and dozens of workshops in the city, and even produced a compact disc called *Voices of Washington*, Horwitz said.

"This is at the very heart of preventing youth and guns from intertwining," Horwitz said. It seems to be having an effect. Horwitz called the early data "incredibly promising." In Washington, D.C., 414 youth not involved with the program were surveyed. Over one-third of the youth could identify the program. The youth in this group were less likely to carry guns than youth who could not identify the program.

The third area where Horwitz feels he's made a contribution is in making sure grassroots groups around the country have a voice. "There's a need for a national grassroots voice, and one of the things we've done is consciously develop that voice as opposed to developing our own voice. Some people say that what we're doing is not best for the organization, but it's best for the movement," he said.

Similarly, Horwitz is sometimes asked why a product liability attorney is working on education programs. "They are both preventive issues," he said. "With litigation, however, you have to wait until someone is injured or killed before you can go forward and prevent someone else from being injured. I am tired of hearing the stories of someone's son or brother being shot. On the other hand, Hands Without Guns is an education program, so the prevention starts before an injury occurs. Taken together, we can save a lot of lives."

"These are not disparate elements—they're working together," he said.

ADDITIONAL READINGS

Educational Fund to End Handgun Violence web site: http://www.gunfree.org

Hands Without Guns web site: http://www.handswithoutguns.org

Horwitz, Joshua M. "*Kelly v. R. G. Industries, Inc.*: A Cause of Action for Assault Weapons." *University of Dayton Law Review* 15 (1989).

Suzanna Gratia Hupp

Witnessing Parents' Shooting Prompted Support for Carry Law

Born: 1959, Friendswood, TX

Education: University of Texas at El Paso; Texas Chiropractic College

Current Positions: Chiropractor; Texas State Representative

On October 16, 1991, Suzanna Gratia Hupp made what she calls the biggest mistake of her life. She obeyed the Texas law that prohibited her from carrying a concealed handgun with her, leaving her .38 revolver in her car. How could she have known that minutes later 23-year-old George Jo Hennard would ram his truck into the restaurant where she was eating and start shooting? When it was finally over, Hennard had injured 20 and killed 23, including Hupp's father and mother.

Hupp had received her first handgun for self-protection when she was 21. Because she didn't want to risk losing her chiropractor's license, she obeyed the concealed carry prohibition.

On a bright and sunny day, she and her parents decided to go to the nearby Luby's Cafeteria in Killeen. Because of the large crowd, they couldn't sit at their usual table. They dined with the manager, a friend of Hupp's. Just as he moved away from the table to check on things in the kitchen, "this guy crashes his truck through the window. Where he drove in is where we usually sat," she said.

Her first reaction was to go over and help the people who were knocked over by the truck. But even while the truck was still bouncing to a standstill, she heard gunshots. She and her parents got down on the floor, pulling the table on its side in front of them.

"At first I thought it was a robbery. I was expecting to hear him tell us to put our wallets on the tables. My next thought was this was a terrorist attack or a hit on someone important in the crowd. But the shooting continued. It took a good 45 seconds to realize that he was walking around shooting people," she said. Indeed, he was walking over to people calmly, taking aim, and firing.

"I very clearly thought, 'I got this turkey.' The circumstances were perfect. He was up and everyone else was down. I had the table in front of me. He was maybe 15 feet away and I've hit much smaller targets at greater distances. I reached for my purse and that's when I realized my mistake. My gun was 100 yards away, completely useless. What could I do? Throw my purse at him?"

Her attention turned toward her father, who looked like he was getting up. She grabbed his shirt, and forcefully told him to stay down. "But when my dad saw what he thought was a chance, he ran at him." Hennard shot her father in the chest, and he went down in the aisle in front of her. He was still alive, but Hupp knew he wouldn't survive.

"Instead of coming directly at us, he angled to my left. As he was continuing around the room, we heard another window crash at the back of the building. I thought, 'Oh no, here comes another one,' but people were getting out that way. When he had his back turned toward us, I grabbed my mother by the shirt collar and told her to come on," Hupp said.

As she ran, she kept waiting to feel the impact of a gunshot. As a child, she'd been shot in the arm unintentionally by another child, so she remembered that what you feel first is impact, not pain. "My feet grew wings and I made it out that back window. My manager friend had just come out of the kitchen area, glad to see I was all right. I turned to say something to my mother, but she wasn't there," Hupp recalled.

Her parents had celebrated their 47th wedding anniversary two weeks earlier, and "my mother wasn't going anywhere without my father," she said. Instead of running, she crawled over to where her husband lay and cradled his head. Hennard walked up to her, and she looked up at him and then put her head down as he put the gun to her head and pulled the trigger. Hupp learned that story later, from a police officer friend who witnessed the scene in the middle of the pandemonium.

Hupp and the others ran to an apartment building across the street. "I had cuts all over me and someone gave me a washcloth to clean up. Then I went upstairs and made three telephone calls—to my sister's house, my brother's house, and my clinic, telling my staff to tell my brother and sister to get down here in case they called. When I was done, Hennard was still shooting," she said.

Before his ammunition ran out, he killed himself.

Hupp and her brother and sister decided they would talk to the press about the event. "Initially, you don't want to talk, but as a family we decided they're going to print a story because it's their job. If they do it wrong and nobody spoke out, it's not their fault. I wasn't mad at Hennard. That would be like being mad at a rabid dog. You don't get mad at it, you must kill it. We're not talking about a career criminal, but about someone who went insane. I was mad at my legislators because they had legislated me out of my right to protect myself and my family."

Hupp took her testimony to state legislative committees weighing a concealed carry law. One committee chairman told her it was her testimony that swung his vote to support the law that passed in 1995.

Being in the public light as much as she was brought Hupp local attention and respect. She parlayed that into a successful bid for a seat in the Texas House of Representatives. "I concentrated my platform on other basic rights; anyone who was going to vote for me based on gun issues already knew who I was," she said.

In Texas, the legislature meets every other year for 140 days. In the 1997 session, Hupp introduced a bill to lower the minimum age requirement for a concealed handgun permit from 21 years to 18 years. The bill would also have repealed the prohibition on concealed handgun permit holders carrying their legal gun on the campus of a public institution of higher education. "It doesn't apply to private campuses; I'm a believer in private property rights," she said. The bill was voted out of committee, but the session calendar ran out of time.

The bill wasn't voted on during the session, but Hupp isn't deterred. "I'm going to be like a Chihuahua on the heels of people trying to usurp our rights," she said, predicting she'll reintroduce that bill and others like it. "The incidence of violent crime on public university campuses is incredible. To strip these men and women of their right to self-protection is unconscionable. Quite frankly, I won't rest until we restore Second Amendment rights across that board."

Right to carry laws are a step in that direction, but Hupp is adamant: "Gun rights are not up to local control, not any more than we would leave any other constitutional right up to local control. Any usurpation of individual rights really gripes me," she said.

The moment she reached for her gun and found it wasn't there "brought that point home to me. It made things crystal clear."

Hupp feels fairly certain she could have stopped Hennard. Early in the incident, there was that moment when she felt she could have gotten off a clean shot and not endangered anyone else. By the time police arrived, the scene had become chaotic, with patrons scrambling to get out of the restaurant.

"A gun is not a guarantee. Is it possible I could have missed? Possibly. Would my revolver have jammed? It's possible. But it would have changed the odds. A gun is a tool you can use that will change the odds in many scenarios. Now that I'm a mother, the idea of being in a situation where someone threatens my children's lives and me not being able to impact that, makes me almost physically ill," she said.

She was helpless once and that was enough. "I had made an incredibly stupid decision. I'd rather be sitting in jail with a felony offense on my head and have my parents alive to see their grandchildren."

ADDITIONAL READINGS

Annin, P. " 'You Could See the Hate.' " *Newsweek*, October 28, 1991.

Bilski, A. "Tragedy in Texas: A Shooting Spree Leaves 23 People Dead." *Maclean's*, October 28, 1991.

Chin, P. "A Texas Massacre." *People Weekly*, November 4, 1991.

Woodbury, R. "Ten Minutes in Hell." *Time*, October 28, 1991.

See also "Handguns in America," a four-part series consisting of 24 articles that ran in Hearst newspapers October 19–22, 1997, especially "Texas Massacre Leads to Legal Concealed Weapons," by Ralph Winingham, October 20, 1997. The entire set of stories are available on line at http://www.examiner.com/guns/guns.html.

Phillip B. Journey

Political Power on the State Level

Born: 1956, Kansas City, KS

Education: Washburn University, Topeka; J.D., Oklahoma City University School of Law

Current Positions: Practicing Attorney; President, Kansas Second Amendment Society; Director at Large, Kansas State Rifle Association

Phillip B. Journey has shown that he can motivate voters. He's been a successful political player in Kansas, so much so that in 1993 the National Rifle Association's Firearms Civil Rights Defense Fund named him local activist of the year, giving him the prestigious Harlon B. Carter/George S. Knight Award. He took half of the award money and sent it back to the NRA to sign his wife up as a life member.

While he has been successful at turning out votes for gun rights legislators, he said it's always a tough fight. "Volunteers on the gun issue are the most foul weather political activists working. When things are good, they'd rather buy a box of ammo and go to the range. It's only when they get spanked that they work."

And gun owners generally work to protect their own interests. Shotgunners might not turn out for a handgun issue. "They don't see what's happening around the nation. I read three newspapers a day and when I'm preparing for my radio or TV show, I review up to 15 newspapers in a day," he said.

That way he learns what the issues are in California and New York, for example, because he knows that what's going on elsewhere can quickly pick up a head of steam. That's how the assault weapons ban came to pass, he noted. A few small cities in California banned assault weapons. When there were enough to reach a critical mass, the state followed suit. New Jersey passed a similar law. A few high

Phillip B. Journey.

profile incidents fueled the spark, and suddenly the bill was before the U.S. Congress.

The old adage, "An ounce of prevention is worth a pound of cure," absolutely applies to gun control, he said. And another, "Slow and steady wins the race," serves as an important strategy lesson. "Politics changes in small increments. Look at right to carry laws, for example. Many in the gun rights movement want Vermont's law where you don't need to be licensed to carry. But that's not politically do-able in Kansas. In our political situation, it's too big of a change.

Just as our opponents have nibbled at our freedoms, we have to take back that ground a little piece at a time."

That's one reason Journey creates a five-year plan, split up in two two and one-half year election cycles. Just as one is wrapping up, the other is starting. That allows him to look ahead, determining where and when opportunities exist.

Journey's interest in gun issues picked up in law school. "We had to write a dissertation and rather than regurgitate what I had learned, I decided to study what they had not taught me in three semesters of constitutional law. I picked the gun issue and read 2,000 pages of Congressional testimony. It was supposed to be a short paper, and I wrote 75 pages with 400 footnotes. In essence, I've never stopped. I determined that the modern interpretation of the Second Amendment [as guaranteeing a collective right rather than an individual right] was a big lie. I decided at that time it would be my cross to bear for life."

Journey's focus has been more local than national, although he did serve on the NRA's board of directors from 1995 to 1998. "My first term on the NRA's board was a great honor. It was at the same time one of the most rewarding and frustrating things I have ever done in my life. It is a place where not only does one have access to some of the best staff and information on the issue, but one may also contribute in some meaningful way to the cause. It is tragic that I was caught up in the struggles for power that have been going on for so many decades, but it seems to be the nature of the beast." He said he hopes to be reelected some day.

In his dealings with the issue on the national scene, he observed that the rhetoric at times goes too far. "There are people involved in this issue who don't seem to get along with people on the other side. These are our opponents, not our enemies, and there's a great distinction. The absolutist philosophy taken by some gun rights activists is a detriment. We build a public perception that we're intolerant. It allows our opponents to label us as extremists and that hurts us in the general population," he said.

Journey is a director at large of the Kansas State Rifle Association and president of the Kansas Second Amendment Society, a political action committee (PAC) with nearly 500 members. That is where he has had his greatest success. "In 1994, we were the first U.S. Congressional district to elect a pro-gun conservative congressman. We were ahead of the state," he said. Democrat Dan Glickman was ousted by Todd Tiahrt, one of the nation's strongest pro-gun congressmen. "That election night was the most exciting night of my career. Tiahrt gave our PAC credit, in the *Chicago Tribune*. We developed a coalition of homeschoolers, pro-lifers, and gun rights activists and kept the Libertarian candidate out of the race. That was the biggest upset in the nation on election night."

In 1996 he was asked to be a delegate to the Republican National Convention. "I was able to help nominally in platform issues, but moreover, it allowed me to network with others who hadn't been exposed to this issue. If you can convince one politician, that is someone who may be there for you for the next decade," he said.

It's no quick process. "That's one reason I've been doing television for seven years. I don't get paid for it, but I think it has resulted in my Congressional district being two years ahead of the rest in Kansas. Now I'm on the number one talk radio station in the state and every weekend my show is broadcast to six Congressional districts."

In 1996 just nine of the state senators supported right to carry legislation. By early 1998, it was 22, and Journey was hoping to pick up another five seats in the state senate in the November 2000 election. A right to carry bill did pass the state legislature in 1997, but was vetoed by Governor Bill Graves. That was a disappointment to Journey and his co-workers. They were among those who worked to get Graves elected governor in 1994, in his run against Congressman Jim Slattery, who had cast the deciding vote on the assault weapons ban.

In 1998 Governor Graves defeated pro-gun Republican Party chair David Miller two to one. That defeat set the right to carry issue in Kansas back considerably. "The conservative coalition of 1994 did not stay a cohesive unit as in the past. The struggle between purist and pragmatic forces in all issue groups raises its head from time to time, and in 1998 in Kansas, Governor Graves ran a well-funded campaign that divided conservatives with his support for our range protection legislation and signing a moderately pro-life bill."

Aside from his activism, Journey is a practicing attorney who handles a caseload of 2,000 to 3,000 criminal cases per year. Two days a week, he serves as a public defender in Wichita. "The Bill of Rights is my life. If I can defend the Bill of Rights for the least of us, I do it for all of us," he said.

Some of the cases he handles involve gun issues. The state does not preempt localities from passing their own gun regulations, and several towns and cities have done so. "Even though someone traveling through might be in compliance with the state law, they can get arrested in these localities," he said. One of his clients, a Salina resident, recently got a dismissal on just such a case after being charged with negligent storage of a firearm. "We win some, we lose some."

It's the same way in politics. And Journey keeps playing to win.

ADDITIONAL READING

Hart, Timothy. "KCTU-TV Earns a Place in Television, Internet History." *Wichita Business Journal*, February 16, 1988.

Jo Ann Karn

Giving Children a Voice and an Outlet

Born: 1933, Centerville, IN

Education: College courses taken at University of Denver, Earlham College (Richmond, IN), Hope College, and Davenport College (Holland, MI)

Current Position: Director, Hands Without Guns, Holland, MI

It was just a small announcement in the Presbyterian Church's "Justice Jottings": the Citizens Conference to Stop Gun Violence would be held in Washington, D.C. Although she had essentially no first-hand knowledge of gun violence, Jo Ann Karn heard a still, small voice that told her to go to the conference.

Once there, the Holland, Michigan, grandmother of eight attended a seminar on the Hands Without Guns program, which had just been launched in Boston. She saw the video made by the youths and thought, "This is something I have to do."

"In the past six or seven years, this predominantly white Dutch Reformed community had become a more mixed community. Over

Jo Ann Karn.

many years, migrant workers stayed, the Asian community grew, and clashes between cultures arose. We began to have problems, and I felt the community was ignoring it," she said.

"We needed something positive," she said, and the Hands Without Guns program fit the bill. Still, she wasn't exactly excited about the idea of starting the program herself. "It has been a journey of faith for me. I felt that God was pushing me to do this and I resisted until I couldn't ignore it anymore." That moment came during a Sunday sermon in which the minister said, "If you're asked by God to do things, he doesn't send you in alone," she recalled.

Then she plunged in. She called Joshua Horwitz (see profile), the director of the Educational Fund to End Handgun Violence, which promotes the program. He gave her direction, but questioned whether Holland really needed such a program. After all, the other cities where the program was taking off—Boston and Chicago—had much more serious violent crime problems.

But Karn was convinced that the youth in Holland needed a positive outlet. She began the long process of starting an organization from nothing. She talked to schools, community organizations, youth centers. She began fund-raising and received just enough money from a community foundation to hire a youth coordinator.

The first meeting between the program's organizers and the five high school students who had pledged some involvement "was an eye-opening experience. These kids told me things about the community that we didn't know. They said there were two gangs in town threatening each other and that it would be a bad summer. They also said they thought they were good role models, but didn't feel they had a voice," she recalled.

A few months later, Horwitz and Jim Wine, a filmmaker, were back in Holland for three days of filming. Filming took place at youth clubs, a learning center, and a local park. Wine turned those clips into eleven video spots and three full-page print advertisements that appear in English and Spanish newspapers. The youth designed two of the ads and translated them into Spanish.

The youth coordinator started working on a calendar of events for the summer. The first year, 5,500 copies were printed and were distributed through some of the schools. The second year, the youth did the calendar in its entirety and distributed 6,200 copies. Things started to pick up. Another community group offered the group some office space. Until then, they had operated out of a walk-in closet in Karn's condo.

The group received a $6,000 grant from a local company to do three 60-second radio spots. Those spots were written and produced by the youth and ran for two weeks in the summer of 1998.

Despite the growing interest, it hasn't been clear sailing. Karn has run into opposition from schools and individuals worried that the program's name would imply that gun violence was a common problem. For example, a press release announcing the Hands Without Guns kickoff mentioned a recent drive-by shooting. No one disputed that the shooting took place, but police weren't happy it was emphasized. Karn said that attitude is exactly what made her want to do this in the first place. There were problems in the community, but leaders were choosing to ignore them.

After the group received some television coverage, Karn began getting telephone calls from NRA members in the community. "The callers were initially concerned that we were trying to take their guns away, but when I explained that the program was an alternative for the youth, they could see the value of it."

In fact, Holland's Hands Without Guns group had even considered changing the name, believing that most of the opposition stemmed from it. "But the youth said 'No. This is what we're about, so don't change it.' "

One visit to a high school came shortly after four local youth were involved in a robbery during which another youth was killed. The offenders had attended the high school, and the victim's younger sister was still a student there. "That day, 72 kids signed up to become involved with Hands Without Guns. These young people were going to school with a girl whose brother was killed by someone they knew. They said, 'I'll do anything to keep guns out of kids' hands.' "

Indeed, it's been the youth who have kept the project moving along, she said. "It has given them a voice, a voice many people in the community still don't want to hear. The youth trust us and they now believe they can make a difference. Before, they wanted to but didn't believe they could."

For example, a girl featured in one of the TV spots was walking to a friend's apartment. She saw some guys hanging out nearby and knew they were gang members. They started calling after her, "You're a real star." She thought they were jeering her, so she kept on walking. But one walked over and grabbed her. He said, "I saw your ad and you made me think about what I've been doing."

"Kids listen to each other," Karn said.

And they respond to the trust and respect they receive from adults involved in this program. When Karn went on vacation, she gave her house key to the group who was putting out the newsletter so that they could access the computer. They were surprised by the move, but she wasn't. "I've never known them as children. I see them as the adults they're becoming, and they haven't had a lot of that."

"I've never felt alone," said Karn of her odyssey. She has never regretted listening to that voice that moved her. "I've met some wonderful young people with wonderful ideas. My only regret would have been if I missed the calling and had stayed at my house."

ADDITIONAL READINGS

Hands Without Guns web site: www.handswithoutguns.org
Kresnak, Jack. "Small Town Youths' Anti-Violence Crusade Reaches Kids, Riles NRA." *Youth Today* (American Youth Work Center, Washington, D.C.), June 1998.

Don B. Kates, Jr.

Science and History Don't Support Gun Control

Born: 1941, Los Angeles, CA
Education: Reed College; LI.B., Yale University
Current Position: Attorney, Novato, CA

In the summer of 1964, Don B. Kates was a civil rights worker in North and South Carolina. "I had to carry guns to protect myself and the people I was trying to help," he said. From there, he spent the next 10 years working as a legal services attorney, helping the poor with issues ranging from civil liberties infringements to housing and welfare.

From 1976 to 1979, he taught law at St. Louis University. "One of the courses I taught was criminal law and I became more interested in the area of firearms policy," he said. But there was no specific moment when he realized that his research and writings on firearms would take hold of his career. "The first ten years of my legal practice and most of my law school work revolved around civil rights and liberties. Firearms policy was a natural outgrowth."

During the 20 years he's been writing on and researching the topic, Kates has seen the debate take on different forms. Although gun control supporters and opponents are still vociferous in their arguments, Kates feels that a "neutral academic discourse" has evolved. "Reasonably neutral scholars were willing to have their minds changed by facts. They have brought about enormous change," said Kates, specifically citing work by Gary Kleck and James D. Wright (see profiles). "They both started out on the other side [pro-gun control] but found that the facts couldn't support the positions that were routinely offered."

Similarly, Kates saw his own views change. "In the area of constitutional law, I started out on the other side. I assumed it was true that the Second Amendment of the Constitution contained no indi-

Don B. Kates, Jr. Courtesy of Stephanie Turner, The Recorder.

vidual rights. But today, there is basically no dissent among law professors who have worked in this area that the Second Amendment is an individual right. That's something that could not have been said 25 years ago," he said.

Indeed, Kates feels his most significant contribution to the gun control debate has been to help clarify the issue. His study, "Handgun Prohibition and the Original Understanding of the Second Amendment," published in 1983, is "the leading law review article on the subject." It is a basic compendium. He believes it has influenced nearly a generation of law school professors.

A similar work was produced by attorney Stephen P. Halbrook (see profile). "But Halbrook put his work into a book, *That Every Man Be Armed*, and mine was a law review article. So Halbrook's work is better known outside law schools," Kates noted.

Kates also sees as his contribution changing some of the focus of the early debate. "Early on, a substitutionist argument for banning handguns was that handguns were more deadly than knives. The theory was that if all handguns disappeared, even if the same number of attacks took place, fewer people would be killed. But shotguns and rifles are enormously deadlier than handguns. So I calculated that even if all handguns disappeared tomorrow and one-half of the attacks that were previously made with handguns were now made with knives and the other half made with shotguns or rifles, the homicide rate would double. Eighty-five percent of those wounded with a handgun recover. But about two-thirds of those wounded with a 12-gauge shotgun or rifle die. The difference between 85 percent recovering and one-third recovering is huge. I helped point out a theoretical defect in the argument," he said.

Kates has also been vocal in his criticism of what he calls shoddy research. That's particularly true of public health professionals "for whom banning guns is a quasi-religious objective. Because they believe they represent a higher moral consciousness, they see no problem with rearranging facts to suit their purpose," he said, with sarcasm and anger apparent in his voice. "Their motives are for social betterment based on a quasi-religious faith that self-defense is morally wrong, and the possession of weapons for self-defense is morally wrong and they are going to prove how these evil things [guns] are socially deleterious."

He sees part of his role as debunking the premises, methodology, and conclusions of these researchers. "Researchers who are unable to address issues in a scientific manner have no place in this debate. For example, there has been a 170 percent increase in the number of handguns over the past two decades, but there has been a decrease in deaths by gun accidents by two-thirds. There are only two ways that can be accounted for. First, handguns have replaced long guns as weapons kept in the home for self-defense, and handguns are much safer in various ways. The other is the effect of the National

Rifle Association's safety education programs. But you will find no discussion of any of this in the public health literature," he said.

Kates' interest in the gun debate continues, but "I'm more and more interested in the basic philosophical questions and I'm not sure that's where the debate is heading. For example, is the world safer when the government has a monopoly on arms. That is implicit in the anti-gun view," he said, "notwithstanding that during this century various governments have killed upwards of 120 million of their unarmed people in genocides, politicides and the like." Look at Cambodia, Burundi, and Rwanda, he said. "It is only by not counting murders committed by the supposedly civilized, responsible governments that Europe is deemed to have a lower murder rate than the U.S. rather than a much higher rate."

The inverse correlation is the question of whether the world is safer with more people owning guns. "That features freedom of choice as a value, but nonetheless, the notion is that you have a deterrent effect if criminals know people are armed. Of course, it would be desirable to take guns away from dangerous people. Unfortunately, that doesn't seem possible, at least not by direct legislation," he said.

The problems with the criminal justice system complicate that. "We don't have enough jail cells to enforce the gun laws we now have. Criminals know that being caught with a gun isn't an important offense. They know they won't be punished," he said.

If there were enough federal cells to jail criminals guilty of violating federal laws, "you could substantially reduce gun violence," he added. But until such time, "it is clear there are people who are not susceptible to the law at all."

That brings Kates to another disturbing conclusion. "The people who are least likely to obey [gun restrictions] are the ones most needing to be disarmed. Even among criminals, those who could be dissuaded from having guns would be the least dangerous criminals," he argued. It's a classic Catch-22, but one to which Kates seems willing to devote more thought and research.

ADDITIONAL READINGS

Kates, Don B., Jr. "Firearms and Firearms Regulation: Old Premises, New Research" (symposium). *Law and Policy Quarterly* 5 (1983).
———. "Gun Control" (symposium). *Law and Contemporary Problems* 49 (1986): 1–267.

————. *Guns, Murders, and the Constitution: A Realistic Assessment of Gun Control*. San Francisco: Pacific Research Institute for Public Policy, 1990.

————. "Handgun Prohibition and the Original Meaning of the Second Amendment." *Michigan Law Review* 82 (1983).

————. *Restricting Handguns: The Liberal Skeptics Speak Out*. Croton-on-Hudson, N.Y.: North River Press, 1979.

————. "The Second Amendment and the Ideology of Self-Protection." *Constitutional Commentary* 9 (1992).

————. "The Value of Civilian Arms Possession as Deterrent to Crime or Defense Against Crime." *American Journal of Criminal Law* 18 (1991).

Kates, Don B., Jr., with Randy E. Barnett. "Under Fire: The New Consensus on the Second Amendment." *Emory Law Journal* 45 (1996): 1139–1259.

Kates, Don B., Jr., and Gary Kleck. *The Great American Gun Debate: Essays in Firearms and Violence*. San Francisco: Pacific Research, 1997.

Kates, Don B., Jr., and Daniel D. Polsby. "Of Genocide and Disarmament." *Journal of Criminal Law and Criminology* 86 (1995): 247–256.

Kates, Don B., Jr., and Glenn Harlan Reynolds. "The Second Amendment and States' Rights: A Thought Experiment." *William and Mary Law Review* 36 (1995): 1737–1768.

Kates, Don B., Jr., Henry E. Schaffer, John K. Lattimer, George B. Murray, and Edwin H. Cassem. "Guns and Public Health: Epidemic of Violence or Pandemic of Propaganda?" *Tennessee Law Review* 62 (Spring 1995).

Gary Kleck

Defensive Gun Uses Are More Prevalent than Previously Thought

Born: 1951, Lombard, IL

Education: University of Illinois; Ph.D., University of Illinois at Urbana

Current Position: Professor of Criminology and Criminal Justice, Florida State University

Gary Kleck.

Criminologist Gary Kleck started out as a "mild pro–gun control liberal." While writing his dissertation on the deterrent effect of the death penalty, initial indications were that more guns produced more homicides. "But then I did a little further research and extended the time period and those findings disappeared. At a minimum, that told me that the rationale wasn't that solid," he said.

He began to review other research and found that there wasn't much at all in this area. What there was was "pseudopropagandistic. It simply concluded that if you have more deadly weapons, you'll have more deadly events. I had a professor [David Bordua] who taught me to be skeptical," Kleck said.

As he began doing his own research, he found that there wasn't any foundation that the existing assumption was self-evident. "I also started thinking seriously about the premises of the anti–gun control arguments. It wasn't a bizarre idea because many criminologists believe that most laws don't have a measurable effect on crime."

Kleck was interested in what he saw as the central issue of the gun control debate—the self-defense uses of guns. "I started out by looking at other people's work on the subject, and then around 1987 I started doing original research. The question was whether the self-defense use of guns was effective. Would you be less likely to be injured or lose property? The finding was that, yes, you are less likely to be injured or lose property—more so than any other strategy, including nonresistance. Then I made it more complicated by controlling for a variety of factors, but the result was that although gun use was less common, it was the most effective method of self-defense," Kleck said.

So then the big question became, how common is the use of guns for self-defense? According to the survey Kleck used to judge the effectiveness of guns as a self-defense strategy, they were used fewer than 100,000 times each year. "But when you look at the variety of national surveys, you got wildly different results. Some indicated the defensive uses were enormously larger. Why was there this contradiction? Could it be resolved by a better survey?"

Kleck set out to find out. He developed his own national survey, which included 5,000 cases. "We had a long series of questions specifically designed to find out what people meant when they said that they had used a gun defensively," he said. That was important because critics of self-defense use studies argued that people were answering positively just because they had access to a gun, or because some vague threat, such as a suspicious noise, had been thwarted.

"That turns out not to be the case," Kleck said. "The vast majority of people who say yes have the same notion that we did. At a minimum, you had to have had the gun with you and you had to have confronted and threatened someone with it. That person had to be someone who was committing a crime or who you believed was committing a crime. If you used that definition as a minimum standard, there were about 2.5 million defensive gun uses per year. On occasion, there would actually be a shooting," he added.

Kleck said there are significant reasons why his studies showed more defensive gun uses than some other victim surveys—especially those conducted by the federal government. "The federal government's victim surveys are not anonymous surveys. While the surveyors promise confidentiality, they ask for your name and address and telephone number. Remember that most defensive gun use is in public places. Usually, it's illegal to carry a gun there unless you've got a permit. So respondents are being asked to confess to a crime. That would discourage the vast majority of people from reporting a defensive use of a gun," Kleck said.

In fact, if anything, Kleck said he expects the numbers to be low rather than high—"unless this phenomenon is totally different from all other crime-related research. For every individual who claims a false positive, there will be many more who will not confess to what might be an unlawful possession of firearms."

Kleck doesn't push his research into the role of advocacy. "I don't draw any particularly firm policy conclusions from the studies. I don't think it implies that we should get rid of any laws or that it precludes other regulatory measures. However, it does show that there is a serious cost to gun prohibitions because they apply to everybody, including noncriminals and potential victims. A ban that is applied to everyone across the board will disarm a larger share of noncriminals and victims than criminals," he said.

His point is to warn those who might believe there is no cost to disarming the population. However, Kleck realizes that his research is being used to fuel the debate. "I anticipate that people will draw policy conclusions beyond the evidence. When people ask, or when I get the chance to write about it, I say that the only justifiable conclusion is the cost of prohibition."

His evolving views on gun control were "no road to Damascus conversion. The self-defense issue was utterly essential to the gun control debate. If you find there's an association between high violence and high gun ownership rates, why is that? Could it be that more violence causes more people to get guns? The question was clearly central to the political issue. In reviewing previous research, I found that scholars hadn't taken the issue very seriously," he said.

In 1991 Kleck published *Point Blank: Guns and Violence in America*, which has been termed the seminal work on guns and crime. In 1996 he updated the research in his follow-up volume, *Targeting Guns*.

With Don Kates, he edited *The Great American Gun Debate*, a series of separate contributions. Kleck's segments deal mostly with self-defense, and he also contributed a chapter on how the mass media handle the gun control issue.

"The major flaws in crime reporting, in general, are sins of omission. There's not a strong bias in content analysis. When the bias does show up, it favors pro–gun control positions, but it is relatively mild. The real problems are in the omissions. Someone thinks facts are irrelevant or coincidental. The omissions seem to be favorable to pro–gun control positions. For example, there was huge news coverage of assault weapons. But assault weapons are almost never used in crime, accounting for less than 2 percent of gun crimes committed. And on the rare occasions where they are used, they seem to have no impact on the outcome. Theoretically they could, so one could imagine a high rate of fire might be relevant, but there have been no such real world incidents. In other words, these incidents continue for a prolonged enough time that someone with a conventional revolver could have fired as many rounds as the person with the assault weapon actually did," he explained.

He cites as an example a national broadcast in which news anchor Dan Rather was talking about semiautomatic assault weapons, which fire one shot with every trigger pull. But the video footage showed a fully automatic machine gun spraying rounds with only one trigger pull. Many viewers were left with the impression that they saw the firepower of a semiautomatic because the difference was never explained, Kleck said.

Kleck has also conducted a case control study to determine whether access to a gun makes it more likely that people will commit homicide. He undertook the study, in part, to broaden the scope of a study by Arthur Kellermann? that concluded that a gun in the home was 43 times more likely to be used in a homicide, suicide, or unintentional death than in a self-defense. "Kellermann's study focused on who becomes victims—and only on homicides in the home. Since only 11 percent of U.S. homicides are domestic homicides, it was an odd narrowing of the focus. I wanted to determine if having a gun around makes it more likely that a person will kill. There is a slight positive association, but it's probably not big enough to suggest a gun effect. As a minimum standard for taking an association seriously, epidemiologists generally employ a risk factor of three. In other words, if smokers are three or more times more likely to suffer bad health than nonsmokers, then the association is likely to survive further statistical controls and turn out to have a genuine causal effect. Our ratio turned out to be 1.38, so it's unlikely to turn out that a gun really increases the likelihood of committing a homicide," he said.

All his research has led Kleck to the following personal policy.

"Our target should be reducing, as best we can, gun possession among high risk individuals. We would best focus on limiting that without trying to reduce the overall number of guns. I favor most prominently controls on who can own or carry guns and better enforcement of those laws. The policy implication is that if someone doesn't have a prior criminal record, they should be allowed to obtain a carry permit. Then focus police enforcement effort on carry laws. If you don't have a permit, you're in violation," he said. Emerging technologies, such as radar-like devices that can detect metals, will make it easier for police to selectively stop and search people. "By arresting people at a higher rate before and after crimes are committed, there will be more impact. The combination of background checks and better enforcement of carry laws is a workable one."

ADDITIONAL READINGS

Kates, Don B. Jr., and Gary Kleck, eds. *The Great American Gun Debate: Essays on Firearms and Violence*. San Francisco: Pacific Research, 1997.

———. "Bad Data and the 'Evil Empire': Interpreting Poll Data on Gun Control." *Violence and Victims* 8 (1994): 367–376.

———. "Guns and Violence: An Interpretive Review of the Field." *Social Pathology* 1 (1995): 12–47.

———. "Handgun-Only Gun Control: A Policy Disaster in the Making." Pp. 167–199 in Kates, *Firearms and Violence*.

———. "Miscounting Suicides." *Suicide and Life-Threatening Behavior* 18 (1988): 219–236.

Kleck, Gary. *Point Blank: Guns and Violence in America*. Hawthorne, N.Y.: Aldine de Gruyter, 1991.

———. "The Relationship Between Gun Ownership Levels and Rates of Violence in the U.S." Pp. 99–135, in Kates, *Firearms and Violence*.

———. *Targeting Guns*. Hawthorne, N.Y.: Aldine de Gruyter, 1997.

Kleck, Gary, and David Bordua. "The Assumptions of Gun Control." In *Firearms and Violence: Issues of Regulation*, ed. Don Kates, Jr. Cambridge, Mass.: Ballinger, 1984.

Kleck, Gary, and Miriam DeLone. "Victim Resistance and Offender Weapon Effects in Robbery." *Journal of Quantitative Criminology* 9: 55–82.

Kleck, Gary, with Marc Gertz. "Armed Resistance to Crime: The Prevalence and Nature of Self-Defense with a Gun." *Journal of Criminal Law and Criminology* 86, no. 1 (Fall 1995): 150–187.

Kleck, Gary, with Karen McElrath. "The Effects of Weaponry on Human Violence." *Social Forces* 69 (1991): 669–692.

Kleck, Gary, with Britt Patterson. "The Impact of Gun Control and Gun

Ownership Levels on Violence Rates." *Journal of Quantitative Criminology* 9 (1993): 249–287.

Kleck, Gary, with Susan Sayles. "Rape and Resistance." *Social Problems* 37 (1990): 149–162.

Neal Knox

Architect of NRA Reforms

Born: 1935, Rush Springs, OK

Education: Abilene Christian University; Midwestern University

Current Positions: Executive Director, Firearms Coalition; NRA board member (1983–1984, 1991–   ). NRA Second and First Vice President (1994–1997); Executive Director of the NRA Institute for Legislative Action (1978–1982)

The moment that Neal Knox committed much of his life to gun rights is clear to him decades later. He was a young sergeant in the Texas National Guard stationed at Fort Sill, Oklahoma, in 1955. He became friends with Charley, a Belgian-American who grew up in Belgium during World War II.

Charley had learned about guns and gun laws from an old master gunsmith. One day, the old man asked his young friend to help him bury all his carefully greased guns, rather than register them under a new law. Charley couldn't understand the old man's conviction that registration would lead to confiscation—until a year or so later, when Germany invaded Belgium.

Early one morning, German SS troops banged on the door of Charley's closest friends, twin boys his age, a brother and sister. The German officer demanded to know why their father hadn't turned in his dutifully registered World War I souvenir pistol. The father said he couldn't find it; the family was given 15 minutes for a final frantic search of their home, then the soldiers ordered the neighborhood,

Neal Knox.

including Charley, to the town square to watch the entire family machine-gunned to death.

"I will never forget Charley telling me that story. We were sitting on opposing bunks on a hot Saturday afternoon. Huge tears were rolling down his cheeks, making silver dollar size splotches on the dusty barracks floor," Knox said. "That was my conversion from a casual gun owner to someone determined to prevent gun laws making such an outrage possible in this country."

Soon after returning from Fort Sill, he told the president of his Abilene, Texas, gun club that he wanted to be on its firearms legislation committee. The president replied, "We don't have one; you're now the chairman."

That's when Knox joined the National Rifle Association and started studying the gun control issue. "I had never before read the Second Amendment. I was delighted that the U.S. Constitution prohibited laws like Belgium's," he said. "There was no battle to fight, I thought. Was I wrong!"

Knox's interest in guns started early. He bought his first BB gun when he was five, and when he was nine he received a .22 rifle, which he wasn't allowed to take out alone until he was thirteen. In college he met, and later married, Jay Janen Shirley, whose mother, a single parent, had also given her a .22 rifle for her ninth Christmas. "She was undoubtedly the only girl in Abilene Christian with a rifle in her dorm closet." After their marriage, they began hand loading their own ammunition, and shooting became their main hobby.

An avid reader of gun magazines and technical firearms books, Knox decided he wanted to write about guns, "so I could try out all the latest products, while getting paid for it." The problem was he knew guns, but didn't know writing.

So he left his Houston petroleum products marketing job and went to work as wire editor for his hometown newspaper in Vernon, Texas. That led to a stint as a reporter, editor and gun columnist for a larger paper in Wichita Falls. "I quickly adapted to newspapering, and loved it," he said.

He also achieved his goal of writing articles on hunting, firearms, and gun legislation for outdoor magazines. He was hired to start *Gun Week*, he suspects, partially because few newspaper people knew guns and because of a study he wrote for *Guns & Ammo* magazine (June/July 1966) detailing the failure of gun laws to reduce crime. Knox believes it was the first scholarly research on the issue, and changed the debate from pure emotion to arguing on the basis of objective, empirical evidence. "It predated Professor James D. Wright's massive Justice Department–funded studies by 15 years, but showed the same thing—that gun laws don't work."

That has remained a continuing theme in Knox's writings and Congressional testimony ever since. As editor of *Gun Week*, during the intense debate over the Gun Control Act of 1968 (GCA '68) fueled by big city riots and the assassinations of President John F. Kennedy, Senator Robert F. Kennedy, and Reverend Martin Luther

King, Jr., Knox got his first up-close look at the NRA—and was disappointed.

"Senator Tom Dodd (sponsor of GCA '68) used to blame the failures of his bills on 'the well-organized, well-funded NRA.' Would that we had been," Knox said. "NRA had not one registered lobbyist, or anything approaching an organized lobbying effort." He began looking for ways to make the NRA more representative of its members, for the overwhelming majority wanted "defense of gun rights" to be the organization's top priority. But the NRA board and staff were focused primarily on bull's-eye competition that attracted only a fraction of the membership.

When GCA '68 passed, Knox became editor and publisher of *Handloader* and *Rifle*, two technical firearms magazines. "I again had time to shoot, even to win a national championship, to write about new products, and to appear as an 'expert firearms witness' in court, but I also stayed active in the legislative arena, frequently attending hearings and meetings in Washington, D.C."

In 1973 the NRA's director, Congressman John Dingell, a liberal Democrat from Michigan, and Harlon Carter, former NRA president and former chief of the U.S. Border Patrol, were primarily responsible for the creation of the NRA's first lobbying unit. But the competitive-shooting oriented NRA officers and staff "strangled the baby in its cradle by denying it adequate funding."

In 1975, after the formation of the National Coalition to Ban Handguns (now the Coalition to Stop Gun Violence) and the National Council to Control Handguns (now Handgun Control, Inc.), Carter and Dingell pushed through the NRA's powerful lobbying arm, the Institute for Legislative Action (ILA), which was independent of the rest of the organization, could do its own fund-raising, and reported directly to the 75-member NRA board.

Two days after the NRA Executive Committee gave preliminary approval to ILA, Carter called and said, as Knox recalls the conversation, "The key to its success is who we get as executive director."

"I agree," Knox replied. "How about you?"

"No way; how about you?"

"No way," Knox responded.

Eventually Knox and an NRA search committee prevailed on Carter to take the job of organizing a 50-person lobbying operation. Carter stayed for 17 months, until October 1976 and the defeat of a broad

Saturday night special bill that opponents said would eliminate production of over half the handguns then made.

"Harlon achieved this," Knox said, "despite an ongoing bureaucratic war with directors, officers, and staff who resented the upstart outfit that had been given NRA's highest-profile mission. The NRA establishment feared that active lobbying would endanger their close ties with the Army's Civilian Marksmanship Program (which supported NRA-style competition) and would steal assets and member support from their own pet projects, bull's-eye shooting and a wildlife conservation center in the Rocky Mountains, where they planned to move NRA Headquarters."

Knox feared that without Carter's strong presence the fledgling NRA-ILA would be swallowed up in bureaucratic infighting. He began talking with other legislative activists around the nation about building a member demand that the NRA make protection of gun rights its first priority, insist that the NRA remain based in Washington, and reform the director election process to empower the members.

The New York laws under which the NRA was incorporated in 1871 give the members total control of the association during their annual meeting. They could even amend the bylaws, but members had never before exercised that power. Carter was dubious that any significant member action could be accomplished, feeling that ILA should be protected through the 75-member board, which might react negatively to an organized member movement, Knox recalled.

"Harlon was right about the board's reaction, but wrong about his ability to sway them to give ILA first priority," Knox said. The day before the annual meeting in May 1977 in Cincinnati, the board rejected a series of modest member proposals. That night at a packed meeting across the river in Florence, Kentucky, members from around the country demanded that leaders of the group put together a much broader package of bylaw amendments.

Those bylaw amendments were intended to correct the immediate problems, such as stopping the move from Washington, while making the NRA more representative of the diverse firearms interests of the membership, which shared the single unifying goal of preserving the guns which were key to each member's area of interest. Knox's group worked most of the night and much of the next day on the new package.

"The only way to get NRA back on track quickly was if Harlon would accept the post of executive vice president," Knox said, "but until a few hours before that night's annual meeting, I had never talked to him about it. He accepted, but only if he were in charge of all of NRA, both ILA and NRA's other operations."

"I agreed, for all of NRA should be focused on the Second Amendment, whether we were promoting hunting, collecting, bull's-eye, or some of the many other shooting games," Knox said. "But we knew if we weren't careful we would find ourselves right back where we were, with business as usual at NRA as soon as Harlon again retired."

The leaders wrote a bylaw amendment giving Carter what he desired, but with a safeguard requiring that the NRA executive vice president be elected by the members on the floor of the annual meeting.

"Harlon didn't see that proposal until I introduced our package that night. He called me down from the dais to read it, decided he could accept it, and in the wee hours the members fired all the officers and elected Harlon," Knox said. "As I wrote in my next column, it was the dawning of a new day in NRA."

Knox is adamant that he did not plan what became known as the "Cincinnati Member Revolution" in order for him to take the reins of the NRA, as has often been reported. "As editor of *Handloader* and *Rifle*, living in a small town in the beautiful Arizona mountains, and flying myself to shoots and other firearms events all over the country in the company's twin-engine plane, I had the job of my dreams."

But nearly a year later, after Carter dismissed his replacement as the executive director of ILA, he prevailed on Knox to come to Washington to take over the reins of ILA "for a few days" until he could find a permanent director. "The few days was stretched to a month, then three; finally I accepted the job for two years, but stayed more than four."

Knox had intended to "put ILA on offense, then go home after kicking the boulder off the mountain," he said. Two days after becoming director, Knox spent $300,000 for mailgrams to NRA members in key districts urging them to bombard Defense Department committee members with letters and calls. Their message was against the destruction of World War II rifles so that NRA members could continue to buy them.

"It stopped the rifle destruction, but more importantly, told Congress NRA was going to fight for every inch. Stunned congressmen asked some of my friends, 'If that new guy at NRA will do this to save a few junk rifles, what will he do about something important?' They didn't know that we had fired our most powerful weapon, and couldn't afford to send mailgrams to the entire membership," Knox said.

The next week, Knox "declared war" on the Bureau of Alcohol, Tobacco and Firearms with the objective, he said, of "focusing on the way BATF was enforcing the Gun Control Act. We then intended to challenge the broadly written law itself—which invited civil liberties abuses by any agency which enforced it."

But while mounting that offense, ILA had to fight off a series of bills from the pro–gun control Jimmy Carter administration, including gun registration regulations proposed by BATF—which were later withdrawn.

"The uncharacteristic aggressiveness from NRA slowed the Congressional anti-gun efforts while we unlimbered ILA's new political action committee," Knox said. "That fall we bumped several foes out of Congress, and scared many more."

"That legislative and political offensive not only surprised Congress but upset many on the NRA board, who were more comfortable with the NRA tradition of only opposing new gun laws, and being careful not to offend the Washington Establishment."

During the following year, with a somewhat friendlier Congress, NRA-ILA engineered hearings on BATF's enforcement methods, which convinced powerful Democrats such as Senators Birch Bayh and Dennis DeConcini (both sometimes advocates of restrictive gun laws) that there were problems with both the agency and the law. Then ILA convinced Democratic Congressman Harold Volkmer and Republican Senator James McClure to introduce the long-planned revision of GCA '68.

The McClure-Volkmer bill was eventually co-sponsored by almost half the Congress and specifically endorsed by Republican presidential candidate Ronald Reagan. NRA-ILA and its political action committee went all out to reelect supporters of the bill and defeat its opponents. Knox said that shortly after the 1980 election, Reagan pollster Richard Wirthlin told him that ILA's efforts—which totaled nearly 4 million mailings plus radio and print ads in several states—were a major factor in the Reagan landslide and in giving Republicans control of the Senate.

Reagan's election proved to be a mixed blessing for Knox and the

NRA. In December 1981 the Reagan administration began negotiations with Senator McClure, Representative Volkmer, and the NRA to scale back their bill. The congressmen resisted changes.

Although 56 (of 100) senators were by then co-sponsors, the Senate leadership wouldn't call the bill to a vote. Knox continued to press for passage, particularly angering Senators Bob Dole and Strom Thurmond, he said. A week after the April 1982 annual NRA meetings, where both he and Carter were lauded by the members, Knox was fired.

The following year, with NRA members continuing to demand passage of McClure-Volkmer, Knox was elected to the NRA board by members' petition. His successor at ILA then agreed to a series of what Knox called "gutting" amendments. Knox lobbied against those weakening amendments "as a private citizen," but the board expelled him for opposing ILA's compromise.

In 1985 Knox ran for executive vice president against Harlon Carter's successor, Ray Arnett, and was defeated at the annual meeting. Knox's campaign manager was Tanya Metaksa, now NRA-ILA director, who had served as Knox's deputy at ILA. In 1991 he again ran for the board, but with a slate of candidates, 11 of whom, including Metaksa, were elected with the support of Harlon Carter. Knox's group swung the board balance to elect ILA director Wayne LaPierre as executive vice president.

In 1994 Knox was elected second vice president, and first vice president in 1996. That year, conflicts arose with LaPierre and President Marion Hammer, mainly over financial matters. Those grew into a public dispute in which Hammer and LaPierre urged members to oppose the vice presidents and six Knox supporters in the 1997 director elections; five were defeated.

At the annual meeting, actor Charlton Heston announced as a director candidate, was elected from the floor with the support of Hammer and LaPierre, and two days later defeated Knox as first vice president by four votes.

While Knox remains on the NRA board, his influence was diminished by the defeat of all candidates he supported in 1998. Now Knox focuses more on his own work, writing for various magazines and preparing a book. He also publishes a newsletter, the *Hard Corps Report*, which both applauds and chastises the NRA according to his view of how diligently the association is defending the Second Amendment, as he has done for decades.

Knox is proud of his contributions to the NRA and the gun rights movement. "What I brought to NRA was emphasis on the restoration of gun rights, instead of merely defending against further encroachments. My writings concerning the failures of gun laws triggered far more research by recognized experts, and my support for scholarly studies of the Second Amendment, both at ILA and as a trustee of the NRA Foundation, has helped win the intellectual debate in the law journals. I continue to insist on the right of NRA members to elect leaders who will defend their Second Amendment rights," he said.

"No city, no state, no nation has ever reduced its crime rate by passing a gun law. Their premise is that bad guys will obey gun laws while violating laws against rape, robbery and murder," he said. "Public realization of that illogic is why the anti–gun rights crowd has repackaged its nostrums as 'public safety.' But those folks have little real interest in safety or they would be promoting federal laws mandating swimming pool covers and other protections against far more accidents than involve guns."

"We still see government agencies continuously pushing for gun registration laws, most recently the FBI's announced intention to computerize the names of law-abiding firearms purchasers through the ill-advised 'Instant Check' system, despite Congress' repeated rejections of registration and the Brady Act's specific prohibition against keeping such records," Knox said. "Registration of guns or their owners is an assault on the Second Amendment and an insult to freedom-loving Americans."

ADDITIONAL READINGS

Knox, Neal. "Lapsing Freedom Insurance." *Guns & Ammo*, March 1991.
———. "Lessons of Tiananmen Square." *Guns & Ammo*, September 1989.
———. "Lock and Load" (on trigger locks). *George*, February 1998.
———. "Second Amendment—Bill of Rights 200th Anniversary." National Public Radio broadcast, December 19, 1991.
———. "What N.Y.C. Needs: More Guns." *New York Daily News*, January 12, 1994.
———. Web site: http://www.nealknox.com

Larson, Erik. "True Believer: Harder Line Prevails as Neal Knox Gains Control over NRA." *Wall Street Journal*, October 26, 1993.

David B. Kopel

Research and Experience Taught Him to Revise Former Pro-Control Stance

---

Born: 1960, Denver, CO

Education: B.A., Brown University, 1982; J.D., University of Michigan Law School, 1985

Current Positions: Author; Research Director, Independence Institute; Associate Policy Analyst, Cato Institute

---

Many young people carry the opinions of their parents into adulthood. Others see their own views evolve to the opposite side. David B. Kopel belongs to the second group—at least on firearms policy.

The son of a Colorado state legislator, Kopel said he and his father shared a view of gun policy "typical of urban liberal Democrats. He supported any gun control measure that came along, although pushing such legislation was never one of his passions."

Kopel accepted that view, with growing hesitation, until he was in law school and sought out the company of some of the premiere gun control opponents and legal scholars in the country. Now he's the author of several studies and a book examining gun control policies and the effectiveness of right to carry and other gun control laws.

As a child, the only toy guns he played with were those that came as standard issue for G. I. Joe and other action figures. "But this policy was subverted by my grandfather's gift of an old west revolver toy," he recalled.

"My first memory of real guns was looking at the enormous gun collection mounted on the wall of the father of one of my kindergarten friends. Both my parents and I thought that such an interest in guns—and such a very large display of them—was certainly not a sign of anything good," he said.

David B. Kopel.

He remembers an argument he had with a math teacher in fifth grade. The ex-Marine teacher was lambasting a letter to the editor advocating gun control. The teacher brought up the Second Amendment, the first time Kopel had heard that argument. Up until that moment, Kopel said he had been in favor of total prohibition. "I fell back to the position that even if the government couldn't ban all guns, it could at least require every gun buyer to pass a psychiatric test."

Although his opinion didn't change for another 10 years, in retrospect, Kopel said, "there was a long-term trend at work whose full implications were not yet apparent." At the age of 14, he read *The Gulag Archipelago* by Aleksandr Solzhenitsyn shortly after it was first published in the United States. "It instantly converted me from a George McGovern Democrat to a Scoop Jackson Democrat, at least on foreign policy. While gun control remained a very secondary issue for me, foreign policy was at the top of the charts. Thinking hawkish thoughts about the legitimacy and efficacy of the use of force for national defense against an evil dictatorship doubtless planted some seeds about the value of force in personal defense. Thomas Paine drew a similar parallel, although I was years away from reading any Paine," he recalled.

The evolution in his thinking continued. In college, he read an article in *Esquire* by a man who bought a gun after he had called 911 only to get a busy signal. He felt sympathetic to the man's response.

"But the key gun policy experience for me came a couple years later, when as a law student I was serving on the junior staff of the *Michigan Law Review*. The main job of the junior staff is to 'cite-check' law review articles, to ensure the accuracy of the citations. It is a very tedious process. I found myself cite-checking an article called 'Handgun Prohibition and the Original Meaning of the Second Amendment' by attorney Don Kates. The Kates article mustered a wide variety of sources to show, quite convincingly (at least to me), that the Second Amendment was intended to guarantee an individual right to arms," he said. By his third year of law school, Kopel was writing political columns for school newspapers—several on the right to arms.

"While working at my first law job, I also did some freelance writing. I followed a variety of leads, including animal rights (a cause that I picked up in 1984, and still strongly support), anti-Communism, world hunger and food aid (I had run the campus chapter of Oxfam in college), and gun control policy. The guy I contacted to pursue the gun issue was, of course, Don Kates (see profile). And it was largely because of his great encouragement and tremendous support that I started to go further and further into gun policy," he said.

First, Kates suggested they co-author an article for the *National Law Journal* or a similar publication along the lines of "Why Liberals Should Oppose Gun Control." The article was never published, but it became the core of Kopel's first major work on gun policy, a 52-page Cato Institute policy analysis called "Trust the People: The Case against Gun Control."

Kates also invited him to present a paper at an academic conference in Montreal. Kopel said, "I misunderstood the topic that Kates had assigned, and (never having attended such a conference before) grossly misunderstood the level of quality expected for conference papers. The result was a 100-page paper, where 10 pages would have done. But the paper, 'Foreign Gun Control Through American Eyes,' became the foundation for my first book, a study of gun control in eight democracies, *The Samurai, the Mountie, and the Cowboy: Should America Adopt the Gun Controls of Other Democracies?*"

The Cato paper and *The Samurai* had taken him very far up the gun policy learning curve. "As a young lawyer eager to help shape public policy, I found myself considered a national expert on an important subject," he said.

It helped, certainly, that the Second Amendment turned out to be a field relatively open to new scholarship. "I never thought that the Second Amendment was more important than any other civil liberty. While I love the First Amendment just as much as the Second, the First Amendment has been thickly covered by a prodigious amount of scholarship. The opportunity to contribute was much greater for the Second Amendment."

"The more I do public policy, the more I see how the whole Constitution fits together so well. A lot of the conflict over the Second Amendment could be resolved by paying attention to the rest of the Constitution. In particular, by remembering that the Constitution only gives Congress authority over certain subjects, and not a general police power. The Congressional power to raise revenue through taxation and to regulate interstate commerce should never have been allowed to become pretexts for federal control of simple gun possession within a single state."

Kopel considers the vast expansion of federal criminal power "a huge civil liberties problem, and not just for gun owners. My latest book, *No More Wacos: What's Wrong with Federal Law Enforcement and How to Fix It*, actually says very little about gun control policy, and instead points to the dangers of federalizing all sorts of crimes which are not properly within Congressional jurisdiction."

Kopel's interest in guns and gun control is primarily academic. Actually owning and shooting guns was a relatively incidental part of the process for him, he said. He didn't buy his first gun until he was 25. At age 33 he took a six-day class in defensive handgun training. Until then, he had fired only a few hundred shots in his life. "I like owning guns, but don't find the time to shoot them more than a few times a year. Hunting holds no interest for me, although I don't denigrate people who enjoy it. From my animal rights perspective, responsible hunting is a much smaller problem than factory farming,'' he said.

It frustrates him that the gun control debate produces so much acrimony, direct-mail nastiness, and demonization—on both sides of the issue. In a way, that surprises him. Taken individually, people he has met on either side of the issue seem friendly.

"One of my goals—which I do not always succeed in living up to—is to lower the temperature of the gun control debate. A more temperate discussion would generate less needless friction, fear, and animosity. One of the long-term ways to accomplish this is to get away from 'winner-take-all' contests at the federal level, and allow the states to serve their natural function as laboratories for democracy, and venues for diversity. Montana and New York City don't need to have the same gun laws, manufactured in Washington, D.C. Of course any state or local gun law should still be consistent with the state constitution, as well as with Bill of Rights standards of due process and the Second Amendment," he said.

Kopel, a former assistant attorney general for the state of Colorado, was presented a Bill of Rights Award in September 1997 by the Second Amendment Foundation for his "exemplary contributions in the field of communications, in talented defense of the Bill of Rights."

Some elements of Kopel's story come full circle. Remember the kindergarten pal whose father displayed his gun collection on the wall? Three decades later, Kopel found himself back in touch with the man, who was serving as president of the Colorado Gun Collectors Association. Kopel used an item from his collection as evidence in some gun control litigation. And by the mid-1990s, Kopel's father, who had such an early influence on Kopel's views, came to share his son's view on firearms policy. It's just one example of how time and one's experiences can change a person's outlook on a public policy issue like gun control.

ADDITIONAL READINGS

Blackman, Paul, and David B. Kopel. *No More Wacos: What's Wrong with Federal Law Enforcement and How to Fix It.* Buffalo: Prometheus Books, 1997.

Cramer, Clayton E., and David B. Kopel. " 'Shall Issue': The New Wave of Concealed Handgun Permit Laws." *Tennessee Law Review* 62 (1995).

Cramer, Clayton E., David B. Kopel, and Scott Hattrup. "A Tale of Three

Cities: The Right to Bear Arms in State Courts." *Temple Law Review* 68 (1995).

Gardiner, Richard, and David B. Kopel. "The Sullivan Principles: Protecting the Second Amendment from Abuse of Product Liability Law." *Seton Hall Legislative Journal* 19 (1995).

Gottlieb, Alan, and David B. Kopel. *More Things You Can Do to Defend Your Gun Rights.* Bellevue, Wash.: Merril Press, 1995.

Independence Institute web site: http://i2i.org

Kopel, David B. "The Allure of Foreign Gun Laws." *Journal of the Medical Association of Georgia* 83 (March 1994).

———. *Gun Control in Great Britain: Saving Lives or Constricting Liberty?* Chicago: University of Illinois at Chicago, Office of International Criminal Justice, 1992.

———. "Guns, Germs, and Science: Public Health Approaches to Gun Control." *Journal of the Medical Association of Georgia* 84 (June 1995).

———. *Guns: Who Should Have Them?* Buffalo, NY: Prometheus Books, 1995.

———. "The Ideology of Guns and Gun Control in the United States." *Quarterly Journal of Ideology* 18 (1995).

———. "Massaging the Medium: Reducing Media Violence without Infringing the First Amendment." *Kansas Journal of Law and Public Policy* 4 (1995).

———. "Rational Basis Analysis of 'Assault Weapon' Prohibition." *Journal of Contemporary Law* 20 (1994).

———. *The Samurai, the Mountie and the Cowboy: Should America Adopt the Gun Controls of Other Democracies?* Buffalo: Prometheus Books, 1992.

———. "The Untold Triumph of Concealed Carry Permits." *Policy Review: The Journal of American Citizenship*, no. 78 (July–August 1996).

Kopel, David B., and Chris Little. "Communitarians, Neorepublicans, and Guns: Assessing the Case for Firearms Prohibition." *Maryland Law Review* 56 (1997).

Kopel, David B., and Joseph Olson. "Preventing a Reign of Terror: Civil Liberties Implications of Terrorism Legislation." *Oklahoma City Law Review* 21 (1996).

Martha J. Langelan

Guns Are False Security, Says Self-Defense Instructor

Born: 1949, Toledo, OH

Education: Syracuse University

Current Positions: President, Langelan & Associates; Self-Defense
Instructor; Sexual Harassment Prevention Expert

Barely 5'3", Marty Langelan felt vulnerable in college when she was
walking from a night class to her dorm. "What could be more basic
than the simple human right to walk down the street without fear?
I hated feeling afraid. I didn't want to become any predator's prey,"
she said. So she signed up for a judo class at her YWCA. She found
she had a talent for martial arts and continued the training with karate
and other classes, eventually achieving a variety of belts in different
martial arts.

She opted for martial arts over a handgun because self-defense
skills are more accessible. "I could carry martial arts with me at all
times. I wouldn't need to reach into a glove compartment or purse.
Once I learned it, it was mine. It was something I could actually
use," she said. Most important, "it's something that cannot be used
against you."

She feels that way today, more than 20 years later. The only difference is her increased opposition to guns as a viable self-defense
method. Her views stem from her experience working with assault
survivors at the D.C. Rape Crisis Center. When Langelan came to
Washington in 1976 as a government economist, leaders at the Rape
Crisis Center asked her to teach their self-defense courses. She continues to serve as the primary instructor for the center, and has
branched out, teaching self-defense courses to children, senior citizens, deaf and disabled people, high school and college students, and
neighborhood groups in community centers and church basements.

"My classes are particularly designed for people who are small and not terribly strong. The escape methods I teach rely on leverage, not brute strength. Muscle mass to muscle mass, most women can't compete. But with these techniques, we can," she said. "I tell my students, 'We don't have to be bigger than the attacker—we just have to be smarter. And that's not hard!' " She estimated that 5,000 to 6,000 women and children take at least one of her basic courses each year.

As president of her own consulting firm, she provides sexual harassment prevention training, reviews equal employment opportunity (EEO) policies and procedures in the workplace, and teaches corporate and government seminars on EEO issues, workplace violence, conflict resolution skills, and employee safety.

In all of her self-defense classes, Langelan stresses that firearms are more of a risk than a help. "I came to the conclusion, after working with women at the Rape Crisis Center and battered women's shelters, that the presence of a weapon is a significant risk to women. If there was a weapon available during an assault—whether the attacker was a stranger or an acquaintance—the likelihood that the male would use the weapon was great, and the likelihood that the woman would be able to get to it, retain it, and use it, was small," she said.

Moreover, she said the incidence of injury and death increases when a weapon is involved. "In my experience with thousands of women, it's clear to me that we are safer without a gun."

Langelan said that gun advocates haven't analyzed the way assaults actually place. "It's dangerous—and deeply disrespectful—to tell women to rely on a self-defense method that won't work in a real assault."

First of all, there's the timing. "In real life, attacks happen so fast that in the majority of cases, a woman doesn't have time to get to the weapon. And even if she can get her hand on a loaded gun, it's hard to hold onto it when someone is trying to take it from you. The third factor is psychological: many women are unwilling to pull the trigger." Noting that 70 percent of sexual assaults are "acquaintance rapes," the odds grow even slimmer, she said. "Women are reluctant to use a firearm in general, but become extremely reluctant to shoot someone they know. In the most frequent kinds of attacks on women—acquaintance rapes and domestic violence—guns don't help; they hurt."

In addition, guns "add a layer of psychological trauma to a rape victim's recovery. Rape is a horrible crime. A typical rape may go on for two or three hours, sometimes six hours. It's hard enough to recover from such a deep and traumatic violation. Many women suffer post-traumatic stress. But when a woman has her own weapon used against her, it adds an even deeper level of distress," she said.

Langelan heard it from the women themselves when she was counseling rape victims; she hears it from the counselors now. Women who were unable to fend off a rapist with a gun, and had it used against them, feel as if they provided the rapist with more power over them. The victims often blame themselves. "It's hard to recover from a rape under the best of circumstances; it's that much harder for a woman whose own gun was used against her," she said.

Langelan advises women not to rely on gadgets but on their own resources and creativity. The first homework assignment she gives her classes is to practice observation circles. "Start with a circle 10 feet around you and see who's in that space. Practice identifying three things about every man you see in that space. 'Blue sweater, glasses, ring, whatever.' When you get good at that, expand your circle to 20 feet around you. This is your early warning system."

"Look at his body language; is it tense or aggressive? Many assailants unconsciously signal their hostile intentions. Trust your instincts," Langelan emphasizes. "If a situation feels creepy, it *is* creepy. Get yourself out of there fast. Don't wait to react—get to a safe place with people and lights."

Women should recognize the stages of an attack, Langelan said. First, there's the planning stage, as the rapist is checking out the area and looking for opportunities. Often, the next step is "rape-testing," the use of harassment—an unwelcome verbal or physical intrusion— to select targets for assault. He may say something crude or invade a woman's space, to test her reactions. "Rapists are not looking for a fair fight," Langelan said. "An attacker is looking for someone he can intimidate. The testing stage is a critical intervention point. A clear, strong verbal response to the initial intrusion can prevent an attack."

For example, an appropriate response to a suggestive comment might be, "Stop harassing women. No one likes it." "Use a calm, matter-of-fact tone of voice—no threats, no obscenities, no insults, and no verbal fluff or deferential language. Just a plain, direct statement and command. At that intervention point, verbal self-defense is the most efficient way to make it clear that *you* are *not* an easy target," she said. "A gun is completely useless."

In fact, brandishing a gun could have an entirely unwanted effect. "Guns are very valuable. If you flash one on the street, the guy might come after you just to get it. It's like flashing a gold watch," she said.

The next stage is the beginning of the attack. "All the research indicates that the first minute or two of an attack is the best time for women to resist. The assailant hasn't fully invested himself in the effort and women have good odds of escaping. Women who resist verbally and physically at this point—yelling and using a combination of tactics to break free—are less likely to be raped or otherwise injured," she said.

Here again, Langelan said, guns are ineffective. "It happens so fast. If you didn't realize you were being tested, suddenly someone is on you. You don't have two minutes to reach for a gun. You don't even have two seconds. There is no opportunity to locate a firearm, but there is an opportunity to fight back."

Indeed, because guns can lead to a false sense of security, women might be less observant in the first place. "Women endanger themselves by relying on guns instead of being alert to what is happening around them," she said.

Langelan does teach women to use weapons—but weapons can be whatever item is nearby. That's homework assignment number two for the women who take her classes. Langelan calls this the "what if" exercise. Look around you and identify ways to escape, which way to run (toward people and lights), and potential weapons in everyday situations. In an office building, even something as utilitarian as a stapler could be used for self-defense. In a laundry room, reach for the bleach, soap powder, or laundry basket to defend yourself. One graduate of her class successfully used a wicker laundry basket to fight off an attacker armed with a knife in a laundry room. Another quickly scanned the laundry room, noted the way the dryer doors opened, and moved toward a dryer. As the attacker came closer, she swung open the dryer door, hard, into his face. She knocked him out cold, said Langelan.

"Another woman was stopped with her car window open in a parking garage. A man came up, grabbed the door and ordered her out of the car. She escaped after she grabbed the car ashtray, full of her brother's cigarette butts, and smashed it in the assailant's face. That's the kind of weapon women use in real life. I think it's terrific, the way women use their creativity to fight back," she said.

Langelan has written a book, *Back Off!*, which includes nearly 100 real-life success stories from women of all ages (8 to 83) who used effective verbal and physical tactics to prevent attacks. She has just completed her second book, focusing on techniques that work for older people. "Eighteen percent of sexual assaults are on women over 60," she said. "But canes, walkers, and wheelchairs are great self-defense weapons."

"We have to look at what happens in real life. Step by step, how do you stop an attack before it starts or cut it off as early as possible once it has begun? I focus on what actually works. Having a gun on the scene doesn't help at any of the critical junctures of intervention. It's worse than useless—it actually puts the woman in even greater danger."

"The pro-gun advocates are living in some kind of Wild West fantasy. They ignore all the solid research on violence against women, from incest to battering to acquaintance rape. They don't bother to educate themselves about women's real experiences. There is an appalling amount of violence against women and children in our society—but it is unrealistic and completely irresponsible to tell women that a gun will be any use at all," Langelan said.

ADDITIONAL READINGS

Brink, Susan. "The Case for Fighting Off a Rapist." *U.S. News & World Report*, December 20, 1993.

Dana, Carol. "Talking Back to Street Harassers." *Washington Post*, August 19, 1986.

Langelan, Martha J. *Back Off! How to Confront and Stop Sexual Harassment and Harassers*. New York: Simon & Schuster, 1993.

———. "Her Say: The Rape Issue and Fighting Back." *Chicago Tribune*, November 7, 1993.

———. *Smart Self-Defense Strategies for Seniors*. Forthcoming.

Metz, Holly. "Stopping Sexual Harassment." *The Progressive*, April 1994.

Karen L. MacNutt

Complex Laws Intimidate Law Abiding, Attorney Argues

Born: 1948, Boston, MA

Education: University of Massachusetts, Amherst; J.D., Boston University; Advanced degree in military law, Judge Advocate General School, U.S. Army

Current Positions: Attorney; Legal Editor, *Women & Guns*

In her 1998 race for attorney general for the state of Massachusetts, Karen L. MacNutt thought gun control was a nonissue for most people. But since she was running for the seat most recently held by Scott Harshbarger, the attorney general who crafted consumer protection legislation banning "junk guns," comparisons were natural.

"My platform was based on the death penalty, health care problems, and consumer fraud. Gun control is an issue for those who wish to push for it, and for those who are affected by it. But it does little for the people in between. Most gun control initiatives have little to do with getting the community involved with law enforcement and in that way taking care of itself," she said. "Gun control, as advocated, is not directed at the criminal, but at the average citizen. It renders people more vulnerable to crime while empowering the criminal."

While it might not have been an issue during the months she was in the race in her run for the highest law enforcement position in the state, it is certainly a passion. Finding a common ground for debating the issue, however, has proven difficult. "Some gun control advocates mask their true agenda in terms of 'reasonableness.' They're afraid to say they don't think anyone should have a gun. So the discussion is nonspecific. Sometimes they talk about crime, sometimes gun safety. If you're talking about drowning, people don't complain about water safety, but some anti-gun people do complain about teaching gun safety," she said. It wouldn't be so bad if they came

Karen L. MacNutt.

right out and called for outright bans. "That's a legitimate view, but they should be open about it from the start."

"If there was more intellectual honesty on the other side, you might find people on the pro-gun side willing to compromise more. Instead, they're constantly being asked to sacrifice and never get anything in return," she said.

Sportsmen in the state feel like they've been burned before when they tried to compromise. "We started out supporting a mandatory year in jail for committing a crime with a gun. Then it was shifted to a year in jail if you didn't have a license. Then it shifted again, so if you used a gun for any purpose other than what was stated on your license, you could be arrested and charged as if you didn't have a license." She has known of people who were arrested because their license said "target shooting" and they stopped for a pizza on the way home from the range.

She has represented people who have been charged with violating the Bartley-Fox Act. The Massachusetts law is among the more restrictive firearms-carrying regulations in the country, imposing a mandatory jail term for anyone carrying a handgun without a license. "The bulk of those charged were out of state travelers who frequently didn't know the law existed or were erroneously told that their own state's license would cover them here. It doesn't. That begs the question why, when one's own police chief says the person is approved to carry a gun, should police in another jurisdiction put them in jail? People who travel interstate should be able to take with them any property which they're licensed to have," she said.

Because it's a harsh law, MacNutt said innocent people are getting caught by it. Too many of the gun control laws ensnare the law-abiding instead of stopping the criminals, she said. "As restrictions get more and more complex, it gets more difficult for anyone to comply. It's almost a campaign of intimidation, directed not at the people committing crimes but [at] those who are trying to comply with the law."

That includes people like MacNutt herself. A target shooter, MacNutt owns an M1A1 rifle—which could be called an assault weapon. It's a big rifle: eight and a half pounds, about 40 inches long. It has some of the features often ascribed to assault weapons: a flash suppressor, for example. That's on there not to make the gun look menacing, she noted, but to protect the user from the flash of gas that gets blown back after shooting the gun.

So she has a rifle permit and a special permit from the city of Boston because it's an assault rifle. "I can't sell it. I can't leave it to anyone. I can't get it repaired. I can't really use it, and they're telling me that's a reasonable control," she said.

Why then does she keep it? Why did she select such a rifle for target shooting? She's certainly not alone. "Service rifle" is an Olympic event. Shooting a full-sized rifle at a target 600 yards away is "a sport of concentration. If you're good at target shooting, you've learned to control your mind and body to concentrate solely on the target. It's almost meditation in terms of relaxation. There's a sense of self-fulfillment and competing with yourself. It's like asking why people bowl. There are many social enjoyable things we do as hobbies. If you're not hurting anyone, it's no one's business why you're doing it," she argued.

MacNutt has found another outlet related to firearms—she writes about them. As legal editor for *Women & Guns*, her articles appear in nearly every issue. Her articles range from issues of traveling with guns to fantasy pieces, poking fun at gun control activists. "I was one of the early writers urging people not to join militia groups. It's not because I think they're dangerous, but that they're stupid and counterproductive. People who subscribe to that philosophy have abandoned the political process. We can't do that. It's what makes the country work. Rather than abandon it, get involved," she said.

MacNutt talks the talk and walks the walk. She has also run for state representative and for a council seat in the city of Boston. She lost both elections, but she enjoyed the experience. She thinks her stance on gun control helped her more than it hindered her. "The newspapers tend to print what they want. They wanted to target me as a one-issue fringe candidate, but that wasn't what I was about. The major problems weren't firearms, but the lack of good jobs and an infrastructure friendly to business." Most of the reporters came to realize that her platform was deeper than one issue, she said.

Still, her gun control views gave her a boost. "I met a tremendous number of people through my interest in guns. Gun ownership runs across the spectrum. At a shooting range, you'll see a judge next to a ditch digger. A lot of people in law enforcement and many small business owners are interested in competitive shooting," she said. "They all get together and talk about their hobby."

That's the kind of rapport she wishes gun control advocates could develop with gun owners. "The big problem with folks who don't know gun owners is that they typecast them. That's the first step to a persecution. When you turn a person into a thing, there's no problem legislating against them." And that, she said, leaves well-intentioned gun owners caught up in a tangled web of gun control laws.

ADDITIONAL READINGS

MacNutt, Karen L. *Ladies' Legal Companion*, Randolph, MA: MacNutt Art Trust, 1993.
———. "Legally Speaking" (column). *Women & Guns*, monthly.
———. "Militias: Training for Doomsday . . . or feeding Anti-Gun Strategies." *Gun News Digest*, Summer 1995.
Second Amendment Foundation web site: http://www.saf.org

Carolyn McCarthy

The Journey from Grief to U.S. Congress

Born: 1944, Mineola, NY
Education: Mineola High School
Current Position: U.S. Representative (D-NY)

Up until December 1993, Carolyn McCarthy led a settled life. She and her husband, Dennis, lived in Mineola, New York, where she was born and raised. They had a son, Kevin, who was then 26. She worked as a nurse, and Dennis rode the Long Island Rail Road into New York City to his job at a stock-brokerage firm.

Just weeks earlier, Kevin had started working at the same company with his father, and the two rode to and from work together. Then on the evening of December 7, her peaceful world vanished.

A 34-year-old Jamaican immigrant, Colin Ferguson, was on board the same commuter train as McCarthy's husband and son. While the train rolled toward Long Island, Ferguson rose from his seat and took out a gun and began shooting at the 90 passengers in his car. He fired off the 15 bullets in a single clip, then reloaded and emptied again, walking through the car shooting passengers at point-blank range. He was overpowered by passengers as he tried to reload a second time, but by then 25 people had been shot, and 6 were dead.

Dennis McCarthy was one of those killed. Kevin McCarthy was among the most seriously wounded. A bullet in the head had destroyed part of his brain and left him barely clinging to life.

Carolyn McCarthy came home that night after an evening out with a friend to find her brother, Tom, waiting for her with the news that her husband, the man she called "my best friend," was gone, and that her son was gravely injured.

That day started McCarthy on two journeys—to nurse her son back to health, and later to bring to an end the kind of gun violence that had done so much damage to so many lives. Two and a half years after the shooting, McCarthy took a step she would never have dreamed of: she announced plans to run for Congress in hopes of ousting the incumbent Republican congressman from her district who had voted to repeal the federal ban on assault weapons.

"I've learned a lot in the last two and a half years," McCarthy said in her announcement speech, given on the front lawn of her Mineola home. "I have learned a lot about guns. I have worked for victims' rights. I have learned about passing legislation. I have learned to listen to people."

"That day changed my life forever," she said. "It's a life I know I can never go back to. But one thing I do know is that I want to make sure that no family has to go through what we went through."

Details of how Ferguson was able arm himself shocked McCarthy. Ferguson used a gun he had traveled to California to buy, and was carrying it illegally in New York. The 15-bullet magazine he used with it was legal, making the gun particularly lethal. With a lower-capacity magazine, he would have had to stop shooting sooner and might have been stopped.

The bullets in the gun were an especially deadly variety called "Black Talon." They are designed to open up like a claw on impact in order to do the most damage, and they did that to Kevin. About a seventh of his brain had been blown away; the rest held pieces of bullet and fragments of his shattered skull.

McCarthy devoted herself to becoming her son's nurse. She, along with family and friends, worked with Kevin to help him regain mobility. Doctors had predicted that if he survived, he would be paralyzed.

After the shooting, McCarthy was increasingly in the public eye, speaking on gun control. She worked as an activist to win passage in Congress of the 1994 Violent Crime Control and Law Enforcement Act, which outlawed 19 types of assault weapons and the 15-round magazine that Ferguson had used aboard the train. But the next year, members in a new Republican-led Congress were making plans to repeal the assault weapons ban. Among those supporting the repeal was Dan Frisa, the newly elected Republican congressman from McCarthy's district. The repeal passed in the House but was eventually stopped.

McCarthy decided to challenge Frisa, and the next November she beat him, becoming the newest member of New York's Congressional delegation. She ran as a Democrat even though she was a lifelong Republican. "The Republican leadership in Washington has been taken over by Newt Gingrich and the extreme right," McCarthy said in announcing her candidacy. "Gingrich, our Congressmen and their friends have turned their backs on Republicans like me."

In the summer of 1996 she addressed the Democratic National Convention, telling the audience of her son's "courageous recovery" from his wounds. "He's back at work, but he still spends many hours a day in rehabilitation. It's every mother's dream to be able to stand up on national television and say she's proud of her son. Kevin, I am very proud of you."

Of the shooting, McCarthy said, "On that day, I started a journey, a journey against gun violence in this nation. Today, I am here as a nurse, as a mother, as a person who isn't afraid to speak up about what is going on in this country. Gun violence adds millions of dollars in hospital costs every year and threatens victims' families with a mountain of bills and so much pain. Until our government listens to ordinary people speaking out against gun violence, instead of listening to special interests like the NRA leadership, we are not going to have safety on our streets."

Ferguson's trial for the murders was a bizarre spectacle. He had fired his lawyers and was representing himself in the courtroom, which meant he could cross-examine his own victims. He was found guilty of second-degree murder and sentenced to life in prison. When allowed to make a statement in the court, McCarthy told Ferguson about what his actions had done to her.

"I will give you no hatred. I will give you none of my rage. You took away my husband. You took away my best friend. You will never take away my memory of him. You will be gone from my thoughts forever, and we will learn to love and laugh again."

McCarthy has not concentrated solely on gun control issues. "I see my friends and neighbors, my brothers who are boilermakers, my sister who's a student nurse, working part-time and being a single mother. We all have to pay our mortgages, our monthly bills. We have to put our kids through college, and worry if we will be able to afford to retire," McCarthy said. "These are real issues and they have to be addressed in Washington. I've watched this Congress try to roll back environmental laws and to cut education for our children and Medicare for our seniors. As a practical nurse and as the mother of a child who needs medical attention, I know first hand that we need to reform our health care system. We need to make it more affordable but still have the choice of our doctors and hospitals."

"As a Long Islander, I know the value of the environment. I have seen our waters become cleaner as a result of the Clean Water Act. We need to do more to protect the environment, not less. As someone who has raised a son and who has spoken to hundreds of children about crime, I know the value of good schools. I know that we need to make it easier to get college loans, not harder."

When critics questioned her qualifications for high political office, McCarthy countered by saying that her inexperience would be an asset. "I do not pretend to be an expert on policy, but I understand what the people of our district want and need—and I will fight for those things."

McCarthy has found a new purpose in the life that she rebuilt after the nightmare of that day in December 1993. "Getting involved with politics wasn't anything I ever wanted to do," she said in her convention speech. "But this journey will make a difference when our neighborhoods pull together, when the government listens to us again. When all of us, Democrats and Republicans, come together to solve our problems, not just fight about them."

"We have a responsibility to our children to speak up about what we know is right. And to do what is right. I ask you to join me, and my son Kevin, on that journey."

ADDITIONAL READINGS

Associated Press. "Personal Plea on Gun Ban." *New York Times*, March 22, 1996.

Barry, Dan. "L. I. Widow's Story: Next Stop Washington." *New York Times*, November 7, 1996.

Carolyn McCarthy web page: http://www.house.gov/carolynmccarthy

Dao, James. "A Woman Comes to Politics via Personal Trial." *New York Times*, August 28, 1996.

Haberman, Clyde. "Public Cause Follows Private Tears." *New York Times*, May 29, 1996.

Mandell, Jonathan. "A Widow's Crusade." *Good Housekeeping*, September 1996.

Toner, Robin. "A Democrat, but Not a Typical One: Hurled by Tragedy into Public Life, a Novice Learns to Cope." *New York Times*, October 12, 1996.

Wines, Michael. "As Key Allies of Gun Lobby Lose, Questions Arise about Its Power." *New York Times*, December 24, 1996.

Tanya K. Metaksa

NRA's Top Gun Takes Aim at Gun Controls

Born: 1937, London, England

Education: B.A., Smith College

Current Position: Executive Director, National Rifle Association—
Institute for Legislative Action

When Tanya K. Metaksa became the co-founder and first lobbyist of the Connecticut Sportsmen's Alliance in 1969, she was one of only a handful of women involved in gun rights. When she became executive director of the National Rifle Association's Institute for Legislative Action (ILA) in 1994, she became the first woman to hold that position. Gender has been a motivation, not a hindrance, in her rise as one of the most powerful lobbyists in the country.

"I think it's very important that women are involved. Women have something to offer the shooting fraternity, and it's recognized by those involved in shooting sports or the political struggle that women are essential," she said.

That's why one of her focuses has been on self-defense for women. "Self-defense is the primary civil right," she said. She echoed Charlton Heston, actor and member of the NRA board of directors, who has said that the Second Amendment is really the first amendment of the Bill of Rights. "If you can't defend yourself, you don't have the rights of free speech or any of the others enumerated in the Bill of Rights," she said.

As a woman, with daughters and granddaughters, she is particularly sensitive to women's responsibility to protect themselves. "People should become aware and develop a personal safety strategy. Over the years, I've come to appreciate the fact that women don't pay enough attention to this area of life. That's why we've developed the 'Refuse to Be a Victim' program."

Gun ownership can certainly play a role in one's self-defense strategy, she said. "If one does chose gun ownership, [one] should understand how to use the gun safely and responsibly."

Metaksa, a competitive pistol shooter and an avid shotgunner and bird hunter, said the progression "from shooting enthusias to politico was a natural evolution. My father escaped from Russia after the revolution. He was very much at home here and talked about freedoms and responsibilities that came with being an American. In my case, I took on the political role because there was a need and I just stepped into the breach," she said.

Now, the primary role for the Institute for Legislative Action is "to stop the further erosion of our Second Amendment rights and try to take back by good legislation those rights that have been compromised. Right to carry laws are an example. Those are based on the notion that self-defense is the primary civil right," she said.

The ability to pass right to carry or shall issue laws in 31 states, double the number that had such laws just years before, shows the considerable organization that the Institute for Legislative Action and state NRA affiliates wield. "These laws have changed the dynamics of the argument. It's no longer about whether a shall issue law is a good crime fighting tool, but how much it really saves lives," Metaksa said.

Working for and winning a political goal is a thrill—especially on election night. Metaksa counts November 4, 1997, as one of her proudest moments. In Washington State, a gun registration and licensing proposal was soundly defeated by 71 percent of the voters. "I was in essence the architect of the plan to defeat it. But what was so great about it was the grassroots involvement. NRA members around the state got involved in the political process, and they did it in a magnificent manner. I was surprised and extremely pleased by the margin of the defeat," she said.

Election Day 1994 was another high point. Metaksa was part of the team that changed the makeup of the U.S. Congress and saw NRA gains in state and local elections as well. Metaksa chairs the NRA's Political Victory Fund. All told, 80 percent of NRA-endorsed federal candidates won in 1994.

While the NRA and its Political Victory Fund have seen impressive victories, "there are always challenges," Metaksa said. "We have a challenge to explain to the American people what the NRA member is all about. We're everyone's neighbor, who is interested in everything from church activities to civic groups; we have responsible jobs and we take our responsibility as firearms owners extremely seriously. We've seen the media try to denigrate gun owners and cast them in the same lot as people who are not law-abiding gun owners—criminals."

In fact, the NRA has long promoted strict punishments, such as mandatory sentencing, of those who misuse a firearm in commission of a crime. Metaksa directs CrimeStrike, the division of NRA-ILA devoted to criminal justice reform and victims' rights. "The problem is that prosecutors don't use the punishments. The gun charge is dropped in court, so the effect of having a mandatory sentence is completely ignored. Our criminal justice system is overburdened and our prisons are overcrowded. The solution is that we have to build more prisons, and hire more prosecutors and judges. That way, criminals will be given the sentences they deserve. Once caught, they'll serve time," she said.

Metaksa points to Boston, Massachusetts, as an example. The city has an aggressive and "outstanding program of getting bad guys off the street. It shows us that incarceration works. Then the law-abiding citizens are much safer."

Another item of the ILA's agenda is to block attempts "by those who would deny people the right to keep and bear arms and further constrict our rights—one-gun-a-month laws, expanding prohibitions of gun ownership to juveniles, making it more difficult to purchase guns."

The problem with the one-gun-a-month law is "it doesn't do anything." Such laws have been passed in some states as an attempt to curb gun trafficking. But Metaksa argued that they only serve to potentially criminalize law-abiding citizens. "There was a case where a gun owner bought a gun in February. The same date in March, he came back to the gun store, forgetting that February doesn't have 30 days. Just the act of trying to buy a gun made a criminal out of someone with no criminal intentions. The police came to pick him up at the gun store. It's a waste of resources. Why do we have to track millions of purchases to find the needle in the haystack of one person who is going to break the law?" she wondered.

These views are not hers or the NRA board of directors' alone, she emphasized. "It's important to remember that the NRA is an organization made up of 2.8 to 3 million members. The membership is what drives this organization. We're an inverse pyramid. . . . We're not just a lobbying group; we're a living and breathing organism made up of millions of U.S. citizens who believe in safety, responsibility, and freedom," she said.

ADDITIONAL READINGS

Metaksa, Tanya K. *Safe Not Sorry: Keeping Yourself and Your Family Safe in a Violent Age.* New York: HarperCollins, 1997.
————. "We Kept Our Rights." National Rifle Association, January 1998 (available online at http://www.nra.org/politics96/0198tar.html)
NRA web site: http://www.nra.org
Copies of speeches presented by Metaksa are online at http://www.nra.org/ backgrounder/bghome.html

Bryan Miller

Brother's Death Prompts Gun Control Activism

Born: 1951, Baltimore, MD

Education: B.A., Dickinson College, Carlisle, PA; Master of Science in Foreign Service (MSF), Georgetown University, Washington, DC

Current Position: Executive Director, Ceasefire New Jersey

Gunshot victim Mike Miller was in the right place at the wrong time. The gunman was in the wrong place at the same time.

Mike was a special agent with the FBI, working in the special cold case homicide department at Washington, D.C.'s police headquarters. On November 22, 1994, a suspect in a triple homicide, Bennie Lawson, "was looking to exact some revenge on the chief of the homicide division," said Bryan Miller, recalling the day his younger, and only, brother was killed.

"Lawson got some bad directions inside the District Building and ended up in the cold case homicide squad. He walked in and opened fire. In the ensuing gun battle, he killed two FBI agents, one of whom was my brother, and grievously wounded a third. He killed a D.C. police officer and wounded a civilian bystander. When other officers went into the room, Lawson was dead as well," he said.

Lawson used a TEC-9, often termed an "assault weapon" because of its paramilitary characteristics. He was carrying 50-round ammunition clips.

Miller heard the news that evening while he was fixing dinner for himself and his son. "It was the Tuesday right before Thanksgiving and I was just thinking about what I should pack to go visit my parents. The phone rang and it was my sister. The news was so shocking."

Mike and the rest of Miller's family lived in Maryland. Miller and his son made a visit down there about once a month. This visit would include a funeral instead of the usual basketball games.

Miller is still angry, but he has never focused his anger on the gunman. "In my opinion, Bennie Lawson did something that was suicidal and nuts. I have a hard time being angry at someone who is not responsible for his actions. But I am angry at the gun lobby and the cowardly politicians who allow that lobby to get away with such nonsense laws on assault weapons. These are weapons of mass destruction; they are not for sport or hunting," he said.

"What happened to Mike and his colleagues is completely full of irony in the sense that this man was able to walk into the least likely place in the world, a police headquarters full of trained and armed public servants, and exact that kind of damage. The NRA and its apologists ignore that. This case flies in the face of the argument that people can protect themselves if they're armed. Mike and his colleagues were not only armed, but trained to handle these situations. But in the face of the incredible firepower of a TEC-9, they were helpless."

"The NRA's argument is that the more people we arm, the more polite society will be. That's disproven in a lot of ways, but my brother's case is one of the starkest examples. It's an ignorant argument," Miller said.

Miller has been vocal and visible in his opposition to the NRA. Several months after Mike died, he joined Ceasefire New Jersey, and in September 1996 he quit his career in international business and became the activist organization's executive director.

One of the items on the organization's legislative agenda is a child-proof handgun bill, the first of its kind being considered in any state legislature. The proposal requires that guns sold in the state incorporate some method of ensuring that only authorized persons can fire the gun.

Such technology already exists. Indeed, at least two gun manufacturers have already developed prototypes of childproof handguns. High-tech methods of childproofing handguns include fingerprint recognition, bar code scanning, and using radio frequency–emitting transponders that signal their unique codes to a handgun. The transponders can be embedded in a ring or worn on clothing; the gun cannot be fired unless it detects the radio frequency.

In early 1998, Miller said he was optimistic about the chances for the bill's passage. "The governor has made some favorable comments about the proposal. Its focus isn't gun control so much as gun safety. It's a consumer product safety requirement."

While the bill makes sense to Miller, it doesn't have the wholehearted endorsement of the gun control community. Even Ceasefire directors debated the pros and cons before deciding to lobby for it. Those opposing the measure say it will help gun manufacturers by providing them with an entirely new market. "But what's our role? Are we trying to damage gun manufacturers or lessen gun violence? If this bill is enacted, this technology will have an immediate and measurable impact on gun violence," said Miller, summing up the decision of the group's leadership.

If the bill passes, Miller expects other states to follow suit. Even if they don't, gun manufacturers will have to respond—or give up the New Jersey market. "Although it's a small state geographically, we have a large population," he said, noting that it is one gun manufacturers wouldn't forsake willingly. He cites other measures that began in one state and led to nationwide changes, such as antipollution measures on cars in California and childproof caps on medicine bottles in Illinois.

The group is also focusing its efforts on gun trafficking legislation. New Jersey's restrictions on purchasing guns are relatively strict, but Miller points out that it's a short drive to states with more lenient laws. About 93 percent of guns used in crimes in New Jersey were originally purchased in another state, he said, including many purchased in neighboring Pennsylvania. Gun trafficking bills, such as those that limit gun purchases to one gun a month, are effective, he said. Many of the crime guns in the state were formerly traced to Virginia; that number has dropped off since the state passed its one-gun-a-month law. These laws are designed to minimize "straw" purchases, in which a state resident can purchase many guns and sell them, illegally, in areas with more restrictive laws.

Although the focus of such efforts is to limit criminals' access to guns, Miller is quick to point out that more than half of gun deaths are the result of suicides and unintentional injuries. He said the National Rifle Association has been extremely effective in limiting the debate to issues of crime and criminals, disregarding the positive impact gun control legislation could have on suicides.

"All their arguments are misdirection. About 76 percent of suicide attempts with handguns are successful. Suicide attempts with knives are about 17 percent successful. Guns are the most lethal consumer product you can buy," he said.

Laws such as the childproof handgun legislation would greatly reduce the number of teenage suicides and virtually eliminate unintentional shootings by children, he predicted.

That possibility is what keeps him going. "I love this. I feel this is right for me because it's in memory of my brother, but it's also right for my son. He's a kid growing up in this world and what we're trying to do is good. Finally, it also fits with my skills, so I feel like I'm using my capabilities to a much greater degree than I ever did in the past," he said.

Miller's interest in gun control preceded his brother's shooting. After graduate school, when he was living in Washington, D.C., he became a staff instructor for Close Up Foundation, a group that brings high school students to Washington to study government. He soon became the gun control staff instructor. "I have always believed in the issue because gun violence is insane in this country," he said. "I wish it hadn't taken my brother's death to get me this involved, but sadly it did. Now here I am and I feel good about what I'm doing."

ADDITIONAL READINGS

Center to Prevent Handgun Violence. *When Tragedy Strikes Home...A Dedication to Families and Mothers of Firearms Homicide Everywhere. Bryan Miller's Story.* Washington, D.C. (online at http://www.handguncontrol.org/protecting/D1/miller.htm)

Teret, Stephen. *Personalized Guns: Reducing Gun Deaths Through Design Changes.* Baltimore: Johns Hopkins Center for Gun Policy and Research, 1996.

Diane Nicholl

Background in Target Shooting and Firearms Training Adds to Perspective

Born: 1952, Pampa, TX

Education: B.S., Earth Science, University of Texas at Austin

Current Position: Research Scientist, University of Colorado, Boulder; Firearms Instructor

Firearms were a part of growing up for Diane Nicholl. Family and friends owned guns, and "it was common for people to have unsecured firearms next to the back door, in a glass-front gun cabinet or hanging on the wall. I learned about gun safety at an early age and understood the difference between toy guns and real firearms. There was no doubt in my mind what the consequences would be if I handled a real firearm without adult supervision," she said.

As a young girl, she'd take a .22 caliber rifle into the nearby fields for target practice—and learned she was good. "My walking to and from shooting practice with a rifle over my shoulder did not cause alarm or bring forth a SWAT team response as it probably would today," she said.

Even though guns were common, firearms crimes were not. "All my life, I have lived with firearms and have used them safely for sport and recreation. Not once have I ever considered using a gun to commit a crime. History tells me that since the founding of our country this has been a shared experience for tens of millions of Americans."

Firearms had been a recreational outlet for her, but a few years ago she found herself weighing her options for self-defense. A convict who had just escaped from prison shot and killed several people about a mile from her home. The sheriff's department sent out officers door to door looking for him. "Once the officers had driven away I stood in my kitchen and thought about my options. What

Diane Nicholl.

would I do if he tried to break into my house? Rather than risk confronting this armed murderer, I got in my car and headed for town. Fortunately he was captured later that evening, but it raised a question for me—what if he had not been caught? I could not abandon my home and animals indefinitely, so I had to consider my options for personal safety," she said.

Being a scientist, she took the approach best known to her: research. "I wanted to know as much as possible about the use of lethal force for self-protection and sought out the best defensive firearms training in the country. In addition, I read everything I could find in government publications and criminology about the use of firearms for self-defense. There is a federal depository library nearby, so it was easy to access stacks and stacks of data. What I discovered was that firearms are very effective in stopping violent criminal attacks. Those who used a firearm to resist a criminal attack were less likely to be hurt than those who did not resist. In fact, the best available studies showed it was exceptionally rare for anyone to fire a shot in a self-defense situation. Usually the bad guy would run away or beg the armed person not to shoot them. Given these facts, I am very confident in my decision to include the use of a firearm as one of my personal protection tools," Nicholl said.

She also took the advice of some of her firearms training instructors and began teaching herself. She's now a National Rifle Association certified firearms instructor, Women's Shooting Sports Foundation handgun instructor, and a Colorado certified law enforcement firearms trainer. She teaches special courses for law enforcement firearms trainers and publishes firearms training books as well as a use of force policy. It's hundreds of hours of volunteer work each year, but well worth it, she said, "because it is important to me that everyone who wants to is able to learn about firearms safety. I am also the founder of the Annie Oakley Society that provides women an opportunity to maintain and improve their shooting skills."

Although training others has rewards of its own, Nicholl felt she had to expand her influence. "Increasingly during the past few years, guns and gun owners are being portrayed as presenting a danger to the general public. As a law-abiding person, I feel violated when I am likened to criminals because of the mere possession of firearms, or worse, I am criminalized. It seems that the intent of those who support gun control is to create a thought process which they are promoting as the new American morality—firearms are inherently evil and so are their owners. If I am demonized for exercising my Second Amendment right, who will be the next target?" she wondered.

She is sympathetic to some gun control supporters. "I have compassion for those who have lost a loved one in a tragedy involving firearms and realize that if all one knows of firearms is death, destruction, and mayhem, they will support any means of removing firearms from our society in order to feel safe. However, when you look beyond the emotional media sound bites and dig into detailed criminological studies, FBI reports, and data from the U.S. Department of Justice, it becomes clear that guns in the hands of responsible law-abiding people do not present a danger to the general public or law enforcement," she said.

Her knowledge of firearms and her experience with training and talking with law enforcement officials about the effectiveness of gun control, combined with the research she has done, have led her to the conclusion that "current gun control measures have done nothing to reduce crime or violent criminal behavior. The law enforcement officers I train from the local to federal level also share this view. Time and time again they tell me about arresting a criminal illegally carrying a gun and that the first thing the prosecutor does is drop the charge of illegal possession of a gun in a plea bargain. What kind of message does this send?"

"Those who find comfort in passing a law making it illegal for anyone under the age of 18 to own a firearm are only kidding themselves if they think it will reduce the number of violent juvenile offenders," she continued. "Such legislation is purely symbolic and distracts us from the real problem, which is why some teenagers choose to ignore our laws prohibiting the taking of innocent life, rape, robbery, or assault."

Her first close encounter with the political process occurred a few years ago when a bill to reform Colorado's concealed weapon permit law was introduced. The intent of the bill was to ensure that there was a statewide uniform process for issuing permits. Under the current statute, permits (which are valid statewide) could be issued by police chiefs and sheriffs. "Some officials refused to issue permits to anyone, while other officials issued thousands of permits. If you lived in a jurisdiction where the official arbitrarily decided not to issue permits, you had little recourse except perhaps to move to a jurisdiction that did. In some cases a permit cost only $25, while other officials charged more than $400. Not exactly a fair system but it only affected gun owners, so there was no hue and cry of injustice by the general public or media," Nicholl explained.

She said the other side argued that more guns on the streets, even in the hands of law-abiding people, would result in more gun violence. "They argued that just because a gun was close at hand, people would be compelled to use it to settle minor arguments. Newspaper editorials helped spread this myth by painting the picture of permit holders whipping out a hidden gun and shooting a waitperson who accidentally spilled water in their lap."

It was as if the editorial predicted what would come next. Nicholl and some friends were having lunch, and the waitress unintentionally dumped a glass of iced tea in someone's lap. "Not one of the five permit holders at the table reached for their gun—we just broke out in laughter! This incident supports the huge body of evidence that allowing law-abiding people to obtain a permit to carry a concealed weapon for personal protection does not endanger public safety or the lives of law enforcement officers," she said.

Several lawmakers refer to Nicholl as "the calm voice of reason" and have come to trust the information she gives on gun control. She said one of the hard political lessons she has learned is that when an issue involves guns, fear inevitably overwhelms facts. Another painful lesson was witnessing people in positions of trust and authority mislead lawmakers about gun control issues, she said. "The first time this happened I thought that I must have misunderstood what a district attorney said during a senate committee hearing. To make sure, I listened to the recording of the session and then contacted his office to request a copy of the material he had referred to as supporting his claim. The paper his office faxed me was not some obscure report that I had overlooked but a government document that I was very familiar with. The data and conclusions were exactly the opposite of what the D.A. had said. I kept staring at the fax in disbelief, wondering how a trained attorney could examine this document and say what he did in his testimony."

"The data and conclusions did not support the statement made by the D.A. that people who try to protect themselves with weapons are much more likely to be hurt or killed than unarmed people. The document only contains data concerning victims who 'took action' or who 'took no action' and the results of doing so. 'Action' is never defined, so it is impossible to know if those who 'took action' were armed. Also, there is no data regarding the type of weapon the victim might have used," she said.

Nicholl said she found this district attorney's personal belief to be in conflict with information found in several government documents. For example, the publication *Guns and Crime: Handgun Victimization, Firearm Self-Defense, and Firearm Theft*, published by the U.S. Department of Justice, states that "a fifth of the victims defending themselves with a firearm suffered an injury, compared to almost half of those who defended themselves with weapons other than a firearm or who had no weapon."

Nicholl approaches the gun control issue the same way she approaches her lab work. "My background and experience in basic research have taught me how to design experiments, collect and analyze data as well as prepare papers for publication. I am very familiar with reading scientific papers and understand the importance of peer reviews and references. An area of the gun control debate that is of great interest to me is the articles published in medical journals. Many of the medical health writers promote the idea that guns are like germs and are responsible for the epidemic of violent criminal acts. Their favorite prescription for relief is strict gun control measures that will eventually eliminate the germs, i.e., guns. The evidence put forth in many of the medical journals supporting more gun control contradicts everything I have read regarding guns and violence in the fields of criminology and sociology," she said. And the more she read, the more it bothered her.

For example, there is the widely publicized claim made in a medical journal that having a gun in one's home increases one's risk of being a homicide victim. "Upon reading the original article, you will find that, yes, there is an increased risk of homicide in a household where members have a criminal history, have been arrested, use illicit drugs, abuse alcohol and where a family member has been hit or hurt in a family fight. However, to try and generalize the risk of firearms ownership in such dysfunctional households with the risk of firearms ownership in all households (approximately half the households in America) is intellectually dishonest. This particular study was soundly refuted a number of years ago, yet the sound bite remains and is continually used by the leading supporters of gun control," she said.

It disturbs her that these studies carry so much weight and are widely accepted as scientific proof by most of the general public and media, who are often ignorant of the contradictory evidence found in criminology journals, she said.

Throughout her work in the gun control debate, Nicholl said she has found fear to be the greatest obstacle she faces. "Suspicion, fear, and sometimes hatred have always been natural responses to the unknown, and I have found that fear is the foundation of almost all the arguments put forth by gun control supporters. By pointing the finger of fear at all guns, gun control supporters are slowly transferring the fear most people have of armed criminals to everyone who owns a gun (except perhaps the military and police). I believe that the key to breaking this cycle of fear is education. You can learn to move beyond fear once you have an understanding of gun safety and know more about the people who own firearms and enjoy the shooting sports," she said.

ADDITIONAL READING

Guns and Crime: Handgun Victimization, Firearm Self-Defense, and Firearm Theft. Washington, D.C.: U.S. Department of Justice, Bureau of Justice Statistics, 1994.

Jay Printz

Sheriff Challenges Brady Law in Supreme Court

Born: 1946, Hamilton, MT

Education: Law enforcement academy training

Current Position: Ravalli County (MT) Sheriff

Sheriff Jay Printz had a problem with the Brady Law, especially the requirement that chief law enforcement officers conduct background checks on handgun purchasers. In fact, it bothered him so much that he took the United States government to court—all the way to the Supreme Court. And he won.

Printz has worked in the sheriff's office in his hometown of Hamilton since 1972. In 1986 he was elected sheriff. Printz had left high school and earned his equivalency diploma even before his classmates graduated. He served in the Marine Corps from 1963 to 1967, including a tour of duty in Vietnam from 1965 to 1966.

"I'm a firm believer in our constitutional rights, but I'm like a lot of people in that I never thought too much about them. When I became sheriff and started realizing that the buck stops at my desk and that I had an obligation in upholding the oath I'd sworn to, it's a bigger responsibility than you originally thought," he said.

So when the Brady bill was being debated, Printz determined its mandate that local law enforcement officers check on handgun pur-

Jay Printz.

chasers' backgrounds to be unconstitutional—and in direct contradiction to the Montana Constitution and with state law, which prohibits officers from conducting such checks. "When Brady was being considered, I wrote letters to my Congressional representatives opposing that kind of feel-good legislation," he said. Having his officers spend time doing background checks would take away from their patrol duties, he argued. And since the mandate came without federal money, his department would have to absorb all the additional costs.

After the bill passed, Printz tried to locate a copy of the law to determine its impact on his department. "I had trouble getting a copy of it, but then all chief law enforcement officers in the state were notified by the Bureau of Alcohol, Tobacco and Firearms [BATF] that they were having a statewide meeting in Helena. They sent out a package of information, including their interpretation of what Brady meant. I still hadn't seen the actual law and I wasn't about to fall in line with BATF's interpretation," he said.

Nonetheless, he attended the meeting and after 45 minutes of listening to BATF's legal counsel "explaining to all us peons what we have to do, I raised my hand and started asking questions," he said. "I told them I thought it was not only unconstitutional, but illegal because under Montana law, officers are prohibited from doing those checks. I had sworn to uphold my state constitution as well as the federal constitution, and carry out state and local laws."

After he had spoken his mind for about 15 minutes, he told those gathered, simply, that he wouldn't follow the new law. Then he left the meeting.

On the 150-mile drive home, he wondered about what he had just done. "I thought, I've stuck my foot in my mouth, now I've got to do something or I'll be charged with failure to carry out a federal law," he recalled. As soon as he got home, he started working the telephones, and after a few calls ended up with the National Rifle Association, of which he is a member.

"I'm not a wealthy man and I knew a court challenge was going to cost," he said. The NRA put him in touch with attorney Stephen P. Halbrook (see profile), who was already mounting a legal challenge against Brady. "Sign me up," Printz told Halbrook.

Shortly thereafter, Printz filed a lawsuit against the United States in a federal district court in Montana. He asked for, and received, a court injunction to prohibit the federal government from prosecuting him for failure to carry out the law during the proceedings.

Printz started to feel some pressure at home. Three of the county commissioners were deliberating whether Printz should be removed as sheriff. They were concerned that his newfound notoriety could cost them federal funding in other areas. Printz stayed put, but two of the commissioners eventually left their positions.

When the ruling came in, the federal judge in Montana sided with Printz. The U.S. government appealed to the Ninth Circuit Court of Appeals, which Printz calls one of the most liberal federal appellate courts. At that time, Printz's case and a similar one from Arizona were combined. That court reversed the lower courts' ruling.

Printz realized he was going to have to fight this all the way to the U.S. Supreme Court. Because the Fifth Circuit Court of Appeals had recently ruled for the sheriff's position, it seemed likely that the Supreme Court would choose to hear the case, because two appellate courts were in conflict.

"I don't know what I would have done if the Supreme Court denied cert. I would probably have had to quit rather than do something that isn't right. Some people thought I had a strong position for what might be seen as a relatively minor intrusion by the federal government, but this intrusion specifically affected me and my office," he said.

The county commissioners paid Printz's way to Washington, D.C., to hear his case argued before the nation's highest court. "I felt good about it from day one. I'm one of those believers that when you're right, you will be vindicated," he said.

The Supreme Court ruled that it was indeed unconstitutional to mandate that local law enforcement officers conduct background checks while not providing the funding to accomplish the added work.

So is there anything of value in the Brady Law? "It's a waste of time and effort and doesn't accomplish anything," said Printz. "It's simply an expansion of federal power beyond its mandates of limited power."

Government has a role to play in interstate commerce of firearms, he said, noting that such laws already exist. But when it comes to intrastate commerce, he draws the line. "I believe this country is a federalized union of 50 states, not a leviathan monster of a federal government. The Constitution was written for a reason and that was to protect the public from big government, from the concentration of power in one central location."

It irks him that every time there's a "hot-button issue, our Congress and national government has to jump in. There are a series of carjackings, and Congress makes it a federal crime to carjack. What's the point? The same thing happened after several tourists were shot in Florida. Now it's a federal crime to shoot tourists. These are state issues, and my big fear is that this is a move toward nationalizing law enforcement," he said.

What is needed, he said, is less "mollycoddling the criminals. We already have laws that add 10 years on if a firearm is used in the commission of a crime, but there's very little effort to prosecute people on additional offenses. By the time criminals are done plea bargaining and receive concurrent or suspended sentences, they're only serving a fraction of their time."

"Why add laws that only affect law-abiding citizens? What good is it to check on law-abiding citizens when we're not being tough enough on the criminals? That's like a schoolteacher punishing the entire class because one kid acts up," he said.

Printz, who has been fighting crime and criminals for nearly three decades, feels that law enforcement is losing ground. But gun controls aren't the answer, he said, noting that he thinks 80 to 90 percent of rank and file law enforcement officers agree. "We are not gun control advocates. Part of the reason is that we're going to be citizens without badges at some point and none of us want things happening to us like having cops kick in your door or conducting searches without warrants. Because of the power law enforcement officers have, for some there's a temptation to abuse it."

He sees a parallel between the inappropriate wielding of power by some law enforcement officers and the inappropriate intrusions of the federal government. "You get arrogant and then you get in trouble. Arrogance corrupts the understanding heart," he said.

ADDITIONAL READING

Printz v. United States, 521 U.S. 98, 138 L. Ed. 2d 914, 65 U.S.L.W. 4731 (June 27, 1997) and 854 F.Supp. 1503 (D.Mont. 1994).

Michael A. Robbins

For Wounded Officer, Prevention Program Is a Labor of Love

Born: 1951, Chicago, IL

Education: Field Combat Medic, U.S. Navy; Gang Crimes Investigation/Chicago Police Department

Current Positions: Executive Director, Help for Survivors; Hands Without Guns

Mike Robbins joined the Chicago Police Department in 1986. His dedication got him noticed, and after a year he was recruited to the Gang Crimes Unit, an elite group of officers. Their task was to investigate gang activity and remove guns from the street.

"This is an aggressive group of men and women, black and white, who approach this issue of gun violence as a threat to the entire community," he said. Robbins joined the Gang South Detail, which gained a reputation even in the Gang Crimes Unit for its proactive work.

It is dangerous work, too. That was brought home to Robbins on September 10, 1994. "My partner and I were responding to several calls of gang disturbance and shots fired. We were met by a sergeant who told us several citizens had observed others with guns and the suspicion was that there was a gang meeting going on."

He approached it just like the military reconnaissance missions he was trained for in Vietnam—do some surveillance, learn what's going on, alert the rest of the team, and develop a strategy for moving in. "I was driving down an alley in an unmarked car, with the lights out. My partner observed an individual with a gun and shouted. I didn't see him, but threw the car into park and was getting ready to jump out. Before I had the chance, a guy ran up and stuck a gun in my face and began shooting. He fired repeatedly. My gun was in my hand, but before I had a chance to respond, he shot me in the arm. He put the gun into my chest and fired several times, point blank," Robbins recalled.

When it was over, Robbins had received 12 gunshot wounds. His partner had 6. Robbins' partner is still on the force; Robbins left the department on disability. He had two gunshot wounds to the chest, one to the stomach, two in the left arm, one in the right arm, three in the left leg, two in the right leg, and one in his left shoulder blade. Three bullets as well as fragments of another still remain in his body because doctors considered removing them to be too dangerous.

Following the shooting, Robbins underwent surgery numerous times to remove most of the bullets and to repair the damage. For a while, he was partially paralyzed from the waist down. "One day they told me I'd be paralyzed; the next they said they might have to amputate my left arm. With a lot of prayer and help, I recovered from the paralysis and through the experience and faith of the doctors, I still have my left arm, although it is an inch shorter," he said. In the aftermath, Robbins also sought counsel from a trauma therapist for post-traumatic stress. "The scene plays over and over in your head, every day."

After months in traction, dependent on his home health nurses for help with the most mundane activities, he began to regain use of his legs. For exercise, he walked back and forth in his bedroom.

When he was able to start going outdoors again, new ambitions stirred him. He contacted his city alderman, telling her he'd be happy to speak out on behalf of gang activity prevention. She put him in touch with the Illinois Council Against Handgun Violence. Although officially still on the police force, he started volunteering some time with the organization, speaking to community groups, teachers, and students about gangs and gun violence.

"I had done a lot of undercover work buying drugs and guns on the street. I had also done several assignments with the Chicago Bureau of Alcohol, Tobacco and Firearms [ATF]. So I was taking this experience of mine into the community and relating to people what was really going on in the street, how dangerous it was," he said.

How dangerous is it? "It is very easy to buy guns on the street from a number of different resources. There are kitchen table gun dealers, people selling guns from cars and in back streets, and those selling guns illegally at gun flea markets," he said.

"The availability and accessibility was wide and pervasive. Individuals find ways to circumvent the law," Robbins said, noting that Chicago has strict handgun laws. "Laws should be in place to allow law enforcement authorities at the local, state and federal level to track firearms from the time they're manufactured to the wholesale distributor to the retail distributor to the individual." The laws that exist are vague and "don't cover enough ground, not letting us know how many or what type of guns someone buys. Usually you cannot find out this information until after there have been homicides."

The technology and software exist, he said, noting that other consumer products that are recalled are done so with extreme specificity. Lot numbers of tainted drugs or foods are immediately traced to the retail outlets to which they were distributed. But similar legislation for guns has been blocked by the gun lobby.

Another source for guns is through burglaries, noted Robbins. Often, police officers are the targets. "Gang members find out whose father is a law enforcement officer, and they may target that house in hopes that the individual keeps one or more guns there. It puts law enforcement officers in a difficult position. You have to decide whether you're going to be a visible officer, who lives right in the beat community, and potentially make yourself a target, or be more quiet about what you do."

"It's not easy being a police officer. It's not like Mayberry. It involves a great deal of public service. You're a social worker, psychologist, judge, and sometimes a target," he said.

In April 1995, Robbins was watching the TV news. The item that caught his interest: the National Rifle Association had sent out a fund-raising letter to its members calling ATF officers "jack booted thugs." President Clinton was responding, and his words echoed in Robbins' head: "Their exercise of freedom of speech makes our silence unforgivable."

Robbins agreed. In his undercover work with the local ATF, the agents had always protected him. "It was an embarrassment to all law enforcement officers," he said.

At the same time, the Illinois Council wanted to present President Clinton with an award for his stand on gun control. The White House agreed, and it was Robbins who made the presentation.

Because of the visibility that Robbins was gaining, he was approached by Tom Vandenberk, chief executive officer of Uhlich Children's Home. Vandenberk's son Tommy was killed in 1992 at a birthday party at a teenager's house. Someone fired into the house; Tommy was the only fatality. Vandenberk wanted to start a victims' advocacy group for parents and wanted Robbins to be part of it.

"At first I was a bit reluctant, even though it seemed exciting. I was still experiencing some trauma from my shooting incident, but because of his persistence, I said OK," he recalled. In May 1996 the Joyce Foundation provided the seed money for the new group, Help for Survivors.

Now the core of that group has taken on another task. It plays a big part in running the Hands Without Guns program. Hands Without Guns provides alternatives to violence for young people. "Help for Survivors was designed to meet the emotional needs of parents who have experienced traumatic loss or injury. But we didn't have anything in existence to help the siblings who had lost brothers and sisters," Robbins said. The Illinois Council had already started a Hands Without Guns program, but being a lobbying group, it didn't have the time or attention to focus on it. Uhlich Children's Home took over its management and the Help for Survivors group became the logical administrators.

Robbins sees his time with young people as a variation on his police work. "In the Gang Crimes Unit, I locked the kids up, but I always spent time trying to talk to them and get them to change their ways before they lost their lives or seriously lost their freedom. But it was talking to them after they had committed the crime. Now I do it before, and hopefully prevent them from committing the crimes," he said. "It's a labor of love. I want to pass on the same second chance I received. I could have spent the rest of my life in a wheelchair."

"What makes us more unique than some advocacy groups is that there is a coming together of parents who have lost their loved ones. There is fellowship and tears and then we like to use the phrase 'healing through action.' After you're done crying, what do you do? We've been active in local, state, and federal politics," he said.

The group is developing a facilitator program, to train parents in enhancing their communications skills so they'll be confident speaking in public.

In 1997, buoyed by the reaction the year before, the group received enough grant money to take 20 Chicago area parents who had lost children to the Citizens Conference to End Handgun Violence event with them. The annual conference sponsored by the Educational Fund to End Handgun Violence started in 1994. "We were able to get them educated on the issue of gun violence and learn what's going on. They've seen what other people are doing, so now back in Chicago, they're working to build a better mousetrap," he said. "It's a slow process, but we'll just keep chipping away at it."

ADDITIONAL READING

Educational Fund to End Handgun Violence. *Kids and Guns: A National Disgrace*. Washington, D.C.: Educational Fund to End Handgun Violence, 1993.

Andrés Soto

Going After Dealers and Their "Commerce of Violence"

Born: 1955, Berkeley, CA

Education: Contra Costa Community College; University of California, Berkeley

Current Position: Policy Director, Pacific Center for Violence Prevention (a program of the Trauma Foundation)

It now costs $1,500 to get a firearms dealer's license in California's Contra Costa County. The thanks—or the blame—goes in part to Andrés Soto and one bloody weekend in 1993 when 22 people were shot over the course of 72 hours in his hometown of Richmond, California.

Another factor was an article in the *Bay Guardian*, looking at who owned gun dealer licenses in Oakland and Berkeley. The paper reported that lots of names and addresses were fake. In fact, one dog had apparently obtained a federal license to sell guns.

Soto obtained a list of federally licensed firearms dealers for the county. "There were 700 dealers in the county, 35 in the city of Richmond alone. The Yellow Pages listed only 2," he said. "That really got us looking around at what was going on."

At the time, Soto was with the county health department, and he compiled a list of dealers and developed model legislation prohibiting gun dealerships in or near residential areas, schools, daycare centers, alcohol sellers, parks, and recreation centers—"until there was virtually no place except commercial and industrial areas. Also, we added [that] there [couldn't] be an overconcentration of dealers in allowed areas and that gun dealers were required to meet certain security features such as alarm and lighting requirements."

The city of Lafayette became the battleground on the gun dealer regulations. After a seven-month process the legislation was passed.

The Trauma Foundation, a private nonprofit group dedicated to injury prevention, took notice of Soto's work and that of his colleagues. One colleague, Eric Gorovitz, had determined that California's preemption law, preventing municipalities from passing laws stricter than the state's, only covered licensing or registration issues. It said nothing about bans. "With that, the city of West Hollywood decided to ban Saturday night specials," Soto said. Saturday night specials are generally defined as cheap, easily concealed handguns.

The city was sued by the California Rifle and Pistol Association. That brought the legislation onto the radar screen of the East Bay Public Safety Corridor Project, which determined that "crime and violence don't know municipal boundaries. They adopted a package of legislation: a junk gun ordinance and a gun dealer ordinance that stated that any business that sells guns or ammunition as any part of its business must pay a higher tax on everything it sells," Soto said. San Francisco had already developed such an ordinance.

General fund tax measures in California are now voted on and must be passed by a majority. The voters resoundingly voted in favor of an end-user tax in San Leandro, home of the largest gun dealer in northern California next to Oakland, Soto said.

That set off a domino effect. San Jose and San Francisco climbed on board. "That shamed Los Angeles, Pomona, and Sacramento into taking action," Soto said. "What we did was start to elevate the issue of guns and gun violence."

That contributed to the Democrats' recapture of the state legislature, he said. Some gun rights legislators were "cited as examples of what happens when Republicans go too far out of the public sentiment. It became a wedge issue."

One of the reasons the effort has been successful in California is because of the coalition building, Soto said. "With law enforcement, victims, and public health representatives, we can reach out from there. The other side could turn out 100 angry guys at a meeting and it could be intimidating [to legislators] and look like potential votes. But we were able to line up a broad coalition, all of whom had something relevant to say. We were seen as reasonable people looking to take reasonable steps for a situation that had gotten out of hand."

That's not always how Soto felt. Growing up in the late 1960s and early 1970s, he came of age in an era of revolutionary politics in the Chicano movement. He sympathized with the calls of "power to the people" and the argument that armed citizens could not be oppressed. But after seeing abject poverty and violence through his involvement with the Farm Workers Union, his politics shifted to the left and his commitment to advocacy grew.

When he joined the county health department in 1991, he became part of a team developing a violence prevention program. "At the time, I hadn't given thought to the difference between violence prevention and crime prevention." But the difference is significant, he said. "Gun control is debated as crime control, when the reality is that most victims of gun violence kill themselves. That aspect would never get discussed if we left it on the crime control level. There's still a lot of shame around suicide."

He takes the issue personally. He has been shot at himself. A musician, Soto was on his way to a rehearsal in an unfamiliar neighborhood. He turned his car around in someone's driveway, and an old man came out of the house and fired his gun at the car. "The local police wanted to charge him only with brandishing a weapon, but the district attorney charged him with unlawful discharge. I worked with the D.A. on that case because the man had three handguns, six rifles and shotguns, and a Thompson submachine gun in his house. He received a felony probation, which meant he had to either turn in his guns destroyed or the police would destroy them," he said.

The list of those he knows who have been shot and killed grows longer the more thought he gives it. "My oldest son's godfather, my compadre, was shot in the chest collecting rent. Another man I knew came back to the area to coach football. He was partying with friends, got high on crack, and shot his wife and himself. A city councilman with cancer killed himself. A friend at community college . . . killed herself two days before Christmas. A kid I played baseball with growing up was shot by police in a much-documented case of police brutality. As Americans, guns and gun violence, by virtue of our being here in the U.S., are woven through our lives," he said.

His interest goes far beyond personal acquaintances. "On a political level, Latino and African Americans have been particularly victimized because of the genocidal activity on the part of unscrupulous business people. I may not be able to convince the homey down the street that he's in a sucker's game, but I can do the work that will ultimately change the environment for those who come up behind him," he said.

"It's important to me that the NRA supporters are just as much the victims as are the people getting killed. They get their emotions worked up on the Second Amendment, but that has nothing to do with it," he said, noting that court decisions and many legal scholars contend that the Second Amendment guarantees a state's right to arm its militia, not an individual's right to carry arms. "But they believe it as a mantra, a religion. Many of these people are not wealthy or powerful, and they're suspicious of government. In that way, they have a lot in common with the urban poor," the very people their activism is hurting, he said.

He believes it's worth the fight. "We're having a tremendous impact on many different levels. We've brought violence prevention from hopelessness to 'let's work on it.' And we've impacted the commerce of violence. The number of local gun dealers in Oakland has gone from 118 to 6. In early April 1998, the last gun dealer in Richmond went out of business. That makes it more difficult for those in an unregulated market. We're seeing a reduction in gun deaths. In Richmond, between 1994 and 1995, there was a 40 percent decline in homicides in one year," he said.

Which to him shows that a $1,500 gun dealer's license can make a whole lot of difference.

ADDITIONAL READINGS

General Accounting Office. *Federal Firearms Licenses: Various Factors Have Contributed to the Decline in the Number of Dealers.* Washington, D.C.: U.S. Government Printing Office, March 1996.

Pacific Center for Violence Prevention: http://www.pcvp.org

Trauma Foundation web site: http://www.traumafdn.org

Violence Policy Center web site: http://www.vpc.org

Violence Policy Center. *More Gun Dealers than Gas Stations.* Washington, D.C.: Violence Policy Center, 1992.

Stephen A. Sposato

Widower Takes on High Profile Action in Assault Weapons Debate

Born: 1957, Long Island, NY

Education: B.S., M.S., Stony Brook University

Current Positions: Telecommunications Engineer; Gun Control Activist

July 1, 1993, started like most any day for Stephen A. Sposato. His wife Jody was due at an attorney's office in downtown San Francisco for a second day of depositions related to a lawsuit in which she was involved. Sposato dropped off their 10-month-old daughter Meghan at her daycare provider's and went off to work himself.

That afternoon, Sposato was attending a training class for which a videotape was going to be shown. While putting the tape in the VCR, he saw a news bulletin on the television: a gunman had gone on a shooting spree at 101 California Street. "I thought what a close call. That's where Jody was this morning," he said. It was already 3 P.M.; her deposition was due to be over by noon.

On went the training tape, and Sposato continued with the session. But the news report echoed in his mind, and a half hour later he left the office to go home. "She wasn't there, but I still thought that was OK because sometimes she ran errands with Meghan. I wasn't really alarmed, but then I heard that the shooting had occurred at the law firm where she was giving her deposition. I started to get a bit of an adrenaline surge," he said.

He started calling around. Her attorney hadn't reported back to his office, either, so now there were two people missing in action. "I called the police and they had no news. I called every hospital in San Francisco, and none had had anyone by that name come in for treatment. I was thinking that was good news," he said.

He kept making phone calls, assuming that she had been detained for questioning. The daycare provider brought Meghan back home, and by the time the evening news came on, Sposato was fighting panic. "During the news, I was trying to keep Meghan quiet so I could look and listen to the television tape to see if I could recognize any of the bodies coming out of the building. It was torture, not knowing. So after a few hours of this, I decided to go down there."

He arranged for someone to watch Meghan and drove downtown. "I couldn't get anywhere near the building, so I parked the car and walked. I went to the main police van, and they told me to wait in the Red Cross van. I sat there, drinking soda after soda. I kept checking my home and office voice mail to see if she left me a message. Finally, when I saw the SWAT team coming out of the building, I asked one of the team members if there was anyone left in the building. 'No one alive,' he said," Sposato recalled.

Jody's attorney's partners joined him, but no one had any answers. One of the investigators told Sposato, "Sometimes these things are best dealt with in the morning. Go home and get a good night's sleep." Sposato was furious at the time, but later realized he was probably spared the news because of all the reporters nearby. As he and the other attorneys started to walk away, two uniformed patrol officers followed them down the sidewalk and gently suggested they might find some answers at the homicide unit. "The coroner's office is there, too," they said.

"Nothing prepares you for the task of identifying someone you love. It was the most traumatic moment of my life. I pray no one ever sees anything like that. They put you in a room with a glass viewing area and ask if you're ready. 'I guess so,' I said. And there was the most important person in my life lying there with the life sucked out of her. Her eyes were open. Her mouth was open. The look on her face was one of trauma and shock. I kicked the wall a bunch of times and yelled, 'Damn the man that did this to you.' The biggest part of you dies in a situation like that," he said. "The world became surreal to me. I was now walking in a nightmare."

Sposato made some phone calls from the coroner's office. He called Jody's mother and father. "Those were two tremendously difficult and bizarre phone calls. I knew what I was going to tell them was going to shatter their lives. It just kept going on. Every time I told another person, it was the glass dropping, shattering, all over again. I called my neighbor when I got home and I could hear her crying through my open window after I told her," he said.

His friend Mike and Jody's friend Becky came over and they spent the night, sitting, crying, waiting for the newspaper to hit the drive-way at 4 A.M. so they could learn more details. The gunman had walked into the office with a handgun and two TEC-DC9 semiau-tomatic assault pistols, often classified as "assault weapons" because of their paramilitary characteristics and firepower capabilities. He was carrying several 50-round ammunition clips. When the rampage was over, eight people were dead and six were wounded. Jody didn't stand a chance. She was shot five times in the back. "It was an ambush," Sposato said.

Sposato's feelings of anger and frustration soon took on a new form. "Out of that pain you get this unbelievable conviction to make sure this never happens to anyone else," he said. It also led to some introspection. "I'm a gun owner. I'm a lifelong Republican. And I realized that not only is there something wrong with the system, but I'm a part of it. After I read the paper and learned how heavily armed this guy was, I wrote President Clinton asking why all these people were dying and how on earth someone can buy this kind of fire-power."

Now he wondered how he could get his letter to the President himself. Through a friend who called Senator Dianne Feinstein's office, and after some telephone tag, he was given Senator Feinstein's home telephone number in Washington, D.C. "It was 11 P.M. Eastern time when I called. I woke her up. I was expecting a butler or maid or answering service to answer, but I got Dianne on the phone," he said. "Talk about a godsend. She was warm and compassionate and she's out to do what's right. She knew about the shooting and said she'd take the letter to President Clinton. I was ecstatic," he recalled. "We also talked about how to influence change, and it was then that Dianne planted the seed with me that I could be part of that change if I so chose."

A few days later, Senator Feinstein called him to ask if he would be interested in testifying before a Senate committee considering an assault weapons ban. Sposato and Jody's father, Larry Jones, took on the task together of preparing the testimony and were ready to testify on August 3. "Just before I testified, I remembered Senator Orrin Hatch [R-UT], the lone committee Republican still in the room, get-ting up and leaving. This is my political party and Republicans were nowhere to be found. Senator Hatch found it more important to eat a bologna sandwich and was not at all interested in what I or the people of this country had to say," Sposato said.

The moment was dramatic. Meghan was in a backpack on her

father's back. "The hearings ran over and we were out of food and diapers and she was crying. I was in the back room and I whispered to her to be quiet for just five minutes. And with some help from above, she was. She quit crying as I opened the doors to have a seat and testify. We made the national news on every network and that was when I realized that I could be an effective spokesperson for this issue. I was still a novice and I didn't know the power of air time," he said.

He continued to be an effective spokesperson, testifying before a U.S. House of Representatives committee weighing a similar bill and attending several press conferences with President Clinton. "I was nervous about meeting the President," he said. "He's the most powerful person in the world so I felt some anxiety. But all I had to do was look at a picture of Jody and Meghan and I remembered who I was and why I was there."

Sposato praised President Clinton for taking on the issue. In fact, he counts him among his few heroes. "My heroes are my father, who dropped out of high school at the age of 17 to join the Navy and fight in World War II, my two uncles who fought in the Battle of the Bulge, and Dianne Feinstein and Bill Clinton because they've taken on this extraordinary issue. He's a very conscientious person and realizes that the laws that govern the gun industry need to be balanced. There are too many people like myself, our daughter, Jody's parents, grandparents, and friends who suffer because a bunch of guys like to plink at beer cans with assault weapons. Just because a few select folks in rural Kentucky think plinking is a 'sport' doesn't mean assault weapons should be legal," he said.

Sposato made one more trip to Washington, D.C., on September 13, 1994, the day President Clinton signed the crime bill containing the assault weapons ban into law. Sposato expected to be in the audience, so he was surprised when he was ushered through another door. He found himself in a room with U.S. Attorney General Janet Reno and House Minority Leader Richard Gephardt. He was told he'd follow the First Lady onto the platform and stand behind the President while he signed the bill. He shared that stage with Mark Klaas, the father of Polly Klaas, the young girl abducted from her home and murdered. President Clinton handed him one of the pens he used to sign the law into effect and he dedicated the crime bill to the memories of Jody Sposato, Polly Klaas, and James Darby, a Louisiana boy killed on his way home from school.

"Jody's mother and sister were in the stands watching this and as

I stood there, I realized there wasn't much more a person can do. Here's the President of the United States signing a law that will ban the kind of weapon that was used to kill your wife and dedicating the bill to her," he recalled.

So Sposato returned to California and "immediately focused my energies on raising my daughter. I'm not out of the gun control issue because I'm very interested in what goes on on the state and federal level," but his speaking engagements are more limited now.

Sposato still owns his guns—a .22 rifle, a Beretta handgun, and his father's M1 from World War II—but he keeps them locked up and off the premises. "I think guns have a place in our society, but there has to be balance," he said. His beef isn't with those kinds of firearms, but with assault weapons. "You don't need assault weapons to defend yourself. You'll wind up shooting your dog or kids before you shoot anyone coming in. If you feel like you need to defend yourself, a 12-gauge shotgun will scare the dickens out of anyone." He has also testified on behalf of legislation to ban "junk guns," and he has campaigned on behalf of politicians who support gun control, like Dianne Feinstein. He did a television ad which aired frequently before the elections in 1996, giving an important edge to Congresswoman Ellen Tauscher, who ran on the pro–gun control issue and upset two-term Republican incumbent Bill Baker.

Sposato is vocal in his opposition to relaxing concealed carrying laws. "Twenty-five percent of the police officers shot in the line of duty are shot with their own guns. What does that tell you about you or me? It would be a lot higher. What's the NRA thinking? They don't give a damn about my wife or my daughter or myself, but about keeping the profit lines open for the billion dollar gun industry," he said.

But gun control activism is no longer consuming him as it did in the months immediately following Jody's death. "Meghan and I went through a couple of dark years. It's hard when you're trying to work a full time job, spend as much time as possible with your daughter, and do gun control. I had no social life for two years, but that was the way I wanted it. I was too depressed, so gun control was a good therapy for me and for my daughter too. She doesn't comprehend what she's done, but she's undefeated against the NRA. Any legislation she's been behind has been a slam dunk. Her message has been, 'What do we need more of in America? Assault weapons or mommies?' "

Sposato remarried in the fall of 1997, but scars remain for him and his daughter. "While I was driving her to school the other day, she asked me when I was going to die. She's also asked when her new mommy is going to die. A five-year-old shouldn't have to worry about that," he said.

ADDITIONAL READINGS

"Center Files Suits Against Assault Weapon Maker for Victims of California Shooting." CPHV Legal Action Project Report, No. 8. Washington, D.C.: Center to Prevent Handgun Violence.

Merrill et al. v. Navegar, Inc. (In Re 101 California Street Litigation) (California Court of Appeal, First Appellate District, Division Two, No. A079863).

Joseph P. Tartaro

Bringing Information to the Grass Roots

Born: 1931, Buffalo, NY

Education: Attended University of Buffalo; Public Information Officers School, Defense Dept.

Current Positions: Editor, *Gun Week* and *Gun News Digest*; President, Second Amendment Foundation

---

"The whole gun control issue feeds up from the grass roots," said Joseph P. Tartaro. "While many of the people at this level might not be as well informed as they should be, the average gun owner, hunter, or collector sees it as a personal issue."

That's where the influence is—and should be, according to Tartaro. People's minds are changed on this issue in normal conversations with each other, not by the "Sunday morning talking heads."

For example, he recalls talking to a police officer on duty during a National Rifle Association annual meeting. "He was telling me that he approves of the efforts to protect guns, but he questioned the organization's stand on Saturday night specials. I told him the service revolver he was wearing—a Smith Chief's Special—would have been banned under a bill proposed at the time." Tartaro believes those

Joseph P. Tartaro.

details, the kinds of things that bring the issue home, are missing from the national debate.

"In my mind, the core elements have to do with self-protection and political freedom. The self-protection issue transcends everything. If you look at every religion, with a few minor exceptions, the idea of individual survival is paramount. Defending yourself and keeping your life rather than giving it up to some predator is a protected concept," he said.

He recalls dozens of conversations with people over the years who tell him that they don't own guns but can conceive of times when they might want one. "They say they want the choice. There's an interesting parallel on a number of civil liberties issues, such as abortion and religious freedom. People have a gut understanding of the issue, but not of the nuances of it."

So Tartaro has seen his mission as bringing information to the people. As executive editor of the *New Gun Week*, the quarterly *Gun News Digest*, and the *Gottlieb-Tartaro Report*, a monthly newsletter co-edited by Alan M. Gottlieb (see profile), he does just that.

His libertarian views come through in his writing and discussion. "I'm convinced the Constitution protects an individual right to keep and bear arms through the Second Amendment. I served in the U.S. Army during the Korean War and have lived through the World War II era and the years in which we've fought against repression and totalitarianism. But we're seeing a greater invasion of individual rights by our government. We are being brought closer to an era of the Hitlers and the Stalins," he said.

For example, the amount of personal information available about an individual once you have that person's Social Security number is astounding, he said. "From that, someone can determine whether you're a legal citizen, if you've paid your alimony or child support, what kind of medications you take. Guns are only a part of it."

Granted, times have changed. When Tartaro was growing up in Buffalo, young people with guns were not an uncommon sight. He recalls a time when he and some teenage friends were planning to go deer hunting after church. Rather than leave their shotguns in the car, they took them into the church with them. "The best looking of us was wearing jeans and an old Army field jacket. Could you imagine the reaction today if a half dozen scruffily dressed teens walked into a church carrying their shotguns?" he asks, laughing at the image. "But we didn't harm anybody. We were minding our business and it was fairly typical for kids to bring their guns to school so they could go shooting after."

That was a time, he said, when common sense guided public policy. National debate around the time of the Gun Control Act of 1968 got his attention. By the mid-1970s, he had written quite a bit on the issue and his work on gun rights was overshadowing his advertising and public relations business. "I increasingly attended scholarly conferences and writers' conferences sponsored by groups like the Second Amendment Foundation. I came to know the players, including some of those who were heavily involved in scholarship on the issue."

Tartaro began editing *Gun Week* in 1979 after a group headed by himself and his late brother, Vincent, and others acquired it from Amos Press, which had founded the weekly in 1966. He continued as editor when the Second Amendment Foundation acquired the title in 1985, and joined the foundation's board of directors later the same year. Since 1986 the foundation has been sponsoring an annual Gun Rights Policy Conference, and in 1990 it launched a series of grass-roots leadership training conferences. "We talk not only about gun rights, but political activism in general because the essentials are the same for every issue," he said.

The most important point in these sessions is this: the media's version of events is truncated. "It's distorted by the journalists' lack of understanding or the willingness of those journalists to accept the 30-second capsule of what the bill is about. Everything is reduced to a catch phrase."

It's a simplistic debate when viewed that way. One side blames guns, seeing them as inherently evil. "Even if good people own guns, they're simply adding to the pool of guns that might be stolen or used irresponsibly. The other side says there are plenty of laws and you're not enforcing them. Make the people who commit the crime be responsible. But that argument has been going on for 34 years," he said.

But there are nuances. Tartaro believes that the public outcry for criminals being punished effectively bubbled up from the grass roots. The NRA's CrimeStrike initiative has helped, he said, but even that might be a reflection of grassroots voices. "My view is not necessarily the NRA view. I'm more of a friend of the criminal defense lawyer than they are. I don't support a monolithic conservative law and order approach to everything."

But without a doubt he supports the right of individuals to have firearms. "People should be able to choose. They should be able to keep them in their homes and use them for any legal purpose. They should be able to bear them. Ideally, I would like the Vermont model, the epitome of 'an armed society is a polite society.' They can carry but few do because they don't feel threatened."

While everyone would like there to be less misuse of firearms, Tartaro believes efforts such as childproof handguns or personalized handguns "don't make a hell of a lot of sense. First of all, all these handguns are expensive. Secondly, it ignores the concepts that there may be more than one person in a household who has a legitimate use. If you talk to police, they all say they want their partners to be able to use their guns if needed," he said.

It comes back to enforcing laws that are deterrents to criminals. New York State has a law that carries a mandatory one-year jail term for carrying an unlicensed firearm. In New York City, the incarceration rate on that law is only about 50 percent. Upstate, it's about 70 percent. "Either way, a miscreant thinks he can probably beat the rap. There's not much disincentive in the law," he said.

But public support seems to be swinging in favor of stiffer sentencing. That's paying off, he said, as some judges are becoming less lenient. And that public support is a direct result of grassroots activism.

ADDITIONAL READINGS

Second Amendment Foundation web site: http://www.saf.org

Tartaro, Joseph P. "The Great Assault Weapon Hoax." *University of Dayton Law Review* 20, no. 2 (December 1994).

———. *Revolt at Cincinnati*. Buffalo, NY: Hawkeye Publishing, 1981.

Patricia Margaret (Peggy) Tartaro

Encouraging Pro-Gun Activists to Expand Their Base

Born: 1955, Buffalo, NY

Education: Attended Buffalo State College

Current Positions: Executive Editor, *Women & Guns*; Managing Editor, *Gun News Digest*

Peggy Tartaro is always looking ahead. Sometimes it's just a week or two ahead, working to get out the next issue of *Women & Guns*, the nation's only magazine about guns for women, by women. But

Patricia Margaret (Peggy) Tartaro.

the rest of the time, she's looking toward the future—and how the players in the gun rights movement can expand their roles.

"Political gun owners have traditionally done a very bad job of presenting themselves as anything but gun owners to those outside the debate," she said. "Failure to recognize and resolve that is, in my opinion, the most serious error gun owners have made in the past 25 years."

To correct that, it must be acknowledged that "success in the sociopolitical debate of gun rights is dependent on a majority of people who either never will be gun owners themselves or will be gun owners in the most casual sense—that is, owning a firearm, but with little, no, or even an adverse interest in the politics." It is also necessary for political gun owners to look beyond the box to expand their base of support.

It's a fairly common problem for any single-issue group, she noted. "The notion of 'ideological purity' strains not only the group's ability to operate in the real political world, but also the ability to build coalitions with outside groups, attract new adherents, and have a voice in the mainstream. But, in gun owners, who have historical precedent for laying particular claim to the notion of 'rugged individualism,' the concept of joining—even to other like-minded individuals—is difficult."

That means that those gun owners who are an integral part of larger organizations, such as Rotary Clubs and PTAs, frequently leave behind "the important baggage of their 'otherness' when entering the political debate," she said. Tartaro emphasizes that this "otherness" is, in fact, critical. In these settings, they frequently miss the perfect opportunity to share their views with people who respect them. She leads frequent sessions training gun activists and reminds them that "they already have entree into a vast array of 'other clubs' in their everyday professional and personal lives. Talking about what we believe to others—talking, rather than arguing—is the key to providing others with the opportunity to first, understand and accept your beliefs and, occasionally, defend those views themselves."

She uses the example of explaining to her non–gun owning hairdresser the assault weapons issue, using a blow dryer as a prop. It's not a perfect analogy, but it gets the point across. Having known each other for 10 years, the women are on friendly terms. The hairdresser asked Tartaro for security tips when opening her own shop, for example. One day, in the midst of the public debate on "assault weapons," the hairdresser asked if these guns were machine guns.

Tartaro recalled the conversation: " 'No,' I said, but felt that even with a brief technical explanation and the fact that 'machine guns' have been regulated since 1934, she was still confused. So I reached down and picked up her hair dryer. Flicking the switch, I said, 'This is how a semiautomatic operates—it doesn't 'fire' until you pull the trigger.' Leaving the dryer running, I said, 'And this would be a machine gun—not a semiautomatic. It 'fires' until you run out of ammunition—or electricity.' "

"Sensing that I was getting through, I continued, 'Your hair dryer is much more professional looking than mine. It's all chrome and black and mine is beige plastic. They operate the same way, but they look different. If they were guns, yours would be the 'assault weapon.' "

Tartaro emphasizes that the debate must be brought to this level of understanding. "The scholarship, the statistics, and the law are on our side, but very few people want to hear about the Federalist Papers or the Lott-Mustard study; instead, if you tell them how it affects them, they are more apt to consider your viewpoint. For most of my career, for example, I have been telling activists to use the word 'choice' in discussions with women, 'choice' being the preeminent woman's political word, regardless of one's position on abortion."

Tartaro would like to see a wider base of support for gun rights—and women have an influence there. "I don't particularly think the gun club setting is more male chauvinistic than, say, a golf or tennis club. I might argue that the rules of formal and informal recreational shooting are more egalitarian than golf or tennis. But, because of a host a reasons, leadership in these types of clubs (and most formal organizations, for that matter) has been vested in men, and until recently, women's participation was limited to 'ladies-day' or 'family membership' type activities. We are confronted then with mainly white men of at least middle class economic status who recognize that they are not a political majority and that they are viewed—and dismissed—as either hobbyists or zealots. I don't feel it's necessary to tell activists that it's important to include women and other non-traditional gun owners, as I believe the majority of them recognize the fundamental truth of that. Instead, I try to present ways in which this can be accomplished."

Will the future hold an increased number of activist women gun owners brought in by the core groups? Or will it continue to be, as it has been in recent years, those women "who have invited themselves in of their own choice?" She has seen a significant change over the years. Women's views about gun ownership are being better represented politically and in the media. "To some extent, in both cases, women are viewed as enough of a novelty that their views may be given more of an opportunity than men's. We have seen this in women's pages' articles, TV talk shows, but also in political situations, especially involving shall-issue statutes."

Aside from training activists through the Leadership Training Conference program sponsored by the Second Amendment Foundation

(SAF) and the Citizens Committee for the Right to Keep and Bear Arms (CCRKBA), Tartaro believes that *Women & Guns* is a valuable tool for reaching out to women. The publication was started in February 1989 by Sonny Jones, an Arkansas freelance gun writer. She attended a Gun Rights Policy Conference sponsored by SAF/CCRKBA in 1988 and returned with the enthusiasm to pursue this pet project, Tartaro said. The first several issues were between 24 and 36 black and white pages, and it was available only through subscription. The Second Amendment Foundation bought the title in October 1989 and Tartaro became associate editor. When Jones left in 1992, Tartaro became editor. The magazine is now available at newsstands.

"We have tried to live up to our mantle of 'the *only* magazine for women gun owners,' by including as much coverage of as many different subjects of interest to women gun owners, ranging from the mechanics and techniques to personalities. The readership's main interest (as surveyed) is personal protection and self-defense, and we skew heavily in that direction. They also are interested in 'gun politics.' The single issue of gun ownership is often at odds with other political interests and concerns of the readership. Gun ownership is a physical, concrete act—owning an object—that has political-social implications far beyond merely identifying or aligning oneself with a particular philosophy."

She doesn't mean to imply that her readers are more liberal than readers of other gun magazines. What she does find is an "intense interest in the image of gun owners," particularly gun-owning women. "Debate erupts occasionally about particular pictures, for example, and readers often call to our attention TV, movie, and book images which they feel either do or don't represent women gun owners well. We very rarely use models in *Women & Guns*, in contrast to most other women's magazines, finding instead, representation of women gun owners in the reality."

Tartaro feels that *Women & Guns* has been her greatest contribution to the gun control debate. "I think it contributes in two ways. First, it provides 'a room of our own' to women gun owners, many of whom have been subscribers since the beginning. It encompasses the idea of sorority as well as a place to work out our own feelings on identity and image. Secondly, the magazine, as a collection of this notion and these people, allows voice in the wider community."

Tartaro's interest in writing on gun issues started years before. In 1979 her father, Joseph P. Tartaro (see profile), and her uncle were among the investors who bought *Gun Week*. "I came to work for them to see if I would like it and started mainly in circulation and advertising. Working at *Gun Week* allowed me to pursue a variety of interests: media, writing, politics."

While the past two decades have seen many changes, some things have stayed the same. "My biggest frustration is that I have seen enormous general apathy for political discourse. Americans are simply not interested in complicated issues unless they have a direct impact on their lives—and even then they want it boiled down, processed, and most of all, solved, quickly. Even issues which do have a direct effect are lost in this process, so that, if you want to talk about gun ownership, the debate is narrowly limited—'assault weapons,' 'junk guns,' the issue du jour—but the larger questions, particularly the role of the individual, are ignored, lost, and even ridiculed."

That's what Peggy Tartaro is trying to change—with the next issue of *Women & Guns* and over the long haul.

ADDITIONAL READINGS

Second Amendment Foundation web site: http://www.saf.org (*Women & Guns* editorials can be accessed through this site.)
Women & Guns, published monthly.

Stephen P. Teret

Law and Public Health Combine in Gun Violence Research

Born: 1945, New York, NY

Education: B.A., St. Lawrence University; J.D., Brooklyn Law School; M.P.H., Johns Hopkins University School of Public Health

Current Positions: Director, The Johns Hopkins Center for Gun Policy and Research; Professor, The Johns Hopkins University School of Public Health

During a visit to a friend's New York City apartment building, Stephen P. Teret saw something very interesting. Before the elevator would respond to any of the button-pushing, the friend had to hold up her key ring to the elevator's electric eye. Only then would it accept the orders.

The elevator's electric eye served as a sort of electronic security guard. Why couldn't the same technology be used to prevent unauthorized individuals from firing guns?, he thought. Indeed, it can, and Teret is among those advocating its widespread use.

Teret began his law career as a legal services attorney, helping the poor in Harlem. After several years, he switched his focus to representing persons seriously injured. During those nine years, he found one universal truth: given the choice, his clients would have preferred to not be injured in the first place rather than receive money as compensation. "That caused me to be interested in prevention," he said.

And so he arrived in Baltimore in 1978, as a master's in public health candidate at the Johns Hopkins University. He stayed on as faculty and is still there now, as director of the Johns Hopkins Center for Gun Policy and Research.

Starting out broadly interested in injury prevention, Teret found himself gravitating toward gun-related injuries. An incident involving family friends, in which their toddler was shot and killed, "cemented my resolve. The boy was at the home of a woman who was providing private day care. She had taken him up to the crib in her bedroom where she'd put him down for a nap. Her four-year-old son came into the room, found the loaded handgun, and unintentionally shot the two-year-old. What to me was the most troublesome question was how a four-year-old was able to operate a handgun."

At the same time, Teret's attention focused on one of his students, Garen Wintemute (see profile). "We were finding we worked well together, and we started to write an article about guns," he said. The two have collaborated through the years—often fielding criticism from anti–gun control activists who argue that the public health community is out of its realm in this issue.

Teret disputes that. "Gun violence is eminently a public health issue because 36,000 people a year die from gun-related injuries. It's the number one cause of death for some segments of the population and it costs billions of dollars annually to treat victims. Of course it's a public health issue, but it's not an exclusive franchise. It is also a criminal justice issue," he said.

What public health adds to the debate is a broader perspective "because the approach looks at all the factors involved. We're interested in not only those pulling the trigger, but the environment in which the incidents occur." For example, he said, criminologists have little interest in the issue of gun-related suicides.

Teret also found that his background in litigation would serve as much of the foundation of his injury prevention work. "Paradoxically, after having come to the School of Public Health, I learned that one of the strongest tools you have is if you can transfer the costs of injury to the manufacturer of the product."

That concept fits firearms well, he said. "Why is the gun made so a child can operate it? Why are other safety design features not a part of every gun? Ultimately, I think litigation or the threat of it causes manufacturers to redesign their products."

Several lawsuits with similar fact patterns provide a good example of a design defect, Teret said. "Two boys play with a semiautomatic pistol and remove the ammunition clip, thinking the gun couldn't fire. One boy pulls the trigger and now another boy is dead." A load indicator, showing that there was still one round of ammunition in the chamber, could have prevented that tragedy, he and the plaintiff's attorneys argue. Other safety designs include a magazine disconnect, making it impossible to fire the gun if the magazine clip isn't in place.

The idea has precedents, said Teret. Between the 1880s and 1940s, gun maker Smith & Wesson made a gun that they claimed no ordinary young child could operate, "but now they don't use the same technology." In fact, he said, the industry has generally abandoned safety concerns. "If you look at changes made in its products over the past 100 years, they have been to increase the lethality of guns. Guns can shoot more ammunition, and they have laser sights, larger projectiles. One reason is that no one has made the industry focus on safety. The Consumer Product Safety Commission has been barred from oversight on firearms." That's why product liability plays such an important role in the firearms debate, he said.

His focus on improved safety design has led to the work on personalized handguns. Using technology similar to that in the New York City elevator, a gun could be made inoperable if an unauthorized person tried to use it. A microchip can be embedded in a bracelet or ring worn by the gun owner. The gun would only work if a sensor in the gun detects the radio frequency emitted by that microchip. In other words, if the gun were stolen, it would be worthless to the thief. If a despondent teenager found it, it couldn't be used in a suicide attempt. And such technology would virtually eliminate incidents in which children unintentionally shoot other children or themselves.

Initially, the cost of handguns employing this new technology could be about 50 percent higher. As it becomes more commonplace, however, the costs should decline, he said.

The Center for Gun Policy and Research has drafted model legislation to require that any new handguns sold incorporate technology to make them personalized. The center was established in early 1995 with funding from the Joyce Foundation to develop and evaluate gun policies and laws for their impact on gun violence.

Teret has focused on guns for much of the past two decades. "There is still plenty to interest me. The challenge hasn't become any smaller. There are still thousands of people dying and there is still strenuous opposition from the National Rifle Association. Every day there is a new challenge," he said. "This is very long term, just as the change in tobacco policy has been measured in decades. It's foolish to think that we can effect changes in three years."

Such a demanding commitment means that other interests are sacrificed. "I used to consider myself a generalist in injury prevention. I looked at toy safety, motor vehicle safety. But I am no longer a generalist. There are new areas of great challenge for public health that I'm interested in, but I haven't found the time to focus on anything else," he said.

ADDITIONAL READINGS

Teret, Stephen P. "The Firearm Injury Reporting System Revisited." *Journal of the American Medical Association* 275, no. 1 (1996).

———. *Personalized Guns: Reducing Gun Deaths Through Design Changes.* Baltimore: Johns Hopkins Center for Gun Policy and Research, 1996.

Teret, Stephen P., and Susan P. Baker. "Children Shooting Guns: A Failure in Product Design." *Injury Prevention* 1 (1995).

Teret, Stephen P., S. DeFrancesco, and L. A. Bailey. "Gun Deaths and Home Rule: A Case for Local Regulation of a Local Public Health Problem." *American Journal of Preventive Medicine* 9 (1993).

Teret, Stephen P., Daniel W. Webster, Jon S. Vernick, Tom W. Smith, Deborah Leff, Garen J. Wintemute, Philip J. Cook, Darnell F. Hawkins, Arthur L. Kellermann, Susan B. Sorenson, and Susan DeFrancesco. "Support for New Policies to Regulate Firearms: Results of Two National Surveys." *New England Journal of Medicine* 399, no. 12 (September 17, 1998).

Teret, Stephen P., and Garen J. Wintemute. "Handgun Injuries: The Epidemiologic Evidence for Assessing Legal Responsibility." *Hamline Law Review* 6 (July 1983).

———. "Polices to Prevent Firearm Injuries." *Health Affairs* 12 (Winter 1993).

Vernick, Jon S., and Stephen P. Teret. "Firearms and Health: The Right to Be Armed with Accurate Information about the Second Amendment." *American Journal of Public Health* 83, no. 12 (1993).

Vernick, Jon S., Stephen P. Teret, and Daniel W. Webster. "Regulating Firearm Advertisements that Promise Home Protection." *Journal of the American Medical Association* 277 (May 7, 1997).

Wintemute, Garen J., Stephen P. Teret, Jess F. Kraus, and Mona W. Wright. "The Choice of Weapons in Firearms Suicides." *American Journal of Public Health* 78, no. 4 (1988).

Wintemute, Garen J., Stephen P. Teret, Jess F. Kraus, Mona A. Wright, and Gretchen Bradfield. "When Children Shoot Children: 88 Unintended Deaths in California." *Journal of the American Medical Association* 257, no. 22 (June 12, 1987).

Lisa S. Thornton

Rehabilitating Young Bodies and Lives

Born: 1961, Pittsburgh, PA

Education: B.A., Fisk University; M.D., University of Michigan Medical School

Current Positions: Director of Pediatric Rehabilitation, Schwab Rehabilitation Hospital and LaRabida Children's Hospital; Assistant Professor of Orthopedics and Pediatrics, University of Chicago

---

The environment in which they live is extraordinary: the mean streets of inner city Chicago, where gangs, guns, and violence are often a part of growing up. Other than that, "they're typical adolescent kids. They're risk takers, they have an attitude, and they can be arrogant," said Lisa S. Thornton, a pediatrician and rehabilitation specialist. She's talking about her patients, many of whom end up with permanent injuries due to gunshot wounds. "These kids happen to be involved in much more lethal circumstances than regular adolescents. That's what sets them up as different"—like a boy who was recently admitted. He was shot four times because he refused to join a gang, she said.

Her patients have many characteristics in common. They're typically 12 to 17 years old, black or Hispanic. Most are shot by someone else. Most of them were aimed at. All are seriously disabled, usually due to a brain injury or spinal cord injury. "I don't see much of the random gun victim patient population." They're not all gang bangers, she said, but some are. Many have been shot before; almost all know someone who has been. They can usually tell her with which weapon they were shot.

Few anticipate this outcome. There's a cavalier attitude that if they get shot at, they'll either be fine or end up dead. "But disability is a possibility. I see profound examples of what can happen when guns get into hands of impulsive adolescents," she said.

Thornton said it's easy for some people to shrug this off as an isolated problem, something that happens only in inner cities. But it's a national problem, she said, noting an estimated 183,000 to 203,000 people in the United States today have a spinal cord injury, and a growing number of those injuries are the result of gunshot wounds. In 1986, only 14 percent of spinal cord injuries were attributed to gunshot wounds. By 1996, 30 percent were. According to the University of Alabama National Spinal Cord Injury Statistical Center in Birmingham, "Interesting trends in the database show the proportions of injuries due to motor vehicle crashes and sporting activities have declined while the proportion of injuries from acts of violence has increased steadily since 1973."

Since damage to the spinal cord can result in paralysis, emergency and lifetime treatment for these patients is extremely expensive. One's chance of recovery hinges on the injury itself, said Thornton. "If the spinal cord is mildly injured, the patient can recover. It's not a matter of how hard they fight for recovery."

According to the National Spinal Cord Injury Statistical Center, the first-year medical costs for high quadriplegia (patients who can't move at all) are $417,000. Each of these patients tallies up an average of $74,707 in medical costs for each year afterward. For paraplegics (those who can move their arms), first-year medical costs average $152,000, with $15,000 per year thereafter. Half of those injured are under age 30. In other words, the lifetime medical cost for a 25-year-old patient is typically $1.3 million.

"It makes me angry because I don't understand this love affair with guns," said Thornton. "Since I've entered pediatrics, I've been amazed by how much we hate our children. We give child safety lip service, but when it comes to saving the lives of kids, we're quick to say, 'I love my gun more.'"

She is perplexed at the ease with which her young patients get their guns. There's a handgun ban in Chicago, but that doesn't stop gun traffickers. "My patients buy from dealers who sell brand new guns out of the trunks of their cars," she said. "We have to drop this love affair with guns, and we need to begin with our children. If that means infringing on what some people feel is their civil liberty, I don't have a problem with that."

She realizes that her patients don't evoke much sympathy. For example, after the Jonesboro, Arkansas, schoolyard shooting and other similar shootings, counselors are brought in to help the students deal with the grief and shock of the violence. "No one ever debriefs these kids," she said of her patients. "No one ever says it's a shame this kind of thing happens in this community. We have to jump on the problems, even when the victims are impoverished or of color." To do that, "someone has to help these young people change their perspective, shift how they think of life."

Sometimes, it takes a life-threatening injury to do that. "Some describe their injuries as their greatest redemption. They say it has changed or saved their lives. If they hadn't been injured, they would have continued in the same behavior. Some of these guys are bright but they're doing really stupid things. After they're injured, they can't do those things anymore," she said.

While becoming paralyzed is a high price to pay for redemption, these young people most often count themselves lucky. "Being paralyzed is not the worst thing. There can be goodness that comes out of it. Many people in rehab are nurtured in ways they have never been before. There are people touching them every day, people concerned with their progress and their vocational training. While they're in the hospital, they complete their GED [graduate equivalency degree]. For some, it's the thing that saves them," she said.

The national statistics reflect what Thornton sees in her typical patients. According to the National Spinal Cord Injury Institute, among persons injured between 1973 and 1978, 77.5 percent were Caucasian, 13.5 percent were African American, 6 percent were Hispanic, 2 percent were American Indian, and 0.8 percent were Asian. But that is changing. Among those injured since 1990, Caucasians accounted for 56.2 percent, while African Americans made up 28.7 percent, 10.5 percent were Hispanic, 0.4 percent were American Indian, and 2.1 percent were Asian. In other words, the percentage of spinal cord injuries among most minority populations is increasing rapidly.

"It gets disconcerting to see this over and over again," Thornton said. "I can't judge the person who is doing the illicit activity. I don't know all the reasons these people are out there. For me, it's less the fact that they got shot, [than] the reasons why. Why are people shooting at others?"

It's a question she can't answer. There are programs in cities to work with young people to help them find alternatives to violence. If those kinds of programs work, she might see a gradual reduction in the number of young gunshot victims. "A lot of people who are willing to take on such high risk behavior weren't loved. They don't value themselves, so they don't value others," she said. As the mother of a young son, that bothers her deeply. "I wish these kids could feel the love my son does."

ADDITIONAL READINGS

Kizer, Kenneth W. "Hospitalization Charges, Costs and Income for Firearm-Related Injuries at a University Trauma Center." *Journal of the American Medical Association* 273, no. 22 (June 14, 1995).

Powell, Elizabeth C., Karen M. Sheehan, and Katherine Kaufer Christoffel. "Firearm Violence among Youth: Public Health Strategies for Prevention." *Annals of Emergency Medicine* 28 (August 1996).

Spinal Cord Injury Information Network web site: http://www.sci.rehabm.uab.edu/

Joy Turner

Nurse Talks Tough to At-Risk Youth

Born: 1951, Austin, TX
Education: Dominguez High School, Compton, CA
Current Positions: Perinatal Nurse; At-Risk Youth Worker

Joy Turner preaches a kind of in-your-face ministry. After her 19-year-old son Hank was killed in 1989, she found her calling in talking to young men in jails and detention centers. And she is blunt with them.

"I let them know how they destroyed my life. I have a tendency to get raw and graphic. When they start pouting and getting uncomfortable, I tell them I'm giving them the same thing they gave me. There's none of this, 'You poor thing.' They made a choice to do harm. They're accountable for their actions," she said.

She focuses on one of the strongest bonds these young men have—one they often don't acknowledge: their mothers. "Every gang member was raised by a female. When they get hurt, or caught, the first person they call on is their mothers or grandmothers. Many joined a gang because they thought they could find love, but the homeboys aren't there when they get in trouble. 'Who is your homey now?' I ask them. 'It's your mother.' They didn't care enough to stay with her when they were out [on the streets] but they want her to come to the rescue now," she said.

She shows them her family photos—the way things were. Then she holds out a jar filled with broken glass. " 'Fix it,' " she'll tell one of them. " 'Put all the pieces back. Give me my son and my life back. These are the lives you've ruined.' I didn't walk into their lives; they walked into mine."

They can't fix it for her, of course, but they can fix it for themselves. "I tell them even though they're in jail, they have an opportunity to do something good. They can collect some of the pieces that will help them pull their lives back together."

She drives home the point that staying in gangs will just mean trouble. If they insist on staying in a gang, she tells them, "take out a life insurance policy. Don't make your mother or family pay for what you're doing. Don't make them have a car wash or go begging for some money to bury you."

She has buried a son, so she knows how tough it is. Hank was not in a gang; he was a "happy-go-lucky person. He was the family prankster and the busybody. He played football, basketball and baseball," she said.

Hank had been at a house party about a half mile away from the family home on the night he was killed. Someone shot at him from behind a fence; Hank wasn't the intended target. "That doesn't make me feel better," Turner said.

Turner was getting ready for bed when someone came to the door with the news. "As a mother, I was there for the cuts and scrapes and had seen him through all of them. I had no concept of him dying. Even when the hospital called and told me to come right away, I didn't know how serious it was."

One of his main arteries had been severed. He was in surgery for 10 hours and needed 72 pints of blood. Another victim of the same shooting died in the operating room. Turner remembers thinking, "Please don't let my baby die in surgery" because she wanted to see him alive one more time. Hank lived for 10 hours after surgery.

"For the first time in my life I realized that as a parent I couldn't guarantee my children's safety. That devastated me," she said.

Hank's stepbrother was in the army at the time. "The irony is he had gone into the service to get off the streets, but lost his brother to the real war—the war in the streets."

There has been no arrest in Hank's murder. Police have told her the name of the suspect, and at one time they had a witness. But the witness was beat up and became too intimidated to talk, Turner said.

In retrospect, Turner wishes she had been more informed on the pressures of the neighborhood. The signs were subtle as she raised her children on the morals of her parents. "I knew there were bullies in the neighborhood, but that's all I thought they were. I didn't know we bought our house in gang territory and the bullies were killers.

We grew up there and felt comfortable because we knew the neighborhood," she said.

So she talked to her kids about sex, drugs, avoiding fights, and staying out of the way of trouble. "I didn't think they were in any major danger," she said. "Because our home was safe, so were our children. So I thought. What goes on outside had no bearing on what went on inside."

After Hank's death, Turner started looking for ways to assuage her grief and pain. She joined several organizations. Drive By L.A. was started by Lorna Hawkins, who had lost both her sons to gun violence. For a while, Turner was a director and still actively supports the organization. She also joined Women Against Gun Violence and found meaning in talking to at-risk youth through schools and several programs of the California Youth Authority.

She talks straight with young people. As a perinatal nurse, she works with women and high risk pregnant heroin addicts. She sees gang violence and drug addiction as part of the same cycle. Many gang members have mothers who use drugs. She shares this in presentations and counseling sessions. "A mother on drugs cannot love her child emotionally or mentally. It makes it easy to go out in the streets and seek love from another, such as a gang," she said.

"I tell young men, 'You're probably a drug baby.' They don't like what they hear and many respond by saying they don't give a damn about their families, their daddies in particular. I'll tell them, 'Don't you wonder who you look like, where you got your hands? That's why you joined a gang. To feel like you belong.'"

She doesn't tiptoe around with the pregnant mothers either. "I tell them, 'I've seen your baby and if you don't get yourself together, I know what's going to happen. The difference between you and me is that you're giving your baby up; someone took mine. You have no one else to blame.'"

Her confrontation makes an impact on some of the gang members and mothers. Many of the gang members apologize to her for the loss of her son. Some of the mothers do likewise and begin to accept responsibility for the lives they affect. She believes they are sincere because she says she recognizes the liars. "The liars are the ones who are trying to impress someone else."

In order for gang members in the youth authority to participate, they must submit a letter to the jail-based Gang Awareness class, stating why they want to be in the gang class. "If selected, they will see me. I make certain they won't forget me or my pain by holding them accountable for their gang lifestyle," she said. She wants them to understand the cause and effect of their actions.

They are afraid of her not only because she makes them face their actions, but because she holds some of the cards in her hand. She tells them, "I'm in a gang, too. I'm a mother with an attitude, who pays taxes." If they've got a bad attitude in her class, show no remorse, or display no willingness to change their ways, then they have reason to be afraid. "I'll ask them, 'Why do you want to go home . . . ?' If they say they want to get back to their homies, I'll say, 'Keep your ass in here because I don't want you out. When you go before the parole board, I may be the bitch who stops you from leaving here.' If they don't have a plan, then they're more than likely to go back out and continue to gang bang," she said. "These are my tax dollars and I want to see my money working for me, not against me."

None of what Turner does will bring her son back, but she believes it may turn another mother's son around or save him from dying. And that is a job well done, because "the spirit of a life lost will live on," she believes.

ADDITIONAL READINGS

Morrison, Patt. "No One Should Have to Bury Her Child." *Family Circle* (February 1, 1999): 15–6.

Violence Prevention: A Vision of Hope. A final report of Attorney General Daniel E. Lungren's Policy Council on Violence Prevention. Sacramento: State of California, 1995.

Webster, Daniel W., et al. "Weapon Carrying among Inner-City Junior High School Students: Defensive Behavior vs. Aggressive Delinquency." *American Journal of Public Health* 83, no. 11 (November 1993).

Linda M. Vasquez

Providing Youth Alternatives to Violence

Born: 1960, Ft. Worth, TX

Education: B.A., M.S., Oklahoma State University; M.S.W., Ph.D. candidate, University of Southern Mississippi

Current Positions: Pursuing her doctorate full time; Board of Directors, Educational Fund to End Handgun Violence. Former Youth Development/Evaluation Coordinator for the Mississippi Commission for Volunteer Service

Conflict is natural. So is anger. It's helping young people learn how to deal with them without resorting to a gun that occupies much of Linda Vasquez's time. A social worker, therapeutic recreation specialist, and youth advocate, Vasquez believes the answer lies in providing alternatives, positive outlets for energy and helping youth find their voice. These education and prevention programs go beyond encouraging kids not to carry guns, but that is certainly a component.

"Here in Mississippi, a lot of people hunt. We have a strong safety component for hunting, and agencies have implemented the NRA's Eddie the Eagle program for the young children because they often have access to handguns since their parents own them," she said. But they felt that wasn't enough because it wasn't addressing the glamour and power guns represent to older children.

So Vasquez helped develop a program that involved the Hands Without Guns program (see profiles of Joshua Horwitz and Jo Ann Karn). It focuses on conflict resolution and reasons not to carry guns. One of its highlights was a summit conference involving 425 youth and 50 adults in May 1998.

As part of the two-day summit, the youths and adults participated in sessions teaching youth how service learning can be used as a preventive model for youth violence, alcohol, tobacco, and other drug nonuse. The program's purpose was to help youth develop skills,

Linda M. Vasquez.

strategies, and program models to implement in community youth programs.

One example was the ABC coloring book project, which involved junior high English class students and high school art students from around the state. Junior high students submitted written work related to violence prevention, drug use prevention, or volunteerism. High school students submitted artwork on the same topics—based on a letter of the alphabet. Twenty students logged more than 1,000 hours during the 10 months they worked on the project.

The submissions were compiled into two coloring books: "Activities for Better Choices" and "Always Believe in Children." The first stresses alternatives to drug use and violence. The second stresses volunteerism and youth service. The books include contributions from students at 25 schools, and more than 3,000 of the books were distributed across the state.

Mississippi has recently developed a statewide youth commission to work on leadership development. The coloring book was chosen by the older students because they wanted to do something on prevention for younger kids, Vasquez said. "They're becoming trainers themselves."

That's all part of a service learning model, in which youth are trained to go back into the community and work with others, using the same techniques—a ripple effect, with ever widening circles. "A lot of programs that we fund use a service learning model because the power of one does make an impact. Youth being involved makes a difference in the communities and even in their own homes, getting along with their parents and grandparents," she said.

The focus of many of these programs is that there are appropriate ways to express anger. "You don't have to hurt somebody. When these youth have guns or weapons, they are more likely to use them. The best prevention is not to carry handguns," she said.

Vasquez is sympathetic to those who feel that handguns represent protection. Her mother once felt that way. "When we were kids, she had a handgun. But when I was a senior in high school she decided not to have one anymore." She has not regretted that decision, even when she found herself in the midst of a shootout between rival gangs years later. Sitting in her car at a drive up window of a bank, her mother ducked down when the shooting started. She escaped unharmed, said Vasquez, and has never believed that being armed herself would have had any impact on the outcome.

Vasquez knows parental influence can be strong. "Some parents of the youth I work with have guns and carry them in their purses and cars. That's a trying thing when you're working with students and asking them not to carry. But the parents don't want their children carrying, either," she said. It is against federal law for anyone under 21 to own a handgun.

Helping youth see the value of their parents teaches respect. She had worked with a class of eight-year-olds who wrote her letters after her session with them. "They acknowledged their moms and the importance of their parents. They recognized that their parents were the ones who were most significant in their lives and who did a lot for them—from helping with homework to just spending time together." That may seem inconsequential, but those kids who recognize the value of their family and who feel respected in it are much less likely to join a gang, Vasquez said.

Letting young people see their value in the community also has a big impact. Vasquez received some funding through a Corporation for National Service Summer of Safety grant program. Joshua Horwitz of the Educational Fund to End Handgun Violence came to support DREAM of Hattiesburg, Inc., a youth leadership program in which the youth in the area had identified handgun violence as an issue.

Vasquez and Horwitz trained 50 youths in four assisted housing neighborhoods. Those youth then helped conduct summer projects in those neighborhoods. Neighborhood safety fairs, puppet shows, smart choices, recreational activities, plays and skits, art activities, CPR and first aid training were among the activities planned. Some of the programs were ongoing, such as neighborhood safety plans, conflict mediation, neighborhood surveys, and community service.

After that summer safety project, Vasquez joined the board of directors of the Educational Fund to End Handgun Violence. "I bring in the grassroots approach. I am a social worker, but I'm really a community worker and I'd like to think that I advocate for a youth voice. So much of the time, the adults come to the table and don't bring along the youth," she said. Through her regular contact with youth, she can better facilitate their involvement in expressing youth opinions and concerns.

"I like working with the youth because you move beyond yourself. Everything we do impacts and affects others. I've been in prevention for nine years and I hope that those I have been in contact with expand prevention efforts in their own communities," she said.

ADDITIONAL READINGS

Educational Fund to End Handgun Violence. *Kids and Guns: A National Disgrace.* Washington, D.C.: Educational Fund to End Handgun Violence, 1993.

Educational Fund to End Handgun Violence web site: http://www.gunfree. org

Hands Without Guns web site: http://www.handswithoutguns.org

Powell, Elizabeth C., Karen M. Sheehan, and Katherine Kaufer Christoffel. "Firearm Violence among Youth: Public Health Strategies for Prevention." *Annals of Emergency Medicine* 28 (August 1996).

Bob Walker

The Timing Was Right to Join Gun Control Movement

Born: 1951, Ottawa, IL

Education: Rockford College; University of Illinois School of Law

Current Position: President, Handgun Control, Inc.

Bob Walker was working on Capitol Hill in December 1992 when he saw an advertisement in the paper for a position as director of federal legislation for Handgun Control, Inc. (HCI). "I desperately wanted that job," he said. He made a call to a friend who had contacts with HCI and received a phone call the next day from Richard Aborn, then HCI president.

"That afternoon, I met with Richard. We hit it off from the beginning," he said. Walker felt that the timing was right to join the gun control movement. "I had a strong and deep interest in handgun control, and it seemed a propitious time to work for HCI. I knew about the Brady bill and the efforts to ban semiautomatic assault weapons. With a new Democratic President [Clinton] coming in, I felt there was a good chance to pass these bills. I saw it as an excellent opportunity to make a difference. And I couldn't think of a better area to work in."

Walker next met with HCI chair Sarah Brady and shortly thereafter received the job offer. From there, he climbed through the ranks quickly. Within one year, he became the director of legislation and public outreach. Then, in January 1997, he became acting president, and in May of that year the board officially voted him in as president.

While many people come to gun control activism out of some personal tragedy, Walker did not. Even so, he had firsthand knowledge of many of the issues in the gun control debate.

"My father was shot during World War II, in the Battle of the Bulge. He was also with the Illinois State Police for 28 years. When I was about 10 years old, my father was a policeman on the toll road,

Bob Walker. Courtesy of Murray Bognovitz.

making routine traffic stops. One day, he saw someone walking along the side of the road with a white uniform on. It was about three miles away from the Elgin State Mental Hospital. When my father asked the man what he was doing there, he answered, 'I own this road.' While my father was on the radio, calling for help, the man— 200 pounds, 6'4"—opened the car door, wrestled with my father, grabbed his gun, and shot him in the elbow. He nearly bled to death," Walker said.

His father was relatively lucky. He survived, but suffered permanent injury from the shattered elbow. He was taken off road duty and spent the rest of his police career behind a desk.

"That incident introduced me to the trauma and pain that is associated with gunshot wounds. But it didn't leave me anti-gun. I was quite familiar with guns as a child. Even after the shooting, my dad and I went pheasant and deer hunting. I was not afraid of guns and am not afraid of them today, either," he said.

Rather, it was a collection of incidents that led him to his views on gun control. His father's concern for what he might encounter while on duty was the beginning. Later on, a girl whom he had dated in high school committed suicide with a handgun. "I often thought how the tragedy might have been averted if she hadn't had a gun."

"And I, like a number of people of my generation, had strong views formed by the assassinations of John F. Kennedy, Martin Luther King, Jr., and Robert F. Kennedy," he said. He recalled hearing Allard Lowenstein speak in 1969. Lowenstein, a congressman from Manhattan, had solicited Robert F. Kennedy to run for president in 1968. "I remember the speech in which he spoke with great passion about Robert Kennedy, who was killed the year before. He talked about the gun violence problem in Biafra [Nigeria] and the gun violence problem here at home. What was remarkable was that Lowenstein himself was shot and killed in 1974 by a schizophrenic worker, another victim of gun violence. In a nation as great as ours, what a tremendous tragedy that we are so marred by gun violence. We're world leaders in so many areas, including, unfortunately, gun violence."

So he joined HCI, "not out of personal reasons, but out of concern about what gun violence had done to our society and the toll it was taking on our society."

His major contribution to the cause has been to bring some desperately needed legislative skills at a critical time. "Even if we were to win a critical vote, we might have gotten tied up with the crime bill. The whole process could have collapsed. There were critical decisions that had to be made in a hurry about how to put [the] Brady [bill] back on track. I had worked a total of 14 years on the Hill, so that helped me make the right decisions," he said.

Passing legislation is always a tenuous process. For example, the assault weapons ban passed by only two votes in the House of Representatives. "Any small number of missteps could have derailed our effort. By the grace of God, we didn't make those mistakes," he said.

Walker said the most dramatic days of the gun control debate may be behind us for now. "The struggle is turning into a different kind of fight. At the present time, there is no major piece of legislation on the front burner and there may not be for another four or five years. Remember, it took seven years to pass the Brady bill and four years to pass the assault weapons ban. But I'm ready for a protracted fight."

The time is right, he said, for regulation of the gun industry. He said the debate over guns is where the drunk driving and tobacco debates were years ago. "Through a comprehensive strategy, of which legislation is a key element, we'll see increasing attention on the need to reform the gun industry. My job is to help shape that debate, raise consciousness of the problem, and craft effective solutions."

Gun safety is one of those areas. "Guns are the only unregulated consumer product in America. The Consumer Product Safety Commission has no jurisdiction over guns. We also know that many of the deaths involving children are the result of unauthorized use of a gun. Some of the solutions are as simple as childproof triggers, load indicators, or a magazine safety disconnect, so a 12-year-old taking a magazine out can't fire the remaining bullet."

Another area that needs work is gun thefts, Walker said. "Tens of thousands of guns are stolen from manufacturers and dealers. The industry has a responsibility to ensure that guns don't fall into the wrong hands. There must be stronger security measures to guard against theft."

Walker also sees the future taking shape in communities that are using comprehensive strategies to approach gun violence. Even so, he expects federal gun legislation to continue to be an important component in the debate for years to come.

ADDITIONAL READINGS

Center to Prevent Handgun Violence. "Latest Crime Statistics Refute Gun Lobby: More Guns Do Not Make Us Safer" (press release). Center to Prevent Handgun Violence, January 18, 1999.

Handgun Control Inc. web site: http://www.handguncontrol.org

U.S. Department of the Treasury. *The Brady Law: The First 100 Days*. Washington, D.C.: U.S. Government Printing Office, July 27, 1994.

U.S. Department of the Treasury. *One-Year Progress Report: Brady Handgun Violence Prevention Act*. Washington, D.C.: U.S. Government Printing Office, February 28, 1995.

Wines, Michael. "As Key Allies of Gun Lobby Lose, Questions Arise about Its Power." *New York Times*, December 24, 1996.

Douglas S. Weil

Researcher Follows the Trail from Legal to Illegal Markets

Born: 1958, Dallas, TX

Education: B.A., University of California, San Diego; M.S. and Sc.D., Harvard School of Public Health

Current Position: Research Director, Center to Prevent Handgun Violence

---

Douglas S. Weil hadn't expected to find himself stateside again so soon. The former Peace Corps volunteer had spent two years as a health educator in Micronesia. In 1994 he was living in Switzerland with his wife and their one-year-old son. But the opportunity to become research director at the Center to Prevent Handgun Violence had an even greater attraction than experiencing life in foreign countries.

While Weil was working on his doctorate in public health from Harvard School of Public Health, he focused on a variety of health policy issues that combined law, ethics, and public health. "I had focused my early work on drug use and pregnancy, and while I was waiting for some data from New York City on prenatal care and drug use, my advisor suggested I do some work on firearms, specifically who keeps loaded guns," he said.

The study interested him, as did the contrast between the Swiss and American attitudes on guns. Weil's wife was living in Switzerland at the time, and Weil spent two years commuting between Geneva and Boston before moving to Geneva himself for two years. Switzerland is often compared to the United States because men of military age are required to have firearms. "They have firearms, but control of those firearms is very well regulated. Virtually every person I knew who was part of the Swiss Army kept their firearms behind lock and key. Ammunition was sealed and it was a punishable offense to un-seal it," he said.

Aside from the differences in the way firearms are stored, Weil said the other big difference was the attitude toward private gun ownership. "That seemed much less common, certainly much less obvious. People I knew were always shocked by our treatment of firearms. While Switzerland is often brought up as an example of a place where guns in the home are common and bad use is uncommon, the reasons are fairly obvious. They take far more precautions in terms of how they keep and store guns."

On a trip back to the United States, to prepare for defending his doctoral dissertation, Weil was told by his advisor that the Center to Prevent Handgun Violence was creating a research department. He flew down to Washington, D.C., and interviewed with the group the morning after defending his dissertation. About a month later, he came on board.

"Since I've been here, the most important contribution I've made is to demonstrate that regulating the retail sale of guns has a real impact on criminal access and behavior. For example, I evaluated a law passed in Virginia which limits firearm purchases to one gun a month. The analysis was able to demonstrate that law had an impact on gun trafficking along the eastern United States," he said. Another study of his shows that states that were required to conduct background checks under the Brady Law became less important as sources of firearms later used in crimes.

"Both of those results could only happen if criminals are affected by regulations in the retail market. For years the NRA and pro-gun lobby have claimed that outlaws don't obey the laws. But these two studies show that gun controls work," he said.

In doing this kind of research, Weil feels he has contributed a new area to the body of data. "There has been a great deal of research on risks associated with keeping guns in the home, but not much on gun trafficking and the policies that could impact that. Before I came here, I co-authored with David Hemenway a thought piece about changing the technology of guns to make them less lethal. It was one of the early pieces that led to the thought now that we can make guns personalized, reducing unintentional injuries, teen suicides, and unauthorized use by criminals," he said.

As a researcher with a public health background, Weil stands up to the criticisms often lobbed at the public health community for its involvement in the gun control debate. "I would say that the other side, while it takes broad swipes at public health and researchers, has narrowly focused its criticisms against a few studies. What gets lost is that they haven't effectively been able to criticize the good research out there. They'll only say, 'It's bogus.' "

Weil said he thinks that strategy might backfire, because the public health community is responding by replicating the results and fine-tuning the studies. "We now have more work which is becoming indisputable. The studies have become more refined in response to the criticism, and the results hold up."

It also bothers him that researchers' motivations are called into question. "Most researchers don't come to the issue trying to ban guns—or end up there. They are concerned about reducing injuries. What are the risk factors and how can we reduce them? The public health perspective also helps to broaden the focus from criminal aspects to nonfatal gunshot wounds, suicides, and unintentional injuries," he said.

Weil fires back with criticisms of the research produced by the other side. "The pro-gun side doesn't produce a lot of empirical-based research. They tend to try and focus on only the criminal aspects of firearms use. They tend to promote the belief that increased ownership in gun carrying is the best alternative, and they base that belief on studies that have now been thoroughly discredited by a broad range of researchers."

The two sides show a marked difference in attitude and behavior, he said. "My side discusses the problems with our studies. We set out to try to adjust for them in the next study. If our work is discredited, we don't continue to push it as if there weren't questions about it. There's no sense of restraint on the other side in terms of what they're pushing. You have people advocating dangerous policies with no regard for public health and safety."

Weil also noted that the firearms industry has a responsibility. "Gun manufacturers are not innovating for safety. They're producing advertising which suggests guns are truly protective when you bring them into your home. And they're producing firearms that have virtually no . . . private legitimate use but are really attractive to criminals. Those kinds of behaviors are controllable by the industry."

With more discretion from the firearms industry and an effort to produce coordinated gun control policies, there could be a significant reduction in firearms fatalities and crimes, he suggested.

"What I want the world to know is that gun laws which regulate the retail market can make an impact on criminal behavior, that guns flow from the legal market to the illegal market, and that proposals that Handgun Control, Inc., advocates, such as one gun a month, licensing, and registration, can impact that."

When Americans develop an attitude about firearms ownership more similar to that of the Swiss, then the incidence of misuse should drop accordingly, he said.

ADDITIONAL READINGS

Center to Prevent Handgun Violence. "Latest Crime Statistics Refute Gun Lobby: More Guns Do Not Make Us Safer" (press release). Center to Prevent Handgun Violence, January 18, 1999.

Weil, Douglas. "Denying Handguns to Prohibited Purchasers: Quantifying the Impact of the Brady Law" (press release). Washington, D.C., Center to Prevent Handgun Violence, August 26, 1996.

———. "Traffic Stop: How the Brady Act Disrupts Interstate Gun Trafficking." Washington, D.C., Center to Prevent Handgun Violence, September 19, 1997.

Weil, Douglas S., and Rebecca Knox. "Effects of Limiting Handgun Purchases on Interstate Transfer of Firearms." *Journal of the American Medical Association* 275 (June 12, 1996).

Garen J. Wintemute

Emergency Room Physician Studies Guns as Tools of Violence

Born: 1951, Long Beach, CA

Education: Yale University; M.D., University of California School of Medicine; M.P.H., Johns Hopkins University School of Public Health

Current Positions: Emergency Medicine Physician, University of California, Davis Medical Center; Director, Violence Prevention Research Program, UC Davis; Professor of Epidemiology and Preventive Medicine, UC Davis School of Medicine

Garen J. Wintemute.

It was in the fields of Cambodia that Garen J. Wintemute truly grasped the devastation caused by gunfire. An emergency physician, Wintemute had taken a planned six-month leave of absence to attend to the civilian casualties of war. While he had treated occasional gunshot victims before, the work in the trenches was something new.

He returned to the United States wanting to become involved in prevention and international health issues. He quit his job as director of a hospital emergency department in California to attend the School of Public Health at Johns Hopkins University.

In medical school, Wintemute had no particular interest in the gun issue. But at Hopkins, attorney and professor Stephen P. Teret (see profile) helped give him direction. "While I was interested in international health, I didn't think that was a career for me. I had been interested in trauma epidemiology, and Steve was working on a law journal article on using epidemiological evidence on gun violence in court. I began to realize that adding social epidemiology to clinical practice would bring me much closer to what I was looking for in a career. At first, I focused broadly on injuries, such as drowning, motor vehicle accidents, firearms. Then I followed my nose into these kinds of research programs, which have provided me with exciting work for relatively little money," he said.

Funding is scarce, he noted, not because of lack of interest but because of politics. The federal Centers for Disease Control and Prevention (CDC) dole out much of the available federal money for research on injury prevention. That some of this money has been used to fund studies on firearms violence infuriates the powerful National Rifle Association. In 1997 the NRA was successful in essentially blocking the provision of federal money to fund gun research.

What frustrated Wintemute wasn't so much the NRA's campaign— "they were doing what we expected"—but President Bill Clinton's signing the law into effect. Wintemute called that a "betrayal."

Previously, in 1992, the CDC did fund Wintemute's proposal for a five-year Violence Prevention Research Program at the University of California–Davis in Sacramento. The funding was for specific projects having to do with predicting criminal behavior among people who legally buy handguns. "We wanted to determine whether there is any effect after these people purchased a gun or whether the type of gun has an impact. What we found, for example, was that people who purchase an assault weapon—after adjustments have been made for other factors—are more likely to commit a crime—particularly a crime of violence—in the future," than those who purchase other types of handguns, he said.

Their findings were published in July 1998 in the *Annals of Emergency Medicine*. The study found that young adults with a prior criminal history were twice as likely as those with no criminal history to purchase assault-type handguns (4.6 percent and 2 percent, respectively). All these young adults bought their guns legally, stressed Wintemute. "We were particularly struck by the fact that, among those who purchased assault-type handguns and had previously been charged with any crime involving guns or violence, more than half were charged with new crimes involving guns or violence within three years of buying their handguns."

In fact, the assault-type handgun seems to be a significant indicator because researchers found that among those who had previously been charged with any crime involving guns or violence, those who purchased assault-type handguns were two to three times as likely to be charged with new violent or gun crimes as those who purchased other types of handguns.

The program has also received funding from the California Wellness Foundation for scholarly research. That money funded Wintemute's writing of *Ring of Fire*, a study on cheap, easily concealed handguns, often called Saturday night specials. The majority of these guns are made by Southern California manufacturers, located quite near each other. The study focused on the manufacturers because, according to Wintemute, their guns are disproportionately involved in violence and are too unreliable to be useful for defensive purposes.

In the decade that Wintemute has been writing about gun injuries and fatalities, he has invoked the wrath of gun control opponents. Jim Waldorf, president of Lorcin Firearms, called Wintemute "an emergency room doctor turned consumer advocate and part-time protector of society." He called Wintemute's *Ring of Fire* and subsequent newspaper reports on it "the by-product of bogus information and sensationalized stats the Doc prepared under the name of the noble University of California. This was an attempt to add credibility to the good Doc, whose personal agenda has been well documented as a strong anti-gun proponent, bent on putting gun manufacturers out of business, thus denying most Americans the affordable access to self-protection."

Some might find the gun rights lobby an intimidating enemy. "Not me," said Wintemute. In fact, the louder they scream, the more he enjoys it. "They are a great foil. They manifest ignorance and bluster regularly. It's a pleasure to read how silly their pronouncements are. To say that doctors belong in the emergency room [not in the research arena] results from the same line of thinking that holds that women should be barefoot and pregnant."

Indeed, he thinks criminology and epidemiology can complement each other in firearm research. "It's not the case that public health people are invading the criminologists' turf. We work together. Criminologists have been in this field longer, but public health researchers have statistical methods of research that are improvements over what the social scientists have. Now criminologists are starting to approach crime prevention much the same way medicine and public health researchers are trained to do. A great deal of convergent evolution has already occurred."

Even though Wintemute said he derives some personal pleasure from what he terms the antics of the NRA, "I think it's unfortunate that the leadership of the National Rifle Association is unwilling to engage in meaningful discussion about the role firearms play in firearm violence. That's only true of the leadership, not the membership. Many members are in favor of some gun controls."

Even while delving into research, Wintemute said he continues to work 12-hour shifts in the emergency room six to eight times a month. "I love the work. It's one of the busiest Level I trauma centers west of the Mississippi. The work from hour to hour is exciting. It matters to me that I keep a human face on the abstract population studies we do."

The variation also keeps him from burning out, he said. "No two days are the same."

Wintemute doesn't own guns, but does occasionally shoot at a rifle and pistol club on campus—to some surprise from those who know his work. "I present a paradox. I get some raised eyebrows, but no hostility." Because he's a pretty good shot, he has earned some respect, even from those who don't share his views.

The intensity with which Wintemute approaches his research and emergency room work means that there have been sacrifices. He and his wife determined before they were married that they would have no children. "We realized work was more important to me than anything else. Animals are of equal importance to her, so we created a marriage that provided us equal space." They live on a hobby farm with horses, sheep, ducks, chickens, and a turkey. "My wife tells people there are two turkeys," he said, laughing.

Wintemute came to study gun violence because he didn't see himself in an international health career. "But increasingly, gun violence is becoming an international health issue. U.S. gun makers are increasingly seen as suppliers of violence. Military arms that diffuse into civilian societies or guns made for civilians here making their way into other societies are creating similar gun violence problems elsewhere. For example, the guns used in drug violence in Columbia are assault weapons, particularly U.S.-made assault weapons," Wintemute said.

ADDITIONAL READINGS

Golden, Frederic. "Drop Your Guns!" *Heroes of Medicine,* special issue of *Time* (Fall 1997).

Robinson-Haynes, E., and Garen J. Wintemute. *Gun Confiscations: A Case Study of the City of Sacramento in 1995*. Sacramento: Violence Prevention Research Program, 1997.

Romero, Michael P., Garen J. Wintemute, and Jon S. Vernick. "Characteristics of a Gun Exchange Program, and an Assessment of Potential Benefits." *Injury Prevention* 4 (1998).

Teret, Stephen P., Daniel W. Webster, Jon S. Vernick, Tom W. Smith, Deborah Leff, Garen J. Wintemute, Philip J. Cook, Darnell F. Hawkins, Arthur L. Kellermann, Susan B. Sorenson, and Susan DeFrancesco. "Support for New Policies to Regulate Firearms: Results of Two National Surveys." *New England Journal of Medicine* 399, no. 12 (September 17, 1998).

Teret, Stephen P., and Garen J. Wintemute. "Handgun Injuries: The Epidemiologic Evidence for Assessing Legal Responsibility." *Hamline Law Review* 6 (July 1983).

Wintemute, Garen J. *California's Guns and Crime: New Evidence*. Sacramento, CA: Violence Prevention Research Program, 1997.

———. *Does California Have Crime Guns? An Analysis of Justice Department Data*. Sacramento, CA: Violence Prevention Research Program, 1995.

———. "The Relationship Between Firearm Design and Firearm Violence: Handguns in the 1990s." *Journal of the American Medical Association* 275 (June 12, 1996): 1749–1753.

———. *Ring of Fire: The Handgun Makers of Southern California*. Sacramento, CA: Violence Prevention Research Program, 1994.

———. *Trauma in Transition: Trends in Deaths from Firearm and Motor Vehicle Injuries*. Sacramento, CA: Violence Prevention Research Program, 1995.

Wintemute, Garen J., Carrie A. Parham, Mona A. Wright, James J. Beaumont, and Christiana M. Drake. "Weapons of Choice: Previous Criminal History, Later Criminal Activity, and Firearm Preference among Legally Authorized Young Adult Purchasers of Handguns." *Journal of Trauma* 44, no. 1 (January 1998).

Wintemute, Garen J., Christiana M. Drake, James J. Beaumont, Mona A. Wright, and Carrie A. Parham. "Prior Misdemeanor Convistions as a Risk Factor for Later Violent and Firearm-Related Criminal Activity among Authorized Purchasers of Handguns." *Journal of the American Medical Association* 280, no. 24 (December 23/30, 1998).

Wintemute, Garen J., Mona A. Wright, Carrie A. Parham, Christiana M. Drake, and James J. Beaumont. "Criminal Activity and Assault-Type Handguns: A Study of Young Adults." *Annals of Emergency Medicine* 32, no. 1 (July 1998).

Wintemute, Garen J., Stephen P. Teret, Jess F. Kraus, and Mona A. Wright.

"The Choice of Weapons in Firearms Suicides." *American Journal of Public Health* 78, no 4 (July 1988).

Wintemute, Garen J., Stephen P. Teret, Jess F. Kraus, Mona A. Wright, and Gretchen Bradfield. "When Children Shoot Children: 88 Unintended Deaths in California." *Journal of the American Medical Association* 257, no. 22 (June 12, 1987).

Wright, Mona A., Garen J. Wintemute, and Frederick P. Rivera. "Effectiveness of Denial of Handgun Purchase to Persons Believed to Be at High Risk for Firearm Violence." *American Journal of Public Health* 89, no. 1 (January 1999).

James D. Wright

Sociologist Found Studies Changed His Views

Born: 1947, Logansport, IN

Education: Purdue University; M.S. and Ph.D., Sociology, University of Wisconsin, Madison

Current Positions: Professor, Tulane University; Researcher and Author

James D. Wright calls himself a knee-jerk liberal. He rankles at the suggestion that he sides with the National Rifle Association on gun control. Yet his conversion from gun control advocacy to "agnosticism" is often heralded by gun rights activists.

Nonetheless, Wright feels "there is a respectable liberal 'position' on gun control that is entirely compatible with everything I have written on the topic." And he's written some of the weightiest studies.

Some of his earliest writing, such as "Who Owns the Sidearms? The Demography of Gun Control," was strongly pro–gun control. "Like many other observers, I initially thought that the case against guns was pretty obvious—until I had a chance to look more closely at the relevant research literature. That chance to look more closely

James D. Wright.

was the Wright-Rossi literature review that eventually became *Under the Gun*," he said.

Wright hooked up with Peter Rossi in 1975 when Rossi came to the University of Massachusetts. The two were commissioned by the U.S. Department of Justice to review literature, conduct a police department survey, and gather data from Los Angeles Superior Court. What they found was a dearth of good data, making it difficult, if not impossible, to support public policy conclusions or to measure the effectiveness of gun laws. Their study, *Weapons, Crime and Violence in America*, was published in November 1981.

In 1986 they published *Armed and Considered Dangerous: A Survey of Felons and Their Firearms*. Wright counts this among his most important contributions to the gun control debate because "for the first time, somebody looked directly into the belly of the beast—at the armed bad guys themselves—and said here's how it is. How is it? They don't buy guns through normal retail channels; they fear encounters with armed victims; theft is a major means by which their guns enter the illicit market; if they couldn't get handguns, they'd carry sawed-off shoulder weapons instead; they acquire and carry and use guns because they doubt their ability to survive unarmed in the very violent world that they inhabit.''

''I had no idea what to expect from the reports we were writing. I was too green to have much expectation one way or the other! But my earlier writings on the topic certainly generated a lot of attention, and I can't say I was surprised when our reports did likewise.''

The works also made Wright rethink his gun control views. ''Some of the major findings that made me change my mind would include the complete absence of any compelling evidence that 'stricter' gun control laws actually reduced rates of crime and violence; that most guns were owned mainly for sporting and recreational reasons; that most gun owners were middle-aged, middle-class small town and rural Protestants (and thus far removed, demographically, from the average gun abuser),'' he said.

He wrote about his ''conversion'' in an article, ''Second Thoughts about Gun Control,'' in 1988. In it, he outlined the flaws inherent in most regulations restricting either access to guns or types of firearms. He cited the bumper-sticker philosophy, ''When guns are outlawed, only outlaws will have guns.'' ''Sophisticated liberals laugh at the point, but they shouldn't. No matter what laws we enact, they will be obeyed only by the law-abiding. . . . Why should we expect felons to comply with a gun law when they readily violate laws against robbery, assault, and murder?'' he wrote.

Gun restrictions become the breeding ground for black markets, he argued. And restrictions on particular types of guns might hurt those they're intended to help. For example, Saturday night specials, which are often defined as cheaply made small handguns, might be the only affordable self-defense weapons available to low-income people.

Can any gun controls have an impact on crime? Wright said, '' 'Gun control' is too ambiguous a concept to provide a decisive answer to the question. In general, I would say there is very little credible evidence that enacting further and stricter regulations on the general acquisition, ownership, and use of firearms by the public at large results in any notable reduction in rates of crime or violence.''

The question should be, What is the specific problem for which we're offering this proposal as the solution? Tailoring the question to the specific situation is more useful than a broad stroke approach. For example, ''what you would need to do to reduce the use of guns in suicide is very different than what would be needed to stop kids from taking guns to school and very different again from what would be required to reduce carrying behavior among drug dealers. There is not one 'gun problem' in America but a large number of very different problems, each possibly requiring very different solutions. I doubt that there is any one thing, or even any one set of things, that we could enact that would have major salutary effects across the board," he said.

Even trying to assess gun ownership on a risk-benefit analysis proves slippery, Wright said. "The benefits of gun ownership pertain generally to specific individuals who own guns; the costs tend to be social costs borne by all. Moreover, the benefits and costs tend to be incommensurable. I am pretty certain that there is no credible, empirically based answer to this question."

There are simply too many variables to try to assign comparable costs and benefits, either on the smaller, household level, or on a larger societal level. "The benefit to be derived from keeping a gun in the home for protection against crime, to illustrate, is very different if you live in an area with lots of crime than if you live in an area with very little crime. Moreover, most guns are *not* owned for self-defense but for sport and recreational purposes. How do you assign a value to the pleasure derived from collecting antique guns, or from skeet shooting, or from plinking beer cans, or from killing little furry creatures?"

"And likewise the potential risks: If there are children in the home, the risk of a gun accident involving children is much higher than if there are no children in the home. Guns in a home where all the adults are familiar with small arms and their safe operation are presumably less risky than guns kept in homes where nobody knows the first thing about them." As he said, there are too many variables.

The same is true on a larger scale. "One would have to compare the psychological feeling of safety that people derive from keeping guns in their homes versus the loss of human life that results from, say, fatal gun accidents. These costs and benefits cannot be placed on the same scale and therefore cannot be directly compared in a cost-benefit analysis. Yet the costs and the benefits, assuredly, are real."

"I say, 'Let's be very specific about what kind of problem we want to solve, then very careful in analyzing the problem, and based on careful analysis, let's design specific interventions that will ameliorate the problem at hand.' My work and that of a number of others, for example, suggests pretty strongly that a lot of gun violence results from the tendency in some quarters to carry guns pretty much all the time. This is street violence we are talking about, not domestic violence. So, we have clearly described a piece of the problem and we have good evidence of what causes it. Now, since unlicensed gun carrying is already illegal, we don't need new laws to make it illegal; we need to find an effective, and constitutional, way of enforcing the laws that are already on the books."

Wright's areas of study go beyond gun control. He has written on poverty, homelessness, drugs, and many other topics. Issues such as inequality and social stratification have always intrigued him, he said, and gun issues are another topic he studies because it interests him.

Wright has also written an unpublished essay, "Shoot!," on the gun imagery so prevalent in everday language. For example, "My students often tell me they are shooting for an A in my course. The more successful among them submit papers that are right on target or that hit the mark. The less successful craft arguments that are easy to shoot down or to take pot shots at. When I give students worse grades than they think they deserve, I am accused of gunning for them. Usually, I am unpersuaded by their pleas and thus stick to my guns," he wrote. And so he continues to study the sociology of guns and criminals, confident that his aim is true.

ADDITIONAL READINGS

Sheley, Joseph F., Charles J. Brody, James D. Wright, and Marjory A. Williams. "Women and Handguns: Evidence from National Surveys, 1973–1991." *Social Science Research* 23, no. 3 (September 1994): 219–235.

Sheley, Joseph F., and James D. Wright. *In the Line of Fire: Youth, Guns, and Violence in Urban America.* Hawthorne, N.Y.: Aldine de Gruyter, 1995.

———. "Gun Acquisition and Possession in Selected Juvenile Samples." *NIJ Research in Brief* (Washington, D.C.: National Institute of Justice, December 1993). pp. 1–11.

———. "Motivations for Gun Possession and Carrying among Serious Juvenile Offenders." *Behavioral Sciences and the Law* 11 (1993): 375–388.

Sheley, Joseph F., Joshua Zhang, Charles J. Brody and James D. Wright. "Gang Organization, Gang Criminal Activity, and Individual Gang Members' Criminal Behavior." *Social Science Quarterly* 76, no. 1 (March 1995): 53–68.

Sheley, Joseph F., Zina T. McGee, and James D. Wright. "Weapon Related Victimization in Selected Inner-City High School Samples." Rockville, Md.: National Criminal Justice Reference Service, 1995, pp. 1–13.

Wright, James D. "Guns, Crime, and Violence." Chapter 21 in *Criminology: A Contemporary Handbook*, ed. Joseph F. Sheley. 2nd ed. Belmont, Calif.: Wadsworth, 1994.

———. "On the Criminal Acquisition and Use of Guns." In *Technical Aspects of Firearms and Firearms Control: Proceedings from a Conference*, ed. Arthur Kellermann. Forthcoming.

———. "Review of *Guns, Crime, and Freedom*." *Society* 33, no. 6 (September/October 1996).

———. "Second Thoughts about Gun Control." *The Public Interest* 91 (Spring 1988): 23–39.

———. "Ten Essential Observations on Guns in America." *Society* 32, no. 3 (March-April 1995): 63–68.

Wright, James D., and Laurie M. Joyner. "Health Behavior among the Homeless and the Poor." In *Handbook of Health Behavior Research*, ed. David S. Gochman. New York: Plenum, 1995.

Wright, James D., and Peter H. Rossi. *Armed and Considered Dangerous: A Survey of Felons and Their Firearms*. Hawthorne, N.Y.: Aldine, 1986. [2nd expanded ed. published by Aldine de Gruyter, 1994.]

———. "Weapons and Violent Crime." *National Institute of Justice*, U.S. Department of Justice (1978–1980).

Wright, James D., Peter H. Rossi, and Kathleen Daly. *Under the Gun: Weapons, Crime, and Violence in America*. Hawthorne, N.Y.: Aldine de Gruyter, 1983.

Michael D. Yacino

Making Gun Rights His GOAL

Born: 1942, Worcester, MA

Education: Wentworth Institute

Current Position: Executive Director, Gun Owners' Action League (GOAL)

He's the "gun guy." Since 1976 Michael D. Yacino has been walking past and through doors of Massachusetts state legislators wearing his

Michael D. Yacino. Courtesy of Lanny Photographic.

trademark cowboy boots. A veteran lobbyist had told him that he needed a gimmick to attract attention to his stand on gun control. The cowboy boots did the trick. He still wears them today.

Yacino's introduction to the politics of gun control came rather abruptly. He lost his job because of his views. When Yacino returned from service in Vietnam, he was glad to find a job in civil engineering, his field of study. While working there, he also found an outlet for a hobby by creating the Blackstone Valley Junior Sportsmen, an organization to help young people experience the outdoors. The group introduced young people to camping, canoeing, archery, environmental issues, shooting, and habitat and land management.

At this time, around 1970, gun control started heating up as a topic in Massachusetts. Reporters and activists started calling on Yacino to express the views of gun owners. One evening, he was the guest on a radio show in Worcester. The next morning, his boss at the engineering firm called him in and said, "I'll no longer need you," Yacino recalled. "I was running a $15 million contract on the Massachusetts Turnpike. He gave me pay for one day."

Yacino had gone head to head with a state senator on the radio show. That senator was one of his boss's friends. "That's when politics started interesting me," he said. "I joined the National Rifle Association as a life member, I began organizing people in my area, and I later helped create the Gun Owners Action League (GOAL) in 1974. Getting fired was the biggest motivator."

By January 1976, he had quit his next engineering job to dedicate himself to GOAL full time. The timing was fortuitous, as voters were debating a ballot question on a handgun ban. "We were being told we would lose, but we won by more than 70 percent. I think we won because Governor Michael Dukakis said the government wouldn't pay for the guns. It ticked off the taxpayers that the government thought it could take legally owned property and not pay for it. In Massachusetts, we like to think freedom began here. That's why we won as big as we did," he said, comparing the gun ban initiative to the surtax on the colonists in the era of British rule.

Since GOAL has been organized, Yacino said, only one piece of legislation detrimental to law-abiding gun owners has been instituted. That was when the city of Boston passed a ban on seven particular guns. The Bartley-Fox Act, sometimes cited as one of the nation's strictest gun laws because it carries a minimum mandatory penalty of one year for possessing a handgun without a permit, had already been enacted in 1974.

"We have seen some 30 pieces of legislation that reduce some of the harassment that police can put on the law-abiding citizen," he said.

That ratio is a source of great pride to Yacino. So, too, is the citizen activism he's seen develop in the state. For example, in 1985, 5,000 people turned up at the state capitol to argue that there should be an appeal procedure for those denied a gun license. "It was the only license issued by the government that you had no appeal to," he said. The rally had its effect. The following year, the state legislature passed a bill establishing specific criteria for the appeals process. That circumvented what Yacino said was a loophole police sometimes used—failure to act on a license request. "If police refused to respond to an application, the refusal itself became a denial. That was necessary because some judges had said if the police don't act, it's not a denial. They could just be thinking about the application . . . for a very long time."

Yacino took on another issue that some communities are fighting today: the release of names and addresses of all gun owners. He filed for a court injunction when the *Boston Globe* had petitioned for the list of gun owners. "It scared the hell out of me. It would generate a shopping list for every punk who wants to know where to get a gun," Yacino said. Yacino said within 17 hours a bill had passed the state legislature and was on the governor's desk.

"That showed the concern that all the legislators felt. It was not only infringing on the privacy rights of people, but it was a safety and security issue. If they publish a list of gun owners, by virtue of elimination, they publish a list of people who aren't gun owners," he said. He recalls that as a high point of his career. "We had such a great consensus of people, Republicans and Democrats."

Yacino fully supports an individual's decision to carry a gun. He said he has pulled his gun three times to protect himself. "At 5'5", I'm not big enough to fight," he said. One of those occasions was at 1 A.M. in a parking garage. His potential adversary was 6 feet tall and carrying a machete. "When he saw what I had, he left. I wasn't another statistic because I had the gun. No one got hurt. I didn't need to fire the gun and that's the case 98 percent of the time. It simply avoids the crime. I didn't want to be a victim, but I'm not a vigilante." For example, following the man in the parking lot was out of the question. "That's law enforcement's job, not mine," he said.

When he first became a lobbyist, the same mentor who told him to adopt a gimmick gave him one more piece of advice: "Never lie to anybody. The 200 people in the legislature rely on each other. If you lie to one, you've lied to them all."

To this day, Yacino keeps that advice in mind. "Any time I've testified or responded to a request for information, I put it in writing. That takes away the opportunity to misconstrue what I say. Even those people who disagree with me see what I am. I am a hunter, a shooter, a dealer. I am everything I advocate for. That sincerity has helped me immensely in holding conversations with people," he said.

Yacino's convictions go beyond gun control per se. "There are a lot of issues I believe connect themselves over the gun issue. I'm a strong advocate of mandatory sentencing for someone who uses a weapon in the commission of a crime. That raises the severity of the crime. If someone is so disrespectful of human life that they would carry a firearm with the purpose of hurting someone, I feel the gun itself should bring an additional penalty."

The message to the criminal should be that if they do the crime, they'll do the time. In Massachusetts, the bill he is supporting adds 10 years onto a sentence. "In order for society to sustain itself, it needs to remove that person or there's no disincentive to the next guy," he said.

The other part of the equation rests within communities. Yacino is chairman of the state's Neighborhood Crime Watch Commission. He assists the law enforcement community by teaching them techniques to teach citizens to protect themselves. "We want a safer community. We don't want drugs, illegal guns, people stabbing each other. We should be working together, and I've been able to bring people to the table that heretofore were seen as potential enemies," he said.

A certified NRA firearms instructor, Yacino brings his lesson in safe handling of firearms to all ages. GOAL has funded the NRA's Eddie the Eagle gun awareness program for approximately 85,000 young children at 54 schools and 30 police departments in the state. "It's incumbent on us to teach the basics. If at the end, the youngster says 'I don't want to have anything to do with guns,' that's fine. But addressing the issue is a better approach when you're trying to reduce accidents. We're teaching young people there's the potential of danger. If you're not capable of handling a firearm, get away from it and find someone who is."

"It does work. I just heard about two girls, one seven and one five, who saw a gun when they were outside. They knew what to do. The older one stayed to ensure no one touched the gun, while the other went for the minister. Young people like to be responsible. They want people to have some faith in their ability to do the right thing. It doesn't make sense to wait until they're 17 or 18 before introducing them to firearms," he said.

His dedication to GOAL and youth groups has taken its toll. He points to the hours spent on gun control issues as a major contributor to his divorce. "I've been driven to do more and more because it is so important. There were a lot of people who had done nothing

wrong, who had never even gotten a speeding ticket, who were denied a license because the community police chief said no. When
one person's opinion [on gun possession] affects so many people,
someone has to stand up and say that's wrong."

He's been doing that for two decades now. In another five or six
years, he said, he'll be ready to pass the torch on to someone else.
But he'll hold onto the cowboy boots.

ADDITIONAL READINGS

Gun Owners Action League web site: http://www.goal.org
"Suit Challenges Massachusetts Gun Law; Stephen Halbrook Attorney in
        Challenge." *The New Gun Week*, November 10, 1998.
Yacino, Michael D. "Lifestyles" (column). *The Message*, January 1998.

A Summary of Federal Gun Laws

ARMOR PIERCING AMMUNITION

The 1985 Law Enforcement Protection Act makes it unlawful to manufacture, import, sell, or deliver armor piercing ammunition. This law has an exemption for law enforcement officials. This legislation also excludes ammunition designed for sporting rifles.

The Violent Crime Control and Law Enforcement Act of 1994 creates a new definition of "armor piercing ammunition" aimed at eliminating new types of bullets. Now handgun ammunition made of tungsten alloys, steel, iron, brass, bronze, beryllium, copper, or depleted uranium or handgun ammunition larger than .22 caliber where the jacket weighs more than 25 percent of the bullet is banned.

ASSAULT WEAPONS

The Violent Crime Control and Law Enforcement Act of 1994 prohibits the future manufacture, transfer, and possession of semiautomatic assault weapons and ammunition magazines that hold more than 10 rounds. This law has an exemption for law enforcement.

The Violent Crime Control and Law Enforcement Act of 1994 defines assault weapons as (1) 19 named weapon types (see listing below), and (2) guns which have specific assault weapon characteristics.

Named Weapons

1. Norinco, Mitchell, and Poly Technologies Automat Kalashnikovs (all models)
2. Action Arms Israeli Military Industries UZI and Galil
3. Beretta Ar70 (SC-70)

4. Colt AR-15

5. Fabrique National FN/FAL, FN/LAR, and FNC

6. SWD M-10, M-11, M-11/9, and M-12

7. Steyr AUG

8. INTRATEC TEC-9, TEC-DC9, and TEC-22

9. Revolving cylinder shotguns, such as (or similar to) the Street Sweeper and Striker 12

FEDERAL TAXES

There is a 10 percent excise tax on handgun sales and an 11 percent excise tax on long gun and ammunition sales. The tax applies only to the first sale of the gun or ammunition by a manufacturer or importer. Revenues generated by the tax benefit a hunter education and land conservation program.

IMPORTATION OF NONSPORTING WEAPONS (SATURDAY NIGHT SPECIALS)

The Gun Control Act of 1968 outlaws the importation of guns that are not "generally recognized as particularly suitable for, or readily adaptable to, sporting purposes." Under this section of the statute ATF has set up guidelines about which weapons can be imported:

1. Inexpensive, short-barreled handguns with no sporting purpose made from inferior materials, commonly known as Saturday night specials, are permanently excluded from importation.

2. Imported versions of the Street Sweeper are barred from importation.

3. In 1989 the importation of several makes of assault rifles was suspended.

The 1986 Firearms Owners' Protection Act bans the importation of barrels for Saturday night specials.

LICENSING OF MANUFACTURERS

The Gun Control Act of 1968 requires that firearms manufacturers obtain a federal license and pay a fee of $50 per year unless the manufacturer makes "destructive devices" or "armor piercing ammunition," in which case the fee is $1,000 per year. The manufacturer must allow ATF to inspect the premises (including places of storage). Licensed manufacturers must renew their license every three years.

The Gun Control Act of 1968 requires that ammunition manufacturers obtain a federal license and pay a $10 fee per year unless the manufacturer makes "destructive devices" or "armor piercing ammunition," in which case the fee is $1,000 per year.

LICENSING OF GUN DEALERS

The Gun Control Act of 1968 requires that firearms dealers obtain a federal license. The Brady Handgun Violence Prevention Act of 1993 increases the Federal Firearms License (FFL) fee to $200 for three years with an additional $90 for a three-year renewal. Prior to the 1993 law the fee was $10 per year.

In order to obtain a FFL the applicant must be 21 years old. The applicant must not fall into any of the categories of individuals to whom the sale of a firearm is prohibited (see Prohibitions on Firearm Sales, below). The applicant must also intend to engage in the business of selling firearms.

The Violent Crime Control and Law Enforcement Act of 1994 requires that FFLs now be photographed and fingerprinted. This law also increases the amount of time ATF has to complete a background investigation of gun dealer applicants from 45 to 60 days. It also requires that applicants be in compliance with all state and local laws. ATF now has access to a dealer's records whenever a crime gun is traced to that dealer. Dealers must report any theft within 48 hours and respond to trace requests immediately. The chief law enforcement officer in each jurisdiction will receive a list from ATF of gun dealers within his/her jurisdiction.

MACHINE GUNS

The 1934 National Firearms Act requires registration and thorough background checks for those who manufacture, buy, and sell machine guns and sawed-off shotguns.

An amendment to the Firearms Owners' Protection Act of 1986 generally outlaws the sale, transfer, and possession of new machine guns. The transfer of machine guns that were manufactured before May 1986 is permitted, but a fee of $200 is required.

PROHIBITIONS ON FIREARM SALES

Persons to Whom Sale of Firearms Is Prohibited

As stated in the Gun Control Act of 1968 it is unlawful for any person to sell or otherwise dispose of any firearm or ammunition to

1. a person under indictment for, or who has been convicted in, any court of a crime punishable by over a year in prison
2. a fugitive from justice
3. an unlawful user of any controlled substance or a person addicted to any controlled substance
4. a person who has been adjudicated as a mental defective or has been committed to any mental institution
5. a person illegally or unlawfully in the United States
6. a person dishonorably discharged from the armed forces
7. a citizen of the United States who has renounced his/her citizenship
8. a person subject to a court order that restrains him/her from "harassing, stalking or threatening an intimate partner . . . or child."

SALE TO JUVENILES

Shotguns, rifles, and the ammunition for shotguns or rifles can be sold to anyone over 18 years old. It is unlawful for any licensed importer, manufacturer, dealer, or collector to sell or deliver any other type of firearm or ammunition to someone younger than 21 years of age.

The Violent Crime Control and Law Enforcement Act of 1994 made it unlawful for any person to sell, deliver, or otherwise transfer a handgun or ammunition suitable only for a handgun to anyone younger than 18 years old. It is also illegal for persons under the age of 18 to knowingly possess a handgun or ammunition suitable only for a handgun.

BACKGROUND CHECKS AND WAITING PERIODS

The Brady Handgun Violence Prevention Act of 1993 required that the backgrounds of prospective handgun purchasers be checked to ensure that the sale of a handgun to the prospective purchaser is legal. The law provided a five-day waiting period so that law enforcement officials have time to run these background checks. This provision was to expire in five years when a national instant check system should have been established. At that time, Congress and the White House were considering whether to extend some provisions of the act. States that wish to maintain a waiting period may do so.

The Brady Handgun Violence Prevention Act of 1993 authorized spending $200 million a year over five years to computerize criminal background information and to create a national instant check system.

State Firearm Laws

State laws regarding gun possession and carrying can change. State laws are posted on several Internet sites. Many states have their own web sites, as do several of the organizations involved in the gun control debate; see sources listed in Appendix H.

All states are subject to federal laws, such as the ban on the sale of semiautomatic assault weapons.

Alabama

State House: (334) 242–7100

Bans: None

Concealed Carry: Alabama has permissive laws allowing citizens to carry concealed weapons (Alabama law enforcement has some discretionary power).

Licensing/Required Permits: Yes

Preemption: Yes, with regard to handguns

Registration: None

Purchasing Limits: None

Waiting Period: Yes, 48 hours for pistols

Alaska

State Capitol: (907) 465–4648

Bans: None

Concealed Carry: Alaska has permissive laws allowing citizens to carry concealed weapons.

Licensing/Required Permits: None

Preemption: Yes, but preemption may be overridden by local referendum

Purchasing Limits: None

Registration: None

Waiting Period: None

Arizona

State Capitol: (602) 542–4900

Bans: None

Concealed Carry: Arizona has permissive laws allowing citizens to carry concealed weapons.

Felons: Arizona automatically restores to first-time felons the right to own firearms.

Licensing/Required Permits: None

Preemption: Yes

Purchasing Limits: None

School Grounds: Possession of a deadly weapon on school grounds is an act of criminal misconduct.

Waiting Period: None

Arkansas

Senate Capitol: (501) 682–3000

Bans: None

Concealed Carry: Arkansas has permissive laws allowing citizens to carry concealed weapons.

Licensing/Required Permits: None

Preemption: Yes

Purchasing Limits: None

School Grounds: Possession of a firearm on school grounds is a felony offense.

Waiting Period: None

California

State Capitol: (916) 657–9900

Armor-piercing bullets: Possession of any ammunition designed to penetrate metal or armor is a criminal offense.

Bans: Assault Weapons

Concealed Carry: California has restrictive laws allowing citizens to carry concealed weapons only when need is demonstrated.

Licensing/Required Permits: Permit required for purchase of any type of firearm. For a concealable firearm, purchaser must present a firearm safety certificate.

Preemption: Yes, with respect to handguns.

Purchasing Limits: None

Registration: Dealers are required to keep detailed information on firearms sales.

Waiting Period: 15 days for concealable guns. As of January 1, 1996, 15 days for concealable firearms, 10 days for all others.

Numerous local restrictions, including restrictions on firearms dealers.

Colorado

State Capitol: (303) 866–5000

Bans: None

Concealed Carry: Colorado has restrictive laws allowing citizens to carry concealed weapons only when need is demonstrated.

Licensing/Required Permits: None required.

Preemption: None

Purchasing Limits: None

Waiting Period: None, Instant Check

Some localities have added restrictions.

Connecticut

State Capitol: (860) 240–0100

Bans: Assault Weapons

Concealed Carry: Connecticut has permissive laws allowing citizens to carry concealed weapons.

Licensing/Required Permits: Permit required to carry concealed weapons

Preemption: No

Waiting Period: For handgun purchase, no waiting period for persons with a permit, two weeks without permit. For purchase of shotguns or rifles, no waiting period for holders of a valid hunting license; two-week waiting period without a hunting license.

Several localities have greater restrictions.

Delaware

Legislative Hall: (850) 739–4000

Bans: None

Concealed Carry: Delaware has restrictive laws allowing citizens to carry concealed weapons only when need is demonstrated.

Licensing/Required Permits: None

Preemption: No

Purchasing Limits: None

Registration: None

Waiting Period: Three days for purchase of handguns and rifles

Florida

State Capitol: (904) 488–4441

Bans: None

Concealed Carry: Florida has permissive laws allowing citizens to carry concealed weapons.

Licensing/Required Permits: None

Possession by Minors: It is unlawful to store or leave a firearm in any place within the reach or easy access of a minor (person under 16 years of age).

Preemption: Yes

Purchasing Limits: None

Registration: None

Waiting Period: None

Georgia

State Capitol: (404) 656–2000

Bans: None

Concealed Carry: Georgia has permissive laws allowing citizens to carry concealed weapons.

Licensing/Required Permits: None

Possession by Minors: Providing a pistol to a person under 21 years of age is a misdemeanor.

Preemption: Yes

Waiting Period: No state-mandated waiting period exists.

Several counties and cities have more restrictive gun laws on the books, but the state's preemption clause means that many cannot be enforced.

Hawaii

State Capitol: (808) 587–0478

Bans: Assault weapons and silencers

Concealed Carry: Hawaii has restrictive laws allowing citizens to carry concealed weapons only when need is demonstrated.

Licensing/Required Permits: A permit and firearm safety instruction are required for the purchase of all firearms.

Preemption: No

Purchasing Limits: No

Registration: Registration required for all firearms.

Waiting Period: Up to 16 days for all firearms.

Idaho

State Capitol: (208) 334–2000

Bans: None

Concealed Carry: Idaho has permissive laws allowing citizens to carry concealed weapons.

Licensing/Required Permits: No

Preemption: Yes

Registration: None

Illinois

State Capitol: (217) 782–2000

Bans: Short-barreled rifles and shotguns, silencers, and hollow point and armor-piercing ammunition.

Concealed Carry: Carrying of concealed weapons is not allowed.

Licensing/Required Permits: Owners of firearms must have a Firearm Owner's Identification Card.

Possession by Minors: Persons under the age of 18 are prohibited from possessing any concealable firearm. Persons under the age of 21 who have been convicted of a misdemeanor other than a traffic offense are prohibited from possessing firearms or ammunition.

Preemption: No

Purchasing Limits: None

Registration: Dealers who sell concealable guns must keep a register of all firearm sales.

Waiting Period: 72 hours for concealable guns and 24 hours for long guns.

Numerous local restrictions, including handgun bans in Chicago, Morton Grove, East St. Louis, and Evanston.

Indiana

State House: (317) 232–1000

Bans: Armor-piercing handgun ammunition. Dealing in (but not possession of) a sawed-off shotgun.

Concealed Carry: Indiana has permissive laws allowing citizens to carry concealed weapons.

Dealers: Dealers must possess a state license.

Licensing/Required Permits: Application is required for transfer of ownership of firearms.

Preemption: Local governments are prohibited from creating a gun registry.

Waiting Period: Seven working days; no waiting period for those with a permit to carry a concealed weapon.

Gary and East Chicago have bans on assault weapons.

Iowa

State Capitol: (515) 281–5011

Bans: None

Concealed Carry: Iowa has restrictive laws allowing citizens to carry concealed weapons only when need is demonstrated.

Licensing/Required Permits: Annual permit required for pistols and revolvers.

Possession by Minors: Firearm ownership prohibited for persons under 21 years of age.

Preemption: Yes

Purchasing Limits: None

Waiting Period: A three-day waiting period exists for the annual permit.

Kansas

State Capitol: (785) 296–0111

Bans: None

Concealed Carry: Carrying of concealed weapons is not allowed.

Licensing/Required Permits: None

Possession by Minors: Firearm ownership is prohibited for persons under 18 years of age.

Preemption: None

Purchasing Limits: None

Registration: None

Waiting Period: No state-mandated waiting period.

Several localities have passed stricter gun laws, including bans on short-barreled rifles and silencers.

Kentucky

State Capitol: (502) 564–2611

Bans: Armor-piercing ammunition

Concealed Carry: Kentucky has permissive laws allowing citizens to carry concealed weapons.

Licensing/Required Permits: None

Possession by Minors: No law

Preemption: Yes

Purchasing Limits: None

Registration: None

Waiting Period: No state-mandated waiting period

Louisiana

State Capitol: (504) 342–4479

Bans: Armor-piercing ammunition

Concealed Carry: Louisiana has permissive laws allowing citizens to carry concealed weapons.

Dealers: Dealers must keep records of firearm sales.

Licensing/Required Permits: Permit required for manufacturers, importers, businesses, and dealers.

Possession by Minors: Sales to persons under age of 18 are prohibited.

Preemption: Yes

Purchasing Limits: None

Registration: Registration only for a few specific cases including sawed-off shotguns and rifles, any firearm that has had its serial number or mark of identification obliterated, grenade launchers, bazookas, rocket launchers, flame throwers, etc.

Waiting Period: No state-mandated waiting period.

Several localities have stricter laws in place.

Maine

State House Station: (207) 582–9500

Bans: Armor-piercing ammunition

Concealed Carry: Maine has permissive laws allowing citizens to carry concealed weapons. Persons convicted of a crime may apply for restoration of their ability to carry a concealed weapon five years after they have completed their sentence.

Dealers: Dealers must keep records of firearm sales and must provide firearm safety brochure with every purchase.

Licensing/Required Permits: None

Minors: Furnishing a gun to a person under 16 is a crime.

Preemption: Yes

Purchasing Limits: None

Storage: Leaving a gun or ammunition accessible to a child is a crime.

Waiting Period: No state-mandated waiting period.

Maryland

State House: (410) 841–3000

Bans: Assault pistols and Saturday night specials (all handguns must be approved for sale and possession in Maryland by the Handgun Roster Board)

Concealed Carry: Maryland has restrictive laws allowing citizens to carry concealed weapons only when need is demonstrated.

Dealers: A state license is required to sell handguns.

Gun Shows: Firearm sales at gun shows are subject to the waiting period and application process.

Licensing/Required Permits: An application is required for all sales and transfers of handguns. The application has a $10 fee.

Preemption: Yes, with exceptions for local regulations that govern firearm ownership by minors in places of public assembly.

Purchasing Limits: None

Waiting Period: Seven days for handguns and assault rifles.

Several localities have stricter laws in place.

Massachusetts

State House: (617) 722–2000

Bans: None

Concealed Carry: Massachusetts has restrictive laws allowing citizens to carry concealed weapons only when need is demonstrated.

Dealers: Records of sales required.

Licensing/Required Permits: A license to carry or one-time permit to purchase is required in addition to a firearm identification card for firearm purchase.

Possession by Minors: Minors under the age of 15 cannot acquire a firearm identification card. Persons over 15 but under 18 may get a firearm identification card with the written permission of a parent or guardian.

Preemption: None

Purchasing Limits: None

Registration: Within seven days, the purchaser shall register the firearm and report the conditions of sale in writing to the commissioner of public safety.

Waiting Period: Seven-day waiting period for first-time permit applicants.

Boston has a ban on replica firearms.

Michigan

State Capitol: (517) 373–0184

Bans: Armor-piercing ammunition

Concealed Carry: Michigan has restrictive laws allowing citizens to carry concealed weapons only when need is demonstrated.

Dealers: Register of firearm sales required.

Licensing/Required Permits: For every firearm purchase, purchaser is required to obtain a license to purchase from local police. Applicant must pass a basic firearm safety test. One copy of the license must be returned to the police within 10 days after purchase is completed. License expires 10 days after issuance.

Pawnbrokers: Accepting a pistol for resale is a misdemeanor.

Preemption: Yes

Purchasing Limits: None

Resident Requirements: Only residents of the state or contiguous states may purchase rifles or shotguns. Michigan residents may purchase rifles and shotguns within the state or contiguous states.

Waiting Period: None

Minnesota

State Capitol: (612) 296–6013

Bans: Possession and manufacture of Saturday night specials

Concealed Carry: Minnesota has restrictive laws allowing citizens to carry concealed weapons only when need is demonstrated.

Licensing/Required Permits: A transferee permit is required for transfers of ownership of pistols and semiautomatic weapons. A permit to carry also satisfies the permit requirement.

Preemption: Yes

Purchasing Limits: None

Registration: None

Resident Requirements: Only residents of Minnesota or contiguous states may purchase rifles or shotguns. Minnesota residents only may purchase rifles and shotguns within the state or contiguous states.

Waiting Period: Seven-day waiting period for purchase of all firearms. The waiting period may be waived by the sheriff or chief of police for purchasers of rifles or shotguns who have a valid transferee permit or permit to carry.

Mississippi

State Capitol: (601) 359–3770

Bans: None

Concealed Carry: Mississippi has permissive laws allowing citizens to carry concealed weapons.

Dealers: Records of firearm and ammunition sales required.

Licensing/Required Permits: None

Preemption: Yes

Purchasing Limits: None

Registration: None

Waiting Period: No state-mandated waiting period on handgun purchases.

Missouri

State Capitol: (573) 751–2000

Bans: None

Concealed Carry: Carrying of concealed weapons is not allowed.

Licensing/Required Permits: Permit required for transfers of ownership of concealable firearms.

Preemption: None

Purchasing Limits: None

Registration: None

Waiting Period: Up to seven working days for concealable weapons.

Montana

State Capitol: (406) 444–2511

Bans: Silencers, sawed-off shotguns

Concealed Carry: Montana has permissive laws allowing citizens to carry concealed weapons.

Licensing/Required Permits: None

Possession by Minors: Minors under the age of 14 are prohibited from handling guns except under the supervision of a parent/guardian or qualified firearms instructor.

Preemption: Yes

Purchasing Limits: None

Registration: None

Waiting Period: No state-mandated waiting period on handgun purchases.

Nebraska

State Capitol: (402) 471–2311

Bans: None

Concealed Carry: Carrying of concealed weapons is not allowed.

Licensing/Required Permits: Certificate required for purchase of handguns.

Preemption: None

Purchasing Limits: None

Registration: None

Waiting Period: None; instant criminal history record check.

Several localities have stricter laws on the books.

Nevada

State Capitol: (702) 687–5670

Bans: Metal-penetrating handgun ammunition, short-barreled rifles and shotguns

Concealed Carry: Nevada has permissive laws allowing citizens to carry concealed weapons.

Dealers: Dealers must keep records of weapon sales.

Licensing/Required Permits: None

Possession by Minors: Minors under the age of 14 are prohibited from controlling a gun except under the supervision of an adult. Adults who aid or permit minors to gain access to guns are guilty of a misdemeanor. The sale of concealable weapons to persons under 18 years of age is prohibited.

Preemption: None

Purchasing Limits: None

Registration: None

School Grounds: Possession of a dangerous weapon on school grounds is a misdemeanor.

Waiting Period: No state-mandated waiting period.

Several localities have stricter laws on the books.

New Hampshire

State House: (603) 271–1110

Bans: Armor-piercing ammunition

Concealed Carry: New Hampshire has permissive laws allowing citizens to carry concealed weapons.

Dealers: Records of sales must be kept.

Licensing/Required Permits: Yes—sales to nonresidents are subject to the laws of their state of residence.

Preemption: None

Purchasing Limits: None

Registration: None

Residence Requirements: Nonresidents are subject to the laws of their state of residence.

Waiting Period: No state-mandated waiting period.

New Jersey

State House: (609) 292–2121

Bans: Assault weapons, armor-piercing ammunition

Concealed Carry: New Jersey has restrictive laws allowing citizens to carry concealed weapons only when need is demonstrated.

Dealers: Records of handgun sales required.

Licensing/Required Permits: Permit to carry required for handguns; Firearm Purchaser ID card required for shotguns and rifles.

Preemption: Yes

Purchasing Limits: Only one handgun can be purchased per permit.

Registration: Dealers must keep register of handgun sales.

School Grounds: Possession of a gun on school property is a criminal offense.

Waiting Period: Seven-day waiting period to acquire a handgun permit.

New Mexico

State Capitol: (505) 956–4600

Bans: None

Concealed Carry: Carrying of concealed weapons is not allowed.

Licensing/Required Permits: None

Preemption: None

Purchasing Limits: None

Registration: None

Waiting Period: No state-mandated waiting period; the Brady Bill is in effect.

New York

State Capitol: (518) 455–2800

Bans: None

Concealed Carry: New York has restrictive laws allowing citizens to carry concealed weapons only when need is demonstrated.

Dealers: Recordkeeping of transactions is required for firearms dealers and gunsmiths.

Licensing/Required Permits: License required for possession and carrying of firearms. Permits are good for a maximum of three years.

Possession by Minors: Firearm sales to persons under 19 who are not licensed to possess firearms are prohibited.

Preemption: Yes, however, New York City is exempted from state preemption law.

Purchasing Limits: None

Registration: Dealers and gunsmiths must keep register of gun sales.

Waiting Period: Up to six months for permit.

Several local restrictions apply, especially in New York City, which requires its own permit; permits issued elsewhere in the state are not valid in the city. The permit application fee is $170.

North Carolina

State Capitol: (919) 733–4111

Bans: None

Concealed Carry: North Carolina has permissive laws allowing citizens to carry concealed weapons.

Dealers: Recordkeeping of firearm sales required. State dealer's license required.

Licensing/Required Permits: Permit required for sale of firearms.

Possession by Minors: A firearm cannot be stored so that it is accessible to a minor.

Preemption: Yes

Purchasing Limits: None

Registration: None

Waiting Period: Up to 30 days for issuance of a permit.

Several localities require dealer licenses.

North Dakota

State Capitol: (701) 328–2000

Bans: None

Concealed Carry: North Dakota has permissive laws allowing citizens to carry concealed weapons.

Licensing/Required Permits: None

Possession by Minors: Persons under 18 years of age may not possess a handgun except under direct supervision of an adult for handgun safety training, target shooting, or hunting.

Preemption: Yes

Purchasing Limits: None

Registration: None

Waiting Period: No state-mandated waiting period.

Ohio

State House: (614) 466–2000

Bans: None

Concealed Carry: Carrying of concealed weapons is not allowed.

Licensing/Required Permits: License required.

Possession by Minors: Sales of firearms prohibited to persons under 18 years of age. Sales of handguns prohibited to persons under 21 years of age. Persons under 18 may be furnished a firearm for hunting, safety instruction, or marksmanship only under supervision of an adult.

Preemption: None

Purchasing Limits: None

Registration: None

Waiting Period: None

About a dozen localities have stricter laws in place that range from weapons bans on school grounds to recordkeeping requirements and bans on Saturday night specials and assault weapons.

Oklahoma

State Capitol: (405) 521–2011

Bans: Armor-piercing ammunition

Concealed Carry: Oklahoma has permissive laws allowing citizens to carry concealed weapons.

Licensing/Required Permits: None

Possession by Minors: Sale of pistols and revolvers to minors is prohibited.

Preemption: Yes

Purchasing Limits: None

Registration: None

Waiting Period: None

Oregon

State Capitol: (503) 986–1848

Bans: Armor-piercing ammunition, silencers, and short-barreled rifles and shotguns

Concealed Carry: Oregon has permissive laws allowing citizens to carry concealed weapons.

Dealers: Records of firearm sales are required. No state license is required.

Possession by Minors: Possession of handguns by persons under 18 years of age is prohibited. Parents and guardians may transfer possession of shotguns and rifles to a minor under their care.

Preemption: Yes

Purchasing Limits: None

Registration: Dealers are required to keep register of firearm sales. However, Oregon state law specifically forbids the compilation of information on lawful purchases of firearms for purposes other than to determine if the firearm is stolen or has been used in the commission of a crime.

School Grounds: Discharge or attempt to discharge a weapon on school grounds is a felony offense.

Waiting Period: Oregon has a 15-day waiting period and background check system. However, the legislature has approved an instant background check system.

Two localities require local dealer's licenses.

Pennsylvania

Main Capitol Building: (717) 787–2121

Bans: Armor-piercing ammunition

Concealed Carry: Pennsylvania has permissive laws allowing citizens to carry concealed weapons.

Dealers: A dealer license is required to sell firearms. License is renewed annually. Records of firearm sales must be kept.

Licensing/Required Permits: Yes, for purchase of any type of firearm.

Loans of Firearms: Loaning or giving a firearm to any person without following laws on transfer of firearm ownership is prohibited.

Possession by Minors: Delivery of firearms to persons under the age of 18 years is prohibited. To sell, give, or otherwise furnish a "starter pistol" to a person under 18 years of age is prohibited.

Preemption: Yes

Purchasing Limits: None

Registration: None

Waiting Period: 48 hours

Several localities require local permits or local dealer's licenses. Philadelphia has a ban on military-style weapons.

Rhode Island

State House: (401) 277–2653

Bans: Silencers, armor-piercing ammunition

Concealed Carry: Rhode Island has restrictive laws allowing citizens to carry concealed weapons only when need and ability are demonstrated.

Dealers: Dealers must be licensed to sell handguns. Handgun dealer license is renewed on an annual basis. Dealers are required to keep registry of firearm sales.

Licensing/Required Permits: Gun safety education course is required for handgun purchases.

Possession by Minors: Sale of firearms and ammunition to persons under 18 years of age is prohibited except with parent's or guardian's consent. Sale of pistols and revolvers to persons under 21 years of age is prohibited. Persons under 15 years of age may possess or use firearms only if minor has a permit and is in the presence of a qualified adult.

Preemption: Yes

Purchasing Limits: None

Registration: None—expressly prohibited.

Resident Requirements: Only state residents and members of the armed forces stationed in Rhode Island may purchase handguns. Citizens of Rhode Island must fill out a Rhode Island handgun purchase application and go through a background check even when purchasing a concealable firearm from a dealer in another state.

Waiting Period: Seven days for handgun purchases.

South Carolina

State House: (803) 212–6200

Bans: Saturday night specials, sawed-off shotguns and rifles, teflon-coated (armor-piercing) ammunition

Concealed Carry: South Carolina has restrictive laws allowing citizens to carry concealed weapons only when need is demonstrated.

Dealers: State dealer's license required for sale of pistols.

Licensing/Required Permits: Purchasers of pistols must fill out application prior to purchase.

Possession by Minors: Sale and possession of pistols to persons under 22 years of age is prohibited except for temporary possession under the supervision of a parent or adult instructor.

Preemption: Yes

Purchasing Limits: Persons may purchase no more than one pistol per month.

Resident Requirements: Only South Carolina residents and members of the armed forces may buy pistols in South Carolina.

Registration: None

Waiting Period: No state-mandated waiting period.

South Dakota

State Capitol: (605) 773–3011

Bans: Silencers, short-barreled shotguns

Concealed Carry: South Dakota has permissive laws allowing citizens to carry concealed weapons.

Licensing/Required Permits: Pistol permit application or permit to carry required for purchase.

Possession by Minors: None

Preemption: Yes

Purchasing Limits: None

Registration: None

Waiting Period: 48-hour waiting period for the purchase of pistols. Persons with a valid permit to carry a concealed pistol are exempted from the waiting period.

Tennessee

State Capitol: (615) 741–2001

Bans: Silencers, short-barreled rifles and shotguns, hollow-point ammunition

Background Check: A background check is required for all firearm transfers including transactions involving pawnbrokers and transactions between private individuals.

Concealed Carry: Tennessee has permissive laws allowing citizens to carry concealed weapons. Firearms are prohibited where alcohol is sold.

Dealers: Firearms dealers must be licensed by the state.

Licensing/Required Permits: Purchases must fill out an application and submit to a background check to purchase a pistol.

Possession by Minors: The sale, loan, or gift of a firearm to a minor is prohibited except as a loan or gift for hunting or sporting activity.

Preemption: Yes, except ordinances enacted prior to April 8, 1986.

Purchasing Limits: None

Registration: None

Resident Requirements: Tennessee residents eligible to purchase a rifle or shotgun may purchase a rifle or shotgun in a contiguous state. Residents of a contiguous state may purchase a rifle or shotgun in Tennessee providing they are eligible to do so under the laws of their resident state, Tennessee, and the federal government.

Waiting Period: State mandates a waiting period of up to 15 days for a background check.

Several localities have stricter laws, such as Chattanooga's prohibition on the sale of pistols and a few three-day waiting periods on gun sales.

Texas

State Capitol: (512) 463–4630

Bans: Short-barreled rifles and shotguns, silencers, armor-piercing ammunition, and zip guns

Concealed Carry: Texas has permissive laws allowing citizens to carry concealed weapons.

Licensing/Required Permits: None

Possession by Minors: The loan, sale, or gift of a firearm to a person under 18 years of age is prohibited except when the minor's parent or guardian has given consent.

Preemption: Yes

Purchasing Limits: None

Registration: None

Waiting Period: None

Utah

State Capitol: (801) 538–3000

Bans: None

Concealed Carry: Utah has permissive laws allowing any citizen to carry concealed weapons; no license required.

Licensing/Required Permits: None

Possession by Minors: Possession of weapons prohibited for persons under 14 years of age except when accompanied by a parent or guardian or for persons at least 14, but under 18 with the permission of parent or guardian.

Preemption: Yes

Purchasing Limits: None

Registration: None

Waiting Period: None; instant criminal background check performed for handgun purchasers.

Silencers are banned in Salt Lake County.

Vermont

State House: (802) 828–1110

Bans: None

Concealed Carry: Vermont has permissive laws allowing citizens to carry concealed weapons.

Dealers: Records of firearm sales must be kept. Recordkeeping requirement also applies to pawnbrokers.

Licensing/Required Permits: None

Possession by Minors: To sell or furnish a firearm to a person under the age of 16 years is a criminal offense. The possession of a handgun by a person under 16 years of age without the consent of a parent or guardian is prohibited.

Preemption: Yes

Purchasing Limits: None

Registration: None

Waiting Period: None

Virginia

State Capitol: (804) 786–0000

Bans: Toy guns that discharge objects (other than cap pistols), plastic guns, "Streetsweepers"

Concealed Carry: Virginia has permissive laws allowing citizens to carry concealed weapons.

Dealers: Dealers shall keep a register of all short-barreled rifles and shotguns they handle.

Gun Shows: Gun shows are regulated.

Licensing/Required Permits: Purchaser must submit to background check.

Possession by Minors: Transfer of pistols to minors prohibited, except by family members for sporting purposes.

Preemption: Yes

Purchasing Limits: One gun per month, but purchasers can petition the police to have the limit waived if need is demonstrated.

Registration: None

Waiting Period: None

Numerous localities have passed stricter gun control laws, many of which cannot be enforced because of the state preemption law.

Washington

Legislative Building: (360) 753–5000

Bans: None

Concealed Carry: Washington has permissive laws allowing citizens to carry concealed weapons.

Dealers: A state license is required to sell firearms and ammunition. Dealers must notify police of every firearm purchase. Dealers must be licensed to do business in the state of Washington.

Liability: The state and local government are immune from liability if anyone approved for pistol purchase is in fact ineligible.

Licensing/Required Permits: Application required for purchase of pistols. Applicants for concealed carry license must submit to background check.

Possession by Minors: Persons between the ages of 18 and 21 may own a pistol only.

Preemption: Yes

Purchasing Limits: None

Waiting Period: 30-day waiting period for a concealed carry license.

Washington, D.C.

District Building: (202) 724–8000

Bans: Washington, D.C. prohibits the private ownership of all firearms, with narrow exceptions for military, police and security personnel.

Concealed Carry: Carrying of concealed weapons is not allowed.

Licensing/Required Permits: Permit required for purchase of any firearm.

Possession by Minors: Not allowed under 18 years, ages 18–21 only with parental permission.

Preemption: Not Applicable.

Registration: All firearms must be registered.

Waiting Period: For sale of regulated pistols, 48 hours.

West Virginia

State Capitol: (304) 558–3456

Bans: None

Concealed Carry: West Virginia has permissive laws allowing citizens to carry concealed weapons.

Licensing/Required Permits: Permit required for high-powered rifles.

Possession by Minors: None

Preemption: Yes, with regard to regulations limiting ownership.

Purchasing Limits: None

Registration: None

Waiting Period: None

Wisconsin

State Capitol: (608) 266–0382

Bans: Short-barreled rifles and shotguns, silencers

Concealed Carry: Carrying of concealed weapons is not allowed.

Licensing/Required Permits: Background check required for handgun purchases.

Possession by Minors: It is a criminal offense to keep a loaded firearm within easy access of a minor. Minors may possess a firearm with a barrel 12 inches in length or longer.

Preemption: Yes

Purchasing Limits: None

Registration: None

Waiting Period: For handgun purchase, 48 hours from receipt of confirmation number on background check. The federal five-day waiting period is in effect on handgun purchases from pawnbrokers.

Several localities have stricter gun laws in effect, including dealer and permit requirements and a ban on handguns in Madison.

Wyoming

State Capitol: (307) 777–7220

Bans: None

Concealed Carry: Wyoming has permissive laws allowing citizens to carry concealed weapons.

Dealers: Dealers must keep registry of firearm sales.

Licensing/Required Permits: None

Possession by Minors: None

Preemption: None

Purchasing Limits: None

Registration: None, but dealers must keep records of firearm sales.

Waiting Period: None

State Constitutional Clauses on the Right to Keep and Bear Arms

The constitutions or bills of rights in 43 states contain a "right to bear arms" clause. The seven states that do not have a constitutional provision are California, Iowa, Maryland, Minnesota, New Jersey, New York, and Wisconsin.

Alabama: That every citizen has a right to bear arms in defense of himself and the state.—Alabama Constitution: Article I, section 26.

Alaska: A well-regulated militia being necessary to the security of a free state, the right of the people to keep and bear arms shall not be infringed.—Alaska Constitution: Article I, section 19.

Arizona: The right of the individual citizen to bear arms in defense of himself or the State shall not be impaired, but nothing in this section shall be construed as authorizing individuals or corporations to organize, maintain, or employ an armed body of men.—Arizona Constitution: Article 2, section 26.

Arkansas: The citizens of this State shall have the right to keep and bear arms for their common defense.—Arkansas Constitution: Article II, section 5.

Colorado: The right of no person to keep and bear arms in defense of his home, person and property, or in aid of the civil power when thereto legally summoned, shall be called in question; but nothing herein contained shall be construed to justify the practice of carrying concealed weapons.—Colorado Constitution: Article II, section 13.

Connecticut: Every citizen has a right to bear arms in defense of himself and the state.—Connecticut Constitution: Article I, section 15.

Delaware: A person has the right to keep and bear arms for the defense of self, family, home and State, and for hunting and recreational use.—Delaware Constitution: Article I, section 20.

Florida: The right of the people to keep and bear arms in the defense of themselves and of the lawful authority of the state shall not be infringed, except that the manner of bearing arms may be regulated by law.—Florida Constitution: Article I, section 8.

Georgia: The right of the people to keep and bear arms shall not be infringed, but the General Assembly shall have the power to prescribe the manner in which arms may be borne.—Georgia Constitution: Article I, section I, paragraph VIII.

Hawaii: A well-regulated militia being necessary to the security of a free state, the right of the people to keep and bear arms shall not be infringed.—Hawaii Constitution: Article I, section 15.

Idaho: The people have the right to keep and bear arms, which right shall not be abridged; but this provision shall not prevent the passage of laws to govern the carrying of weapons concealed on the person, nor prevent passage of legislation providing minimum sentences for crimes committed while in possession of a firearm, nor prevent passage of legislation providing penalties for the possession of firearms by a convicted felon, nor prevent the passage of legislation punishing the use of a firearm. No law shall impose licensure, registration or special taxation on the ownership for possession of firearms or ammunition. Nor shall any law permit the confiscation of firearms, except those actually used in the commission of a felony.—Idaho Constitution: Article I, section 11.

Illinois: Subject only to the police power, the right of the individual citizen to keep and bear arms shall not be infringed.—Illinois Constitution, Article I, section 22.

Indiana: The people shall have a right to bear arms, for the defense of themselves and the State.—Indiana Constitution: Article I, section 32.

Kansas: The people have the right to bear arms for their defense and security; but standing armies, in time of peace, are dangerous to liberty, and shall not be tolerated, and the military shall be in strict subordination to the civil power.—Kansas Bill of Rights, section 4.

Kentucky: All men are, by nature, free and equal, and have certain inherent and inalienable rights, among which may be reckoned: . . .

Seventh: The right to bear arms in defense of themselves and of the state, subject to the power of the general assembly to enact laws to prevent persons from carrying concealed weapons.—Kentucky Bill of Rights, Section I, paragraph 7.

Louisiana: The right of each citizen to keep and bear arms shall not be abridged, but this provision shall not prevent the passage of laws to prohibit the carrying of weapons concealed on the person.—Louisiana Constitution: Article I, section 11.

Maine: Every citizen has a right to keep and bear arms and this right shall never be questioned.—Maine Constitution, Article I, section 16.

Massachusetts: The people have a right to keep and bear arms for the common defense. And as, in time of peace, armies are dangerous to liberty, they ought not to be maintained without the consent of the legislature; and the military power shall always be held in an exact subordination to the civil authority, and be governed by it.—Massachusetts Declaration of Rights, Part I, Article XVII.

Michigan: Every person has a right to keep and bear arms for the defense of himself and the state.—Michigan Constitution: Article I, section 6.

Mississippi: The right of every citizen to keep and bear arms in the defense of his home, person, or property, or in aid of the civil power when thereto legally summoned, shall not be called in question, but the legislature may regulate or forbid carrying concealed weapons.—Mississippi Constitution: Article 3, section 12.

Missouri: That the right of every citizen to keep and bear arms in defense of his home, person and property, or when lawfully summoned in aid of the civil power, shall not be questioned; but this shall not justify the wearing of concealed weapons.—Missouri Constitution: Article I, section 23.

Montana: The right of any person to keep or bear arms in defense of his own home, person, and property, or in aid of the civil power when thereto legally summoned, shall not be called in question, but nothing herein contained shall be held to permit the carrying of concealed weapons.—Montana Constitution: Article II, section 12.

Nebraska: All persons are by nature free and independent, and have certain inherent and inalienable rights; among these are . . . the right to keep and bear arms for security or defense of self, family, home, and others, and for lawful common defense, hunting, recreational use, and all other lawful purposes, and such rights shall not be denied or infringed by the state or any subdivision thereof.—Nebraska Constitution, Article I, section I.

Nevada: Every citizen has the right to keep and bear arms for security and defense, for lawful hunting and recreational use and for other lawful purposes.—Nevada Constitution, Article 1, section II, paragraph 1.

New Hampshire: All persons have the right to keep and bear arms in defense of themselves, their families, their property, and the state.—New Hampshire Constitution, Part 1, article 2-a.

New Mexico: No law shall abridge the right of the citizen to keep and bear arms for security and defense, for lawful hunting and recreational use and for other lawful purposes, but nothing herein shall be held to permit the carrying of concealed weapons. No municipality or county shall regulate, in any way, an incident of the right to keep and bear arms.—New Mexico Constitution: Article II, section 6.

North Carolina: A well regulated militia being necessary to the security of a free State, the right of the people to keep and bear arms shall not be infringed; and as standing armies in time of peace are dangerous to liberty, they shall not be maintained, and the military shall be kept under strict subordination to, and governed by, the civil power. Nothing herein shall justify the practice of carrying concealed weapons, or prevent the General Assembly from enacting penal statutes against that practice.—North Carolina Constitution: Article I, section 30.

North Dakota: All individuals are by nature equally free and independent and have certain inalienable rights, among which are . . . to keep and bear arms for the defense of their person, family, property, and the state, and for lawful hunting, recreational, and other lawful purposes, which shall not be infringed.—North Dakota Constitution: Article I, section 1.

Ohio: The people have the right to bear arms for their defense and security; but standing armies, in time of peace, are dangerous to liberty, and shall not be kept up; and the military shall be in strict subordination to the civil power.—Ohio Constitution: Article I, section 4.

Oklahoma: The right of a citizen to keep and bear arms in defense of his home, person, or property, or in aid of the civil power when thereunto legally summoned, shall never be prohibited; but nothing herein contained shall prevent the Legislature from regulating the carrying of weapons.—Oklahoma Constitution: Article 2, section 26.

Oregon: The people shall have the right to bear arms for the defense of themselves, and the State, but the Military shall be kept in strict subordination to the civil power.—Oregon Constitution: Article I, section 27.

Pennsylvania: The right of the citizens to bear arms in defense of themselves and the State shall not be questioned.—Pennsylvania Constitution: Article I, section 21.

Rhode Island: The right of the people to keep and bear arms shall not be infringed.—Rhode Island Constitution, Article I, section 22.

South Carolina: A well regulated militia being necessary to the security of a free State, the right of the people to keep and bear arms shall not be infringed. As, in times of peace, armies are dangerous to liberty, they shall not be maintained without the consent of the General Assembly. The military power of the State shall always be held in subordination to the civil authority and be governed by it. No soldier shall in time of peace be quartered in any house without the consent of the owner nor in time or war but in the manner prescribed by law.—South Carolina Constitution: Article I, section 20.

South Dakota: The right of the citizens to bear arms in defense of themselves and the state shall not be denied.—South Dakota Constitution: Article VI, section 24.

Tennessee: That the citizens of this State have a right to keep and to bear arms for their common defense; but the Legislature shall have power, by law, to regulate the wearing of arms with a view to prevent crime.— Tennessee Constitution: Article I, section 26.

Texas: Every Citizen shall have the right to keep and bear arms in lawful defense of himself or the State; but the Legislature shall have power, by law, to regulate the wearing of arms, with a view to prevent crime.— Texas Constitution: Article I, section 23.

Utah: The individual right of the people to keep and bear arms for security and defense of self, family, others, property, or the State, as well as for other lawful purposes shall not be infringed; but nothing herein shall prevent the legislature from defining the lawful use of arms.—Utah Constitution: Article I, section 6.

Vermont: That the people have a right to bear arms for the defense of themselves and the State—and as standing armies in time of peace are dangerous to liberty, they ought not to be kept up; and that the military should be kept under strict subordination to and governed by the civil power.—Vermont Constitution: Chapter I, article 16.

Virginia: That a well regulated militia, composed of the body of the people, trained to arms, is the proper, natural, and safe defense of a free state, therefore, the right of the people to keep and bear arms shall not be infringed; that standing armies, in time of peace, should be avoided as dangerous to liberty; and that in all cases the military should be under strict subordination to, and governed by, the civil power.—Virginia Constitution: Article I, section 13.

Washington: The right of the individual citizen to bear arms in defense of himself, or the state, shall not be impaired, but nothing in this section shall be construed as authorizing individuals or corporations to organize, maintain, or employ an armed body of men.—Washington Constitution: Article I, section 24.

West Virginia: A person has the right to keep and bear arms for the defense of self, family, home and state, and for lawful hunting and recreational use.—West Virginia Constitution: Article III, section 22.

Wyoming: The right of citizens to bear arms in defense of themselves and of the state shall not be denied.—Wyoming Constitution: Article I, section 24.

Profiles Indexed by Pro-Regulation or Anti-Regulation

Several of the people profiled in the book do not categorize themselves as pro-regulation or anti-regulation. That is particularly true of the researchers and academicians. However, their work is generally used as evidence by one side or the other, and that is how the classification has been made for those individuals.

In Support of Stricter Gun Regulations

Michael K. Beard

Carl C. Bell

James and Sarah Brady

Deane Calhoun

Katherine Kaufer Christoffel

Philip J. Cook

Daniel Gross

Scott Harshbarger

Richard and Holley Galland Haymaker

Dennis Henigan

Joshua M. Horwitz

Jo Ann Karn

Martha J. Langelan

Carolyn McCarthy

Bryan Miller

Michael A. Robbins

Andrés Soto

Stephen A. Sposato

Stephen P. Teret

Lisa S. Thornton

Joy Turner

Linda M. Vasquez

Bob Walker

Douglas S. Weil

Garen J. Wintemute

Opposed to Stricter Gun Regulations

Madeleine (Lyn) Bates

Kenneth V. F. Blanchard

Matthew C. C. (Sandy) Chisholm III

Robert J. Cottrol

Preston King Covey

Larry Craig

Miguel A. Faria, Jr.

Richard J. Feldman

Alan M. Gottlieb

Stephen P. Halbrook

Marion P. Hammer

Suzanna Gratia Hupp

Phillip B. Journey

Don B. Kates, Jr.

Gary Kleck

Neal Knox

David B. Kopel

Karen L. MacNutt

Tanya K. Metaksa

Dianne Nicholl

Jay Printz

Joseph P. Tartaro

Patricia Margaret (Peggy) Tartaro

James D. Wright

Michael D. Yacino

APPENDIX E

Profiles Indexed by State

CALIFORNIA

Deane Calhoun

Don B. Kates, Jr.

Andrés Soto

Stephen A. Sposato

Joy Turner

Garen J. Wintemute

COLORADO

David B. Kopel

Diane Nicholl

WASHINGTON, D.C.

Michael K. Beard

James and Sarah Brady

Robert J. Cottrol

Dennis Henigan

Joshua M. Horwitz

Bob Walker

Douglas S. Weil

FLORIDA

Marion P. Hammer

Gary Kleck

GEORGIA

Miguel A. Faria

Richard J. Feldman

IDAHO

Larry Craig

ILLINOIS

Carl C. Bell

Katherine Kaufer Christoffel

Michael A. Robbins

Lisa S. Thornton

KANSAS

Phillip B. Journey

LOUISIANA

Richard and Holley Galland Haymaker

James D. Wright

MARYLAND

Kenneth V. F. Blanchard

Martha J. Langelan

Stephen P. Teret

MASSACHUSETTS

Madeleine (Lyn) Bates
Scott Harshbarger
Karen L. MacNutt
Michael D. Yacino

MICHIGAN

Jo Ann Karn

MISSISSIPPI

Linda M. Vasquez

MONTANA

Jay Printz

NEW JERSEY

Bryan Miller

NEW YORK

Daniel Gross
Carolyn McCarthy
Joseph P. Tartaro
Patricia Margaret (Peggy) Tartaro

NORTH CAROLINA

Philip J. Cook

PENNSYLVANIA

Matthew C. C. (Sandy) Chisholm III
Preston King Covey

TEXAS

Suzanna Gratia Hupp

VIRGINIA

Stephen P. Halbrook
Neal Knox
Tanya K. Metaksa

WASHINGTON

Alan M. Gottlieb

Profiles Indexed by Profession or Interest

CRIMINOLOGY/SOCIOLOGY

Philip J. Cook, Ph.D.

Gary Kleck, Ph.D.

David B. Kopel, J.D.

Douglas S. Weil, M.S., Sc.D.

James D. Wright, Ph.D.

ELECTED OFFICIALS

Larry Craig, U.S. Senator

Scott Harshbarger, Attorney General, Commonwealth of Massachusetts

Suzanna Gratia Hupp, Texas House of Representatives

Carolyn McCarthy, U.S. House of Representatives

GUN DESIGN/SAFETY

Matthew C. C. (Sandy) Chisholm III

Richard J. Feldman, J.D.

Dennis Henigan, J.D.

Joshua M. Horwitz, J.D.

Stephen P. Teret, J.D., M.P.H.

Garen J. Wintemute, M.D., M.P.H.

GUN MANUFACTURERS

Matthew C. C. (Sandy) Chisholm III
Richard J. Feldman, J.D.

LAW ENFORCEMENT (SERVICE AND/OR TRAINING)

Kenneth V.F. Blanchard
Preston King Covey, Ph.D.
Diane Nicholl
Jay Printz
Michael A. Robbins

LOBBYIST ON STATE LEVEL

Marion P. Hammer (FL)
Richard and Holley Galland Haymaker (LA)
Phillip B. Journey, J.D. (KS)
Bryan Miller (NJ)
Diane Nicholl (CO)
Stephen A. Sposato (CA)
Michael D. Yacino (MA)

LOBBYIST OR NATIONAL ORGANIZATION REPRESENTATIVE

Michael K. Beard
Sarah Brady
Richard J. Feldman, J.D.
Alan M. Gottlieb
Marion P. Hammer
Dennis Henigan, J.D.
Joshua M. Horwitz, J.D.
Neal Knox
Tanya K. Metaksa
Joseph P. Tartaro
Patricia Margaret (Peggy) Tartaro
Bob Walker

PHYSICIANS/PUBLIC HEALTH

Carl C. Bell, M.D.

Katherine Kaufer Christoffel, M.D., M.P.H.

Miguel A. Faria, Jr., M.D.

Don B. Kates, Jr., Ll.B.

Diane Nicholl

Andrés Soto

Stephen P. Teret, J.D., M.P.H.

Lisa S. Thornton, M.D.

Douglas S. Weil, M.S., Sc.D.

Garen J. Wintemute, M.D., M.P.H.

SECOND AMENDMENT

Robert J. Cottrol, J.D., Ph.D.

Stephen P. Halbrook, J.D., Ph.D.

Dennis Henigan, J.D.

Joshua M. Horwitz, J.D.

Phillip B. Journey, J.D.

Don B. Kates, Jr., Ll.B.

David B. Kopel, J.D.

Karen L. MacNutt, J.D.

SELF-DEFENSE

Madeleine (Lyn) Bates, Ph.D.

Preston King Covey, Ph.D.

Alan M. Gottlieb

Marion P. Hammer

Martha J. Langelan

Tanya K. Metaksa

Diane Nicholl

VICTIMS

James and Sarah Brady
Daniel Gross
Richard and Holley Galland Haymaker
Suzanna Gratia Hupp
Carolyn McCarthy
Bryan Miller
Michael A. Robbins
Stephen A. Sposato
Joy Turner

YOUTH WORKERS

Deane Calhoun
Marion P. Hammer
Jo Ann Karn
Joy Turner
Linda M. Vasquez

Additional Readings, by Topic

THE SECOND AMENDMENT

History and Development

Atherton, Herbert M., and J. Jackson Barlow. *1791–1991: The Bill of Rights and Beyond*. Washington, D.C.: Commission on the Bicentennial of the United States Constitution, 1991.

Cramer, Clayton E. *For the Defense of Themselves and the State: The Original Intent and Judicial Interpretation of the Right to Keep and Bear Arms*. Westport, Conn.: Praeger, 1994.

Kammen, Michael, ed. *The Origins of the American Constitution: A Documentary History*. New York: Viking Penguin, 1986.

Malcolm, Joyce Lee. *To Keep and Bear Arms: The Origins of an Anglo-American Right*. Cambridge, Mass.: Harvard University Press, 1994.

Northern Kentucky Law Review 10, no. 1 (1982).

U.S. Senate. *The Right to Keep and Bear Arms*. Report of the Subcommittee on the Constitution of the Committee on the Judiciary. Washington, D.C.: U.S. Senate, February 1982.

Veit, Helen E., Kenneth R. Bowling, and Charlene Bangs Bickford, eds. *Creating the Bill of Rights: The Documentary Record from the First Federal Congress*. Baltimore: Johns Hopkins University Press, 1991.

Modern Views

Amar, Akhil. "The Bill of Rights and the 14th Amendment." *Yale Law Journal* 101 (1992).

———. "The Bill of Rights as a Constitution." *Yale Law Journal* 100 (1990).

Bordenet, Bernard J. "The Right to Possess Arms: The Intent of the Framers of the Second Amendment." *University of West Los Angeles Law Review* 21 (1990).

Brown, Wendy. "Guns, Cowboys, Philadelphia Mayors, and Civic Republicanism: On Sanford Levinson, 'The Embarrassing Second Amendment.'" *Yale Law Journal* 99 (1989).

Burger, Warren E. "The Right to Bear Arms." *Parade*, January 14, 1990.

Cantrell, Charles L. "The Right of the Individual to Bear Arms." *Wisconsin Bar Bulletin* 53 (October 1980).

Caplan, David I. "Handgun Control: Constitutional or Unconstitutional?" *North Carolina Central Law Journal* 5 (1976).

———. "Restoring the Balance: Second Amendment Revisited." *Fordham Urban Law Journal* 5 (1976).

———. "The Right of the Individual to Bear Arms: A Recent Judicial Trend." *Detroit College of Law Review* (1982).

Cramer, Clayton E. *For the Defense of Themselves and the State: The Original Intent and Judicial Interpretation of the Right to Keep and Bear Arms.* Westport, Conn.: Praeger, 1994.

———. "The Racist Roots of Gun Control." *Kansas Journal of Law and Public Policy* (Winter 1995).

Cress, Lawrence D. "An Armed Community: The Origins and Meaning of the Right to Bear Arms." *Journal of American History* 71 (1984).

Dowlut, Robert. "The Current Relevancy of Keeping and Bearing Arms." *University of Baltimore Law Forum* 15 (1984).

———. "Federal and State Constitutional Guarantees to Arms." *University of Dayton Law Review* 15 (1989).

———. "The Right to Arms: Does the Constitution or the Predilection of Judges Reign?" *Oklahoma Law Review* 36 (1983).

Dowlut, Robert, and Janet Knoop. "State Constitutions and the Right to Keep and Bear Arms." *Oklahoma City University Law Review* 36 (1982).

Dunlap, Charles J., Jr. "Revolt of the Masses: Armed Civilians and the Insurrectionary Theory of the Second Amendment." *Tennessee Law Review* 62 (1995).

Gifford, Dan. "The Conceptual Foundations of Anglo-American Jurisprudence in Religion and Reason." *Tennessee Law Review* 62 (1995).

Hardy, David T. "Armed Citizens, Citizen Armies: Toward a Jurisprudence of the Second Amendment." *Harvard Journal of Law and Public Policy* 9 (1986): 559–638.

———. *Origin and Development of the Second Amendment.* Southport, Conn.: Blacksmith Corp., 1986.

———. "The Second Amendment and the Historiography of the Bill of Rights." *Journal of Law and Politics* 4 (1987).

Hayes, Stuart R. "The Right to Keep and Bear Arms: A Study in Judicial Misinterpretation." *William and Mary Law Review* 2 (1960).

Henigan, Dennis A., E. Bruce Nicholson, and David Hemenway. *Guns and the Constitution: The Myth of Second Amendment Protection for Firearms in America*. Northampton, Mass.: Aletheia Press, 1995.

Johnson, Nicholas J. "Beyond the Second Amendment: An Individual Right to Arms Viewed Through the Ninth Amendment." *Rutgers Law Journal* 24 (1992).

———. "Shots Across No Man's Land: A Response to Handgun Control, Inc.'s Richard Aborn." *Fordham Urban Law Journal* 22, no. 2 (1995).

Levine, Ronald B., and David B. Saxe. "The Second Amendment: The Right to Bear Arms." *Houston Law Review* 7 (1969).

Levinson, Sanford. "The Embarrassing Second Amendment." *Yale Law Journal* 99 (1989).

Lund, Nelson. "The Second Amendment, Political Liberty, and the Right to Self-Preservation." *Alabama Law Review* 39 (1987).

Malcolm, Joyce Lee. "Essay Review." *George Washington University Law Review* 54 (1986).

———. "The Right of the People to Keep and Bear Arms: The Common Law Tradition." *Hastings Constitutional Law Quarterly* 10, no. 285 (Winter 1983).

———. *To Keep and Bear Arms: The Origins of an Anglo-American Right*. Cambridge, Mass.: Harvard University Press, 1994.

McClure, James A. "Firearms and Federalism." *Idaho Law Review* 7 (1970).

Moncure, Thomas. "Who Is the Militia—The Virginia Ratification Convention and the Right to Bear Arms." *Lincoln Law Review* 19 (1990).

Reynolds, Glenn Harlan. "A Critical Guide to the Second Amendment." *Tennessee Law Review* 62 (Spring 1995).

"The Right to Keep and Bear Arms: A Necessary Constitutional Guarantee or an Outmoded Provision of the Bill of Rights?" (comment). *Albany Law Review* 31 (1967).

Scarry, Elaine. "War and the Social Contract: The Right to Keep and Bear Arms." *Pennsylvania Law Review* 139 (1991).

Shalhope, Robert E. "The Armed Citizen in the Early Republic." *Law and Contemporary Problems* 49 (1986).

———. "The Ideological Origins of the Second Amendment." *Journal of American History* 69 (1982).

Spannaus, Warren. "State Firearms Regulation and the Second Amendment." *Hamline Law Review* 6 (July 1983).

Sprecher, Robert A. "The Lost Amendment." *American Bar Association* 51 (1965) (2 parts).

Van Alstyne, William. "The Second Amendment and the Personal Right to Arms." *Duke Law Journal* 43 (1994).

Whisker, James B. *The Citizen Soldier and United States Military Policy.* Croton-on-Hudson, N.Y.: North River Press, 1979.

———. "Historical Development and Subsequent Erosion of the Right to Keep and Bear Arms." *West Virginia Law Review* 78 (1976).

———. *Our Vanishing Freedom: The Right to Keep and Bear Arms.* McLean, Va.: Heritage House, 1972.

Williams, David C. "Civic Republicanism and the Citizen Militia: The Terrifying Second Amendment." *Yale Law Journal* 101 (1991).

Young, David E., ed. *The Origin of the Second Amendment: A Documentary History of the Bill of Rights, 1787–1792.* Ontonagon, Mich.: Golden Oak Books, 1995.

See also Robert J. Cottrol; Dennis Henigan; Stephen P. Halbrook; Don B. Kates, Jr.

Relevant Court Rulings

Dred Scott v. Sanford, 60 U.S. (19 How.) 417 (1857).

Nunn v. State, 1 Ga. (1 Kel.) 243 (1846).

Miller v. Texas, 153 U.S. 535 (1894).

Presser v. Illinois, 116 U.S. 252 (1886).

Printz v. United States, 521 U.S. 98, 138 L. Ed. 2d 914, 65 U.S.L.W. 4731 (June 27, 1997) and 854 F.Supp. 1503 (D.Mont. 1994).

Quilici v. Village of Morton Grove, 695 F.2d 261 (Thea Cur. 1983).

U.S. v. Cruikshank, 92 U.S. 542 (1875).

U.S. v. Lopez, 115 S. Ct. 1624 131L.Ed 2d 626 (1995). (On Gun Free School Zone Act)

U.S. v. Miller, 307 U.S. 174 (1939).

RIGHT TO CARRY LAWS AND SELF-DEFENSE

Lott, John R., Jr., and David B. Mustard. "Crime, Deterrence, and Right-to-Carry Concealed Handguns." *Journal of Legal Studies* 26 (January 1997).

McDowall, David, Colin Loftin, and Brian Wiersema. "Easing Concealed Firearms Laws: Effects on Homicide in Three States." *Journal of Criminal Law and Criminology* 86 (Fall 1995).

See also Gary Kleck; David Kopel

CRIME AND CRIMINALS' ACCESS TO GUNS

Bordua, David J. "Firearms Ownership and Violent Crime: A Comparison of Illinois Counties." In *The Social Ecology of Crime*, ed. James M. Byrne and Robert J. Sampson. New York: Springer-Verlag, 1986.

Brill, Steven. *Firearm Abuse: A Research and Policy Report*. Washington, D.C.: Police Foundation, 1977.

Crocker, Royce. "Attitudes Toward Gun Control: A Survey." In *Federal Regulation of Firearms*, ed. Harry L. Hogan. Washington, D.C.: U.S. Government Printing Office, 1982.

Deutsch, Stephen Jay, and Francis B. Alt. "The Effect of Massachusetts' Gun Control Law on Gun-Related Crimes in the City of Boston." *Evaluation Quarterly* 1 (1977): 543–568.

DeZee, Matthew R. "Gun Control Legislation: Impact and Ideology." *Law and Policy Quarterly* 5 (1983): 367–379.

Geisel, Martin S., Richard Roll, and R. Stanton Wettick. "The Effectiveness of State and Local Regulations of Handguns." *Duke University Law Journal* 4 (1969).

Hay, Richard, and Richard McCleary. "Box-Tiao Times Series Models for Impact Assessment." *Evaluation Quarterly* 3 (1979): 277–314.

Hemenway, David, Sara J. Solnick, and Deborah R. Azrael. "Firearms and Community Feelings of Safety." *Journal of Criminal Law and Criminology* 86 (1995).

Jung, Roy S., and Leonard A. Jason. "Firearm Violence and the Effects of Gun Control Legislation." *American Journal of Community Psychology* 16 (1988).

Kellermann, Arthur L., et al. "Weapon Involvement in Home Invasion Crime." *Journal of the American Medical Association* 273, no. 22 (June 14, 1995).

Krug, Alan S. "A Statistical Study of the Relationship Between Firearms Licensing Laws and Crime Rates." *Congressional Record*, July 25, 1967.

Lester, David. "The Use of Firearms in Violent Crime." *Crime and Justice* 8 (1985): 115–120.

Loftin, Colin, Milton Heumann, and David McDowall. "Mandatory Sentencing and Firearms Violence: Evaluating an Alternative to Gun Control." *Law and Society Review* 17 (1983).

Loftin, Colin, and David McDowall. "The Deterrent Effects of the Florida Felony Firearm Law." *Journal of Criminal Law and Criminology* 75 (1984).

Magaddino, Joseph P. "An Empirical Analysis of Federal and State Firearm Control Laws." In *Firearms and Violence: Issues of Public Policy*, ed. Don B. Kates, Jr. Cambridge, Mass.: Ballinger, 1984. Pp. 255–258.

Magaddino, Joseph P., and Marshall H. Medoff. "Homicides, Robberies and State 'Cooling-off' Schemes." In *Why Handgun Bans Can't Work*, ed. Don B. Kates, Jr. Bellevue, Wash.: Second Amendment Foundation, 1982. Pp. 101–112.

Markush, Robert E., and Alfred A. Bartolucci. "Firearms and Suicide in the United States." *American Journal of Public Health* 74 (1984).

McDowall, David. "Gun Availability and Robbery Rates: A Panel Study of Large U.S. Cities, 1974–1978." *Law and Policy* 8 (1986).

McPheters, Lee R., Robert Mann, and Don Schlagenhauf. "Economic Response to a Crime Deterrence Program." *Economic Inquiry* 22 (1984).

Medoff, Marshall H., and Joseph P. Magaddino. "Suicides and Firearm Control Laws." *Evaluation Review* 7 (1983).

Murray, Douglas R. "Handguns, Gun Control Laws and Firearm Violence." *Social Problems* 23 (1975).

Newton, George D., and Franklin Zimring. *Firearms and Violence in American Life: A Staff Report to the National Commission on the Causes and Prevention of Violence.* Washington, D.C.: U.S. Government Printing Office, 1969.

Nicholson, Robert, and Anne Garner. "The Analysis of the Firearms Control Act of Washington, D.C." Washington, D.C.: U.S. Conference of Mayors, 1975.

Seitz, Stephen T. "Firearms, Homicides, and Gun Control Effectiveness." *Law and Society Review* 6 (1972).

Smith, Tom W. "The 75% Solution: An Analysis of the Structure of Attitudes on Gun Control, 1959–1977." *Journal of Criminal Law and Criminology* 71 (1980).

Snyder, Jeffrey R. "A Nation of Cowards." *The Public Interest* 113 (1993).

Sommers, Paul M. "Deterrence and Gun Control: An Empirical Analysis." *Atlantic Economic Journal* 8 (1980).

Zimring, Franklin E. "Firearms and Federal Law: The Gun Control Act of 1968." *Journal of Legal Studies* 4 (1975).

———. "Is Gun Control Likely to Reduce Violent Killings?" *University of Chicago Law Review* 35 (1968).

———. "Street Crime and New Guns: Some Implications for Firearms Control." *Journal of Criminal Justice* 4 (1976).

See also Philip Cook; Don B. Kates, Jr.; Gary Kleck; Tanya Metaksa; James D. Wright

BRADY HANDGUN VIOLENCE PREVENTION ACT AND EFFECTIVENESS OF GUN CONTROLS

Jacobs, James B., and Kimberly A. Potter. "Keeping Guns out of the 'Wrong' Hands: The Brady Law and the Limits of Regulation." *Journal of Criminal Law and Criminology* 86 (Fall 1995).

Lacayo, Richard. "Gun Control: A Small-Bore Success." *Time*, February 20, 1995.

McDowall, David, Colin Loftin, and Brian Wiersema. "Additional Discussion about Easing Concealed Firearms Laws." *Journal of Criminal Law and Criminology* 86 (Fall 1995).

McNichol, Tom. "Secret Weapons." *USA Weekend*, December 29–31, 1995.

Polsby, Daniel D. "Daniel D. Polsby Replies." *Journal of Criminal Law and Criminology* 86 (Fall 1995).

———. "Firearms Costs, Firearms Benefits and the Limits of Knowledge." *Journal of Criminal Law and Criminology* 86 (Fall 1995).

———. "The False Promise of Gun Control." *Atlantic Monthly*, March 1994.

U.S. Department of the Treasury. *The Brady Law: The First 100 Days*. Washington, D.C.: U.S. Government Printing Office. July 27, 1994.

U.S. Department of the Treasury. *One-Year Progress Report: Brady Handgun Violence Prevention Act*. Washington, D.C.: Government Printing Office. February 28, 1995.

Witkin, Gordon, and Ted Gest. "Gun Control's Limits." *U.S. News and World Report*, December 6, 1993.

PUBLIC HEALTH

Adler, Karl P. "Firearm Violence and Public Health: Limiting the Availability of Guns." *Journal of the American Medical Association* 271, no. 16 (April 27, 1994).

Carlson, Tucker. "Handgun Control, M.D." *Weekly Standard* (April 15, 1996).

Caruth, W. W. III. "Guns: Health Destroyer or Protector?" *Journal of the Medical Association of Georgia* 83 (March 1994).

Kellermann, Arthur L., and Donald T. Reay. "Protection or Peril?" *New England Journal of Medicine* 314, no. 24 (June 12, 1986).

Kellermann, Arthur, F. P. Rivera, and N. B. Rushforth. "Gun Ownership as a Risk Factor for Homicide in the Home." *New England Journal of Medicine* 329 (1993): 1084–91.

Kizer, Kenneth W., et al. "Hospitalization Charges, Costs, and Income for Firearm-Related Injuries at a University Trauma Center." *Journal of the American Medical Association* 273, no. 22 (June 1995).

Lester, David. "The Relationship Between Gun Control Statutes and Homicide Rates: A Research Note." *Crime and Justice* 4 (1981).

Martin, Michael J., Thomas K. Hunt, and Stephen B. Hulley. "The Cost of Hospitalization for Firearm Injuries." *Journal of the American Medical Association* 260, no. 20 (November 25, 1988).

Suter, Edgar A. "Guns in the Medical Literature—A Failure of Peer Review." *Journal of the American Medical Association of Georgia* 83 (March 1994).

Guns and Suicide

Brent, David A., Joshua A. Perper, Christopher J. Allman, Grace M. Moritz, Mary E. Wartella, and Janice P. Zelenak. "The Presence and Accessibility of Firearms in the Homes of Adolescent Suicides: A Case Control Study." *Journal of the American Medical Association* 266, no. 21 (December 1991).

Kellermann, Arthur L., et al. "Suicide in the Home in Relation to Gun Ownership." *New England Journal of Medicine* 327, no. 7 (August 1992).

Lester, David. "An Availability-Acceptability Theory of Suicide." *Activitas Nervosa Superior* 29 (1987): 164–166.

———. "Gun Control, Gun Ownership, and Suicide Prevention." *Suicide and Life-Threatening Behavior* 18 (1988): 176–180.

———. "Gun Ownership and Suicide in the United States." *Psychological Medicine* 19 (1989).

———. "The Preventive Effect of Strict Gun Control Laws on Suicide and Homicide." *Suicide and Life-Threatening Behavior* 12 (1982).

———. "Restricting the Availability of Guns as a Strategy for Preventing Suicide." *Biology and Society* 5 (1988): 127–129.

Lester, David, and Mary E. Murrell. "The Influences of Gun Control Laws on Suicidal Behavior." *American Journal of Psychiatry* 137 (1980).

Markush, Robert E., and Alfred A. Bartolucci. "Firearms and Suicide in the United States." *American Journal of Public Health* 74, no. 2 (February 1984).

Rosenberg, Mark L., James A. Mercy, and Vernon N. Houk. "Guns and Adolescent Suicides" (editorial). *Journal of the American Medical Association* 26, no. 21 (December 4, 1991).

See also Don B. Kates, Jr.; Diane Nicholl; Miguel A. Faria (gun rights views); Carl C. Bell; Katherine Kaufer Christoffel; Lisa S. Thornton; Stephen P. Teret; Douglas S. Weil; Garen J. Wintemute

CHILDREN AND GUNS

Bjerregaard, Beth, and Alan J. Lizotte. "Gun Ownership and Gang Membership." *Journal of Criminal Law and Criminology* 86 (Fall 1995).

Blackman, Paul H. *Children and Firearms: Lies the CDC Loves.* Washington, D.C.: National Rifle Association Institute for Legislative Action, 1992.

Blumstein, Alfred. "Youth Violence, Guns, and the Illicit-Drug Industry." *Journal of Criminal Law and Criminology* 86 (Fall 1995).

Educational Fund to End Handgun Violence. *Kids and Guns: A National*

Disgrace. Washington, D.C.: Educational Fund to End Handgun Violence, 1993.

Kachur, S. Patrick, Gail M. Stennies, Kenneth E. Powell, William Modzeleski, Ronald Stephens, Rosemary Murphy, Marcei-Jo Kresnow, David Sleet, and Richard Lowry. "School-Associated Violent Deaths in the United States, 1992 to 1994." *Journal of the American Medical Association* 275 (1996).

Sheley, Joseph F., Zina T. McGee, and James D. Wright. "Gun-Related Violence in and around Inner-City Schools." *American Journal of Diseases of Children* 146 (June 1992).

FIREARMS DEALERS

U.S. Government Accounting Office. *Federal Firearms Licenses: Various Factors Have Contributed to the Decline in the Number of Dealers*. Washington, D.C.: U.S. Government Printing Office, March 1996.

Violence Policy Center. *More Gun Dealers than Gas Stations*. Washington, D.C.: Violence Policy Center, 1992.

NATIONAL RIFLE ASSOCIATION

Anderson, Jack. *Inside the NRA: Armed and Dangerous. An Expose*. Beverly Hills, Calif.: Dove Books, 1996.

Davidson, Osha Gray. *Under Fire: The NRA and the Battle for Gun Control*. New York: Henry Holt, 1993.

LaPierre, Wayne. *Guns, Crime, and Freedom*. Washington, D.C.: Regnery, 1994.

Simon, Jonathan. "The NRA under Fire." *Public Citizen* (July/August 1989).

Sugarmann, Josh. *National Rifle Association: Money, Firepower and Fear*. Washington, D.C.: National Press Books, 1992.

Resources

American Shooting Sports Council, Inc.
9 Perimeter Way, Suite C-950
Atlanta, GA 30339
Telephone: (404) 933-0200
http://www.assc.org

Arming Women Against Rape and Endangerment (AWARE)
P.O. Box 242
Bedford, MA 01730-0242
Telephone: (781) 893-0500
http://www.aware.org

Ceasefire Action Network
http://www.gunfree.org.ceasefir.htm

CeaseFire, Inc.
1290 Avenue of the Americas
New York, NY 10104
Telephone: (212) 484-1616
http://www.ceasefire.org

Center to Prevent Handgun Violence
1225 Eye Street, NW, Suite 1100
Washington, DC 20005
Telephone: (202) 898-0792
Fax: (202) 371-9615
http://www.handguncontrol.org

Citizens Committee for the Right to Keep and Bear Arms
Liberty Park

12500 NE 10th Place
Bellevue, WA 98005
Telephone: (206) 454-4911
http://www.ccrkba.org

Coalition to Stop Gun Violence (CSGV)
1000 16th Street NW, Suite 603
Washington, DC 20036
Telephone: (202) 530-0340
http://www.gunfree.org

Congress of Racial Equality
30 Cooper Square
Ninth Floor
New York, NY 10003
Telephone: (212) 598-4000

Eddie the Eagle program. Contact the National Rifle Association

Educational Fund to End Handgun Violence (EFEHV)
1000 16th Street NW, Suite 603
Washington, DC 20036
Telephone: (202) 530-0340
http://www.gunfree.org

Gun Owners of America
8001 Forbes Place, Suite 102
Springfield, VA 22151
Telephone: (703) 321-8585

Handgun Control, Inc. (HCI)
1225 Eye Street NW, Suite 1100
Washington, DC 20005
Telephone: (202) 898-0792
Fax: (202) 371-9615
http://www.handguncontrol.org

Hands Without Guns program. *See* Educational Fund to End Handgun Violence

HELP Network
Children's Memorial Hospital
2300 Children's Plaza
Chicago, Illinois 60614
Telephone: (773) 880-3826
Fax: (773) 880-6615
http://www.guninfo.org

Independence Institute
14142 Denver West Pkwy., Suite 185
Golden, CO 80401
Telephone: (303) 279-6536
http://i2i.org

Jews for the Preservation of Firearms Ownership
2872 South Wentworth Avenue
Milwaukee, WI 53207
Telephone: (414) 769-0760

Johns Hopkins Center for Gun Policy and Research
School of Public Health
624 N. Broadway
Baltimore, MD 21205
Telephone: (410) 955-3995

Join Together
441 Stuart Street
Boston, Massachusetts 02116
Telephone: (617) 437-1500
Fax: (617) 437-9394
http://www.jointogether.org

Law Enforcement Alliance of America
7700 Leesburg Pike
Suite 421
Falls Church, VA 22043
Telephone: (703) 847-2677
http://www.leaa.org

National Rifle Association
11250 Waples Mill Road
Fairfax, VA 22030
Telephone: (703) 267-1000
http://www.nra.org

National Shooting Sports Foundation
555 Danbury Road
Wilton, CT 06897
Telephone: (203) 762-1320

PAX
New York, NY
http://www.paxusa.org

Physicians for Social Responsibility
1101 14th Street NW, Suite 700
Washington, DC 20005
Telephone: (202) 898-0150
Fax: (202) 898-0172
http://www.psr.org

Second Amendment Foundation
12500 N.E. 10th Place
Bellevue, WA 98005
Telephone: (206) 454-7012
http://www.saf.org

Straight Talk About Responsibilities (S.T.A.R.) program. *See* Handgun Control, Inc.

Teens on Target program. *See* Youth ALIVE!

Violence Policy Center (VPC)
1300 N Street, N.W.
Washington, DC 20005
Telephone: (202) 783-4071
http://www.vpc.org

Violence Prevention Research Program
University of California, Davis
2315 Stockton Blvd.
Sacramento, CA 95817
http://edison.ucdmc.ucdavis.edu.80/research/vprp

Youth ALIVE!
3300 Elm Street
Oakland, CA 94609
Telephone: (510) 594-2588

Youth Crime Gun Interdiction Initiative
Bureau of Alcohol, Tobacco, and Firearms
http://www.atf.treas.gov/core/firearms/ycgii/ycgii.htm

Index

About the Author

MARJOLIJN BIJLEFELD is a freelance writer and editor who worked with the Coalition to End Gun Violence and served as the Director of The Educational Fund to End Gun Violence. She is the author of *The Gun Control Debate: A Documentary History* (Greenwood, 1997).